Praise for *Merlin Stone Remembered*

"A beautiful work of love ... celebrating the life of Merlin Stone ... a delight to read!"

—Miriam Robbins Dexter, PhD, author of *Whence the Goddesses*

"This book is paradigm-shifting. It should be read by all those who yearn for miracles, as well as by those who still need proof to believe that they are possible."

—Gloria Orenstein, Professor Emerita, Comparative Literature and Gender Studies, University of Southern California, Los Angeles

"An easy-to-follow book about Merlin Stone, who gave us back women's global spiritual heritage."

—Z Budapest, feminist author, activist, and founder of the Susan B. Anthony Coven

"A lovely and loving tribute to the late Merlin Stone, a foremother of Goddess feminism."

—Judith Laura, author of *Goddess Spirituality for the 21st Century*

"[*Merlin Stone Remembered*] touched me to the core. The book is both humble and powerful ... a peek into the mysterious, private world of this iconic feminist woman who changed history."

—Vicki Noble, feminist shamanic healer and author of *The Double Goddess*

"Merlin Stone is a great inspiration for those of us who want to know not just about history, but also about herstory ... this book about Merlin's life will inspire many."

—Linda Perry Barr, Journalist, WBAI News, Pacifica Radio, New York

"A beautifully crafted tribute to a remarkable person."

—Charlene Spretnak, author of *Lost Goddesses of Early Greece*

"This book is a loving tribute to an Illustrious Ancestress."

—Luisah Teish, author of *Jambalaya: The Natural Woman's Book of Personal Charms and Practical Rituals*

"Lenny's chronicle of their life together was extremely touching."
—Donna Henes, author of *The Queen of My Self*

"*Merlin Stone Remembered* reveals the magic of Goddess Intuition, the power of Ecofeminism, and the love of Nature which Merlin expressed in life and inspired in others."
—Selena Fox, priestess, author, environmentalist, and senior minister for Circle Sanctuary

"Merlin was such a pioneer in remembering Goddess spirituality, and an inspiration for us all … It is great to read something more personal about Merlin's life."
—Kathy Jones, feminist author and Priestess of Avalon

Praise for the work of Merlin Stone

"Merlin was a bright star among us at a very important time in our feminist history."
—Kate Millett, 2013 inductee, National Women's Hall of Fame

"Merlin Stone changed the world."
—Carol P. Christ, author of *Rebirth of the Goddess*

"[*When God Was a Woman*] spoke to me in a very special way … There is a karmic bond between us."
—Erica Jong, feminist and author

"In her defining history of Goddess worship, Stone takes us on an archaeological journey and uncovers the ancient conspiracy that resulted in man's rule over woman."
—*Ms. Magazine*, "Top 100 Feminist Books"

"[Merlin Stone gave us] the feminist vision of Elizabeth Gould and the inspired scholarship of Robert Graves … in a style so lucid that even the most patriarchal of pedants ought to acknowledge defeat."
—Robin Morgan, feminist activist and author of
Sisterhood Is Powerful

"Merlin was one of the most important foremothers of the Women's Spirituality Movement."
—Margot Adler, author of *Drawing Down the Moon*

"Merlin tirelessly dug deep [and] gave us a truly global vision of the Goddess, allowing all the Goddesses a place at the table."
—Flash Silvermoon, author of *The Wise Woman's Tarot*

"Merlin Stone was the first to say it out loud and then get it published—'when god was a woman.' And that summation changed everything. It challenged the unmitigated gall of organized religion, governments, and their enforcers through the ages."
—Mary Beth Edelson, pioneer feminist artist and author

merlin stone
Remembered

About the Authors

DR. CAROL F. THOMAS holds a master of arts degree in American literature from Stetson University, and a master's degree in counseling psychology from the University of Connecticut. She also holds a PhD in literature and psychology from Union Institute and University, and a doctorate in applied theology (DMin) from Pittsburgh's Theological Seminary. She taught women's studies, psychology, and literature at the University of Connecticut, Bowie State, as well as at additional colleges and universities. She also taught creative writing for Saint Leo University and for Gavle University in Storvik, Sweden. During her sojourn of eleven years at the University of Connecticut, she enjoyed private practice as a member of Shoreline Psychiatric Associates. At the Niantic Correctional Institution, she taught for Mohegan College and was instrumental in facilitating the publication of a book of art and poetry written by the incarcerated women and published by the State of Connecticut's Counsel for the Arts. She has published a book on the Women's Movement and three books of poetry. Dr. Thomas's husband is a practicing surgeon, and they have four sons and six grandchildren. She and her husband had a horse ranch in Oklahoma, where they resided for a number of years, and have a home in Ormond-by-the-Sea, Florida, which is now their retirement home.

LEONARD SCHNEIR was born in Brooklyn, New York. He lived at home with his sister, Renée, and his mother, Betty. His father, Irving, a shoe manufacturer, only occasionally lived with them. In 1947, at the age of seven, Lenny's family moved to Kew Gardens, Queens, where he became an expert at roaming the streets, as his memoir amply recounts. He received his bachelor of science in business administration in 1962, from the University of Denver. Thereafter, he served in the army, rising to sergeant E5, honorably discharged in 1968. After a series of jobs, first for his father and at other sales positions, he moved to his home at 184 6th Avenue, New York City, that same year. There, he settled into the life of a professional poker player. Later, he became a major collector of gambling memorabilia in partnership with the American playing-card authority Gene Hochman. As an expert in that area, Lenny authored the book *Gambling Collectibles: A Sure Winner* (Schiffer Publishing: Atglen, PA, 1993). Lenny met Merlin in September 1976, and she moved in soon after. They lived at their Sixth Avenue residence until 2005, at which time they moved to Daytona Beach, Florida. Since Merlin's death, Lenny continues to live in Daytona Beach.

DR. GLORIA F. ORENSTEIN has just retired as Professor of Comparative Literature and Gender Studies (Emerita) from the University of Southern California, Los Angeles. She is the author of *The Reflowering of the Goddess* and *The Theatre of the Marvelous: Surrealism and the Contemporary Stage* and was co-editor of *Reweaving the World: The Emergence of Ecofeminism.* In the seventies, she co-created the Woman's Salon for Literature in New York City. Gloria has lectured widely on surrealism, ecofeminism, salon women, shamanism, and how the Goddess has been reclaimed by contemporary feminist artists and writers. She has also been a student of the Shaman of Samiland, in Lapland, Norway. Most recently she has written for *In Wonderland*, the book that accompanied the exhibition "In Wonderland," on surrealist women artists who migrated from Europe to the Americas, where their work flourished. Now, in retirement, she says she continues to read about everything she wished had been taught in academia but was omitted from the curriculum—including lost civilizations and cosmic mysteries.

DR. DAVID B. AXELROD was born in Beverly, Massachusetts, but settled on Long Island, New York, for forty years after his college studies. He holds a BA from the University of Massachusetts, an MA from The Johns Hopkins University, an MFA from the University of Iowa, and a PhD from Union Institute. Best known as a poet, Dr. Axelrod is the recipient of three Fulbright Awards and author of twenty books of poetry. As a professor in the State University of New York system, he taught creative writing and ran conferences and visiting writers programs. In 1976, he founded Writers Unlimited Agency, Inc., a nonprofit writers cooperative, which he directed until 2009, when he turned the leadership over to his son, Daniel Axelrod, a professional journalist currently completing a PhD at the University of Florida. Dr. Axelrod's three daughters continue to live and work professionally in the New York area. Since 2009, when he moved to Daytona Beach, Florida, he is the founder and director of the Creative Happiness Institute, Inc., a nonprofit, educational organization that presents programs in creative writing and alternative health.

merlin stone

Remembered

HER *life* AND *works*

~

DAVID B. AXELROD

CAROL F. THOMAS

LENNY SCHNEIR

Llewellyn Publications
Woodbury, Minnesota

First Edition
First Printing, 2014

Cover design by Ellen Lawson
Cover photo courtesy of the estate of Merlin Stone
Interior photos courtesy of the estate of Merlin Stone

Color insert image: www.istockphoto.com/#16034084

Llewellyn Publications is a registered trademark of Llewellyn Worldwide Ltd.

"Chapter 10: Unraveling the Myth of Adam and Eve" from *When God Was a Woman* by Merlin Stone, copyright © 1976 by Merlin Stone. Used by permission of Doubleday, an imprint of the Knopf Doubleday Publishing Group, a division of Random House LLC. All rights reserved. Any third party use of this material, outside of this publication, is prohibited. Interested parties must apply directly to Random House LLC for permission.

Library of Congress Cataloging-in-Publication Data (Pending)
ISBN: 978-0-7387-4091-1

Llewellyn Worldwide Ltd. does not participate in, endorse, or have any authority or responsibility concerning private business transactions between our authors and the public.
   All mail addressed to the author is forwarded but the publisher cannot, unless specifically instructed by the author, give out an address or phone number.
   Any Internet references contained in this work are current at publication time, but the publisher cannot guarantee that a specific location will continue to be maintained. Please refer to the publisher's website for links to authors' websites and other sources.

Llewellyn Publications
A Division of Llewellyn Worldwide Ltd.
2143 Wooddale Drive
Woodbury, MN 55125-2989
www.llewellyn.com

Printed in the United States of America

For Merlin Stone,
a most remarkable woman.
With profound and everlasting love.
—LENNY

*"In the beginning, people prayed to the Creatress of Life,
the Mistress of Heaven. At the very dawn of religion,
God was a woman. Do you remember?"*
—MERLIN STONE, *WHEN GOD WAS A WOMAN*

Merlin Stone, 1969.

Contents

Preface
—Carol F. Thomas

THIS BOOK IS LOVINGLY dedicated to Merlin Stone—ardent feminist, artist, sculptor, art historian, persistent, tireless, and courageous traveler, researcher, writer, lecturer, and speaker. Merlin traveled the globe, alone, gathering material to explicate and illuminate what many scholars, psychologists, and historians have called "the biggest hoax" in the universe—the Adam and Eve creation story and the continuing biblical accounts of patriarchy, male dominance, and superiority and mastery as dictated by a father god. Although Stone's observations were formulated in the context of the fifties, sixties, and seventies, she asks an enduring question in the preface to her first book, *When God Was a Woman*: "How did it actually happen? How did men initially gain the control that now allows them to regulate the world in matters as vastly diverse as deciding which wars will be fought ... to what time dinner should be served?" (Stone, xi).

In contemporary American culture, a majority of the population continues to believe in a divine father god who protects them, rewards their behavior, and provides them with a heavenly and eternal life. It was Merlin Stone who, through her hands-on archeological evidence and anthropological findings, revealed that there was an extremely complex socio-religious structure in which women were seen to be the autonomous creators of new life.

Mary Daly published *Beyond God the Father* in 1973. She, along with other authors who called patriarchy into question, were part of a growing movement that encouraged Stone's research to document just how much of our human history has been suppressed. Stone proved that the earliest civilizations considered the woman divine in her role as Goddess and mother of the world. The Goddess was understood to be the sacred, sole creator of human life; she was honored and revered. Later, when male-worshipping religions developed, they sought to erase from history the feminine leadership, perspective, and values that had existed for at least eight thousand years.

As Gloria F. Orenstein explains in her introductory essay for *Merlin Stone Remembered*, Merlin definitively established that there were earlier matrilineal communities. The patriarchs, with their need for male dominance, competition, and tribal warfare, reduced women in every respect, rendering them disenfranchised, unwanted "others." Though much progress has been made since Merlin wrote her groundbreaking books, male "mastery" still continues to this day in corporate and religious institutions.

In her exhumation of women's history, Stone illuminates the crucially important female contributions to the development of humanity that patriarchy has attempted to obliterate. Where is the desire to create nonviolent communities, countries, nations, and peoples? What happened to the wisdom, stateswomanship, intuition, understanding, nurturing, and love that were evidenced in matriarchal societies?

In 1976, Merlin Stone completed a thorough and extensive investigation to discern if the human condition was doomed to the ongoing delusions of divine male protection. Stone's research suggests another way—a way to understand our relation to ourselves, one another, and the planet Earth. The planet—skies, water, soil, and all its inhabitants—is in jeopardy. We need a new origin story inclusive of innovative visions of science, spirituality, human community, and especially gender equality.

At a time when our planet is threatened by various destructive forces, Merlin Stone offers an invitation to discover the tragic transition from matriarchy to patriarchy. There is an alternative way to understand the human condition—cooperative, compassionate, mutually respectful, creative, and inclusive—rewriting the biblical script.

Merlin Stone, long before anyone else dared to suggest that our planet and our very lives were in danger, submitted the need for the gathered wisdom of women of the world to transform our cultures with true planetary and ecological consciousness. Her core values focused on wisdom, knowledge, the tools and paths to autonomy, freedom from oppression, and the courage and conviction to claim one's own voice based on life experiences. May this book remind you of the Goddess in all her diverse manifestations and bring you to an even greater appreciation of the work of Merlin Stone.

Editor's Note
—David B. Axelrod

*W*HEN MY GOOD FRIEND Lenny Schneir asked if I would help with a speech he promised to give at a ceremony to commemorate his life partner, Merlin Stone, I was happy to help. He told me that he had never given a speech. "I don't think I've spoken to more than seven people at a time in my entire life," he said.

After a great success before an audience of nearly one hundred women—many of whom were well-known feminists—Len was inspired to tell his personal story about his life with Merlin. They were as close as any couple could be for thirty-four years. Thus, Len sat and told me story after story. He wrote his notes and together we assembled his memoir.

Thereafter, he asked me to help him compile a book that would celebrate the life and work of Merlin Stone. Understand, however, that I never got to meet Merlin. She passed away just one month before I met Len at a poetry workshop. In fact, Len first got to know me as a poet, then a friend, and when he learned that I also had worked as a professional author in other forms—academic articles, journalism, nonfiction, fiction—he put me to work on this book.

I am also aware of what an honor it is that I have been given the task of shaping this book. I have three daughters, which, in and of itself, requires me to be a feminist. Not that I need to be "required," as my entire life as a student of literature and a poet has been devoted to observing, recording, and empathizing with the human condition—and more pointedly the conditions under which women live and struggle.

As a last word, I'd like to explain the inclusion of various poems in this book. When Merlin contemplated her own mortality, she expressed herself in poetry. In the second of her books on the Goddess, she wrote more than forty poems that are prayers in honor of the Goddess. When I first met Len, he was in mourning for Merlin, and the poem he presented at the workshop was entitled "The Eternal Grief Hotel," which expressed his deep despair. We have included some of his poems in the book, which I regard as an extension of his memoir. Carol F. Thomas, a lifelong feminist author and professor, has always expressed herself through poetry. We feel poetry to be an integral part of life, and thus including poems here is equally central to the purpose of this book. In that spirit, and as a professional poet, I am including a poem of my own, "I Want to Love Your Wife," written shortly after I met Lenny in the spring of 2011. It is one more way for me to thank Len for allowing me to celebrate the work of Merlin Stone. Not long into our friendship, I learned that Merlin and Lenny had been life partners and had not married. Still, I've kept the original title—believing that they could not have been any closer in their relationship than any husband and wife.

I Want to Love Your Wife

This poem was written by David B. Axelrod for Lenny Schneir in honor of Merlin Stone.

I never met her but
I want to love her
at least a little, for you,
my new friend, were
her friend, her fan, her
worshipper, married to her
for thirty-four years
before illness first
weakened her, rendered
her mute, then stole her
from you. When I
search her name
four million links appear.
She was famous,
gorgeous, brilliant,
which you can prove
to me with clippings
in albums, books she
wrote, even her resonant
voice responding to
an interviewer on CD.
I have to love your wife
or we can't be friends.
Not that you've compelled
me. Not that you've
aimed some figurative gun,

but, in fact, her studies of
Goddesses are what I
might read for fun
and also, when I learn
to love your wife,
it will teach that
male-chauvinist bastard,
Death, that he can't win.

introduction

Merlin Stone, circa 1991.

Transforming His/story into Her/story:

MERLIN STONE'S DRAMATIC ENTRANCE
ONTO THE STAGE OF OUR STORY

by Gloria F. Orenstein
Professor Emerita, University of Southern California, Los Angeles

*A*s a professor of women's studies, gender studies, comparative literature, and the arts for the past forty years, I was privileged to have lived through and participated in the birth of the feminist Goddess movement. Whenever people outside of academia and the women's movement ask me, "Gloria, after all you have lived through and learned, what do *you* think is the most important contribution this research has made to *your own* understanding, knowledge, and life so far?" I am taken aback because it is such a difficult question to answer. There have been so many contributions made through research and activism that one cannot prioritize them. However, I can say, definitively, that Merlin Stone's book *When God Was a Woman* had the most profound impact on my teaching and writing—on all that I was involved in since its publication in 1976.

Over the many years I taught women's studies classes, students always asked me if there was any country in which patriarchy did not predominate. For a while, back in the seventies, many of us were looking for cultures that had at least the remains of matriarchal (or matrilineal, matrifocal) societies. These could be places that had vestiges of these structures in place in our contemporary era. Sometimes we located a small culture where women played the roles that men do in our culture today. Perhaps we found one or two, but it wasn't until Merlin Stone's book was published that the actual answer came to light. In the early days of the late sixties and seventies, as Merlin has emphasized, and as was true in my life, I had never been taught anything about the ancient Goddess civilization. One of the most amazing things Merlin told us was that what we used to call a Goddess cult was, in fact, an entire Goddess civilization. Merlin's research in both history and archeology presented vast amounts of information and art from those early eras. That single illustration or photo of a Goddess figurine in the history books was not at all representative of the truth. Using what Merlin revealed to us, we had to transform our notions of Goddess cults into an ever-well-documented understanding of the importance of the Goddess.

I remember sitting and contemplating that transformation for a long time. It was immense, profound, *important*. It was possibly the most important thing I learned from those decades in which new paradigms were being brought to light all the time. I can't say enough about how important it was. For me, it was surely as shocking as it had been for those who first learned that the earth revolved around the sun, and not the other way around, as had been accepted knowledge previously.

For me, it was always Merlin Stone who launched this movement toward revision and pioneering scholarship without tipping over into fantastic claims to paint a more original picture. However, I want to contextualize her moment by mentioning the names of others who either preceded her or wrote on these subjects during the period in which the Goddess movement began to take shape. It is important to review some of the problems critics have identified with earlier studies, which Merlin's book transcended.

One of the earliest books to introduce us to the feminine symbolism of the Stone Age religion was G. Rachel Levy's 1948 book *The Gate of Horn*, first published by Faber and Faber Ltd. in Britain and then republished by Harper and Row in the United States in 1963 under the new title *Religious Conceptions of the Stone Age and Their Influence Upon European Thought*. Ms. Levy was speaking as a professional, and her pronouncements on the importance of understanding the cave as a female womb and the mother as the pregnant Earth

Mother were taken seriously and respected by those in her field. The book cover featured the icon of the Venus of Laussel, who stands with the horn of the moon upraised in her hand, and Levy's title, *The Gate of Horn*, implied entry to the cave of the Great Paleolithic Mother. That cave of the Great Mother was both the womb and the tomb of all life that cycles through the phases of life, birth, and death and awaits rebirth in the cycle of regeneration. The actual Paleolithic figurine of Venus of Laussel provided concrete evidence that proved the veracity of the concept of the Stone Age religion in which the creator was imaged as female and as the Great Mother of all life.

Another early work that attempted to construct a feminine history of culture was the historian Helen Diner's *Mothers and Amazons: The First Feminine History of Culture* (Anchor/Doubleday, 1973). The book was published in German forty years before its translation into English in 1965. The Introduction, by Brigitte Berger, is a critical review that, while evaluating the defects in Diner's scholarship, also appreciates the poetry of the author's vision of our past. Berger criticizes Diner for her generalizations, her lack of scientific knowledge, and the absence of precise documentation. Indeed, I would add that these earliest attempts to put this herstory together, attempts that were done with an absence of sufficient archeological and anthropological material, were often extremist in their conclusions. Diner presents generalized visions of everything that contradicted the patriarchal world in which she was living, and connected those reversals to inflated versions of all she fantasized about this unknown past.

For example, Diner begins by proclaiming that these prehistorical eras were matriarchal, which would imply governance by the female, for which we have no proof. She concludes that life began parthenogenetically, with the asexual creation of humans via the female alone. She declares, "In the beginning, there was woman. The man only appears as the son, as a biologically younger and later phenomenon. The female is the older, the more powerful, and the more aboriginal of the two mysterious, fundamental forms. ... Virgin conception reaches far into our animal ancestry as parthenogenesis. ... The original female in the animal species not only reproduces herself but also is the sole creatress of the male: the male never is anything without the female" (Diner, 1). By calling the many millennia of pre-patriarchal herstory "matriarchal," Diner conflates the differences between matrilineal and matrifocal to "matriarchy," and jumps to an unfounded characterization of the society's organization based upon her emphasis on parthenogenesis. She also hypothesizes a stage of sexual "promiscuity" in early cultures, where rites of initiation and other ritual functions may have explained the liberated sexual behavior better than promiscuity.

While the book has many intriguing aspects, including a herstory of Amazons, Diner then expands her information on diverse groups in multiple cultures into only one type of social organization, and names that a "gynocracy." Her book has clearly inspired the imagination of more contemporary feminists to create stories about the prowess and powers of these ancient warrior heroines. Diner's book serves as an example of earlier writing that presented original and highly speculative ideas challenging our inherited notions of women as the weaker sex and as historically and forever subordinate to men. The problem was that it was unreliable as actual scholarship.

Another precursor to Merlin Stone's study was *The First Sex* by Elizabeth Gould Davis (Penguin Books, 1971). Gould Davis posits the superiority of woman over man, claiming that the male is a mutation and an imperfect female. About the male's single Y chromosome as contrasted with the double Xs of the female, she writes: "It seems very logical that this small and twisted Y chromosome is a genetic error—an accident of nature, and that originally there was only one sex—the female.... The first males were mutants. Freaks produced by some damage to the genes caused perhaps by disease or a radiation bombardment from the sun.... The male sex represents a degeneration and deformity of the female" (Gould Davis, 35).

Gould Davis posits a "gynarchic age," a "Queendom" in which women were dominant, and claims that it was a matriarchal, vegetarian era where there were no animal sacrifices. It was a peace-loving epoch, having no violence, and its supreme deity was a Goddess. In her vision, this paradise on Earth was a golden age for women, where no interest in males or in the paternity of children was demonstrated. It was a world in which men served women and where women, not men, created all the crafts and technologies of civilization. She then refers to these "superior" women as "the ancient mariners," and envisages them as having traveled throughout the world spreading the wisdom and the worship of the Goddess everywhere. Gould Davis leaps from her interpretation of biology to postulate social organization and gender hierarchies throughout time. She seems to write as if any conclusion that would imply the superiority of women over men must, indeed, be valid.

Monica Sjoo's book *The Great Cosmic Mother*, written with Barbara Mor, was almost contemporaneous with that of Merlin Stone's work. The book appeared in a short version in 1975, published in Bristol, England, under the title of *The Great Cosmic Mother of All*. Only in 1987 was it more widely released by Harper and Row, retitled *The Great Cosmic Mother: Rediscovering the Religion of the Earth*. Monica Sjoo, originally from Sweden, was an artist, a writer, and a passionate explorer of the religion of the Great Earth Mother Goddess. Sjoo had personally slept at most of the sacred sites in Britain during all the phases of the moon, at the solstices and the equinoxes, and she recorded her visions and dreams. She also painted them and created a visual art oeuvre of iconic works about each of the sacred sites she explored in Europe. Her book is a passionate overview, with in-depth analyses of both symbols and myths relating to traditional narratives as well as to Sjoo's personal experiences at the sacred sites of the Great Mother. The book contributes to a new conception that includes relating the processes of the female body to the emotional and spiritual processes of both women and the earth. As such, Sjoo was an early ecofeminist, understanding the interrelationship not only of women and the planet but of the interconnectedness of all forms of life on Earth. She makes an important point of conceiving the communal body of women, the village of women, as a holistic body of interconnected energies and forces. This holistic vision places a social importance on the combined strength of the many great women who were our progenitors, our original inventors, healers, shamans, artists, and transmitters of energy and wisdom for generations.

Sjoo also stresses the importance of recognizing the original Black Mother of Africa as a black goddess who was regarded as bisexual and was understood to be self-fertilizing. Mawu-Lisa was both female and male, and was both the Earth and the rainbow. Hence, Sjoo introduces racial diversity and breaks with the white male colonizers' historical stereotypes, in interpreting the power, status, and productivity of women whose ancient prestige relates to the Black Mother Goddess.

Sjoo interweaves many dimensions of women's cultures into the fabric of a vast herstory of the Goddess's role in the creation of civilization. She introduces a consideration of the rituals of women's blood mysteries, of women's ecstatic spiritual healing rituals, and the importance of the moon times and the lunar calendrical cycles, while critically revisiting the patriarchally rendered myths such as the Garden of Eden. She also conceives of the earth as possessing a soul and having her own form of earthly intelligence, with her ley lines and power centers. Sjoo's vision of the earth is one that is close to that of today's Gaia hypothesis. She is angry about the demise of the Goddess civilization, destroyed by patriarchy's violent invasions, and she firmly declares that patriarchy's greatest crime is matricide, with its witch hunts, rapes, stonings, and burnings of women. Finally, she considers the price we have paid for the complete erasure and denial of the thirty thousand years of herstory in which the Great Cosmic Mother of all prevailed—the loss to humanity of millennia of herstory and of all the wisdom that has been omitted from our human legacy. Her personal travels and experiential explorations combined with immense documentation make her book an important reference for understanding the pioneering and visionary originality of another woman artist in search of the hidden history and knowledge of the civilization of the Goddess.

Without pursuing an analysis of these books any further, we can see that although there was some writing that had already attempted to reconstruct a history of women before Merlin's book came out, much more expertise and authority were needed. These books merely launched feminist scholarship on the road to making original assertions, implying that, when necessary, the imagination and fantasy were somehow valid to invoke, in place of actual historical knowledge or other material documentation. The postulates and pronouncements made by these two authors, Elizabeth Gould Davis and Helen Diner, are largely unsubstantiated by valid scientific proof. However, in their time, despite the critical reviews they received, they were, nevertheless, inspiring to feminist authors in terms of rethinking the patriarchally inscribed notions of our origins.

Sometimes women of knowledge and power from other countries knew something about "the Goddess," and when I first heard of her, I was shocked—having only known about gods and goddesses. Thus, when I first met Surrealist artist Leonora Carrington in 1971, she put her fingers up in the sign of the horns of the moon, and I asked her what that meant. She told me, "Those are the holy horns of consecration." I asked her, "Consecration of what?" and she said nonchalantly, "Of *the Goddess!*" In 1971, I could not wrap my mind around the word in the singular. I had only heard of goddesses and the one God. Leonora came from a Celtic background and she had a greater range of knowledge about pre-history, but with all my education, until then, I had never heard of *the Goddess*. I responded, "The who?" Those were my famous last words until Merlin wrote her book and when I first saw her step onto a stage in Santa Cruz, California, in 1978.

Then, suddenly, a plethora of information and strange names of ancient eras of what today we call "herstory" came into view. I began to re-periodize our Western civilization, beginning with the Upper Paleolithic. Thus, as Merlin's book burst forth upon the women's studies scene, I was able to answer my students' questions about whether there had ever been any culture that exhibited non-patriarchal structures. I was so proud to tell them that there was not just a single culture but there were thousands of years of pre- (hence non-) patriarchal civilization in the Western world alone, all of which preceded the eras that had been written about in our history books as the origin of civilization.

Once Merlin Stone provided us with her careful scholarship and a truly feminist (not biased, patriarchal) accounting of ancient Goddess cultures, I and all who found Merlin's work were finally able to understand our herstory and answer the questions of our students. Student papers used to begin by saying: "From the beginning of time immemorial, men were the rulers of civilization." Now I could cross that out and correct my students—giving them hope that what they had taken for unchangeable, absolute truth was now being transformed before their very eyes. We had answers to the questions that had troubled them. Did women ever have power? What importance did women have in civilization over time? Merlin was the pathfinder for these revelations.

At the end of the seventies, I was teaching on the East Coast, and the chairperson of women's studies and English asked me the topic for my next research project. I was so excited to tell her that it would be a book about the reclamation of the ancient Goddess civilization's mythos and ethos as it appears in the creative literary and artistic works of contemporary women artists and writers. They were making a link between gynocentric origins of pre-history—fostering a re-emergence of those symbols, themes, and myths. I borrowed the term "matristic," which Marija Gimbutas (a pioneer in feminist archaeology) had used because we do not have literal documentation about the actual social structures in those ancient cultures. Were the priestesses also queens? Were the figurines and images of goddesses or of women in general? Did priestess queens rule in a matriarchy? We just knew that these pre-patriarchal cultures were centered on a Mother Goddess, the great creator of all life. So the words I would use for the contemporary era, "feminist matristic," came to symbolize that unknown specificity for each culture. I added the word "feminist" to "matristic" when I spoke of such concepts as depicted by contemporary feminist women artists and writers.

When I told my chairperson what I wanted to write about, she looked shocked. "Do you expect me to tell *that* to the dean?" she asked in a tone that indicated I must be living on another planet, as this was so inappropriate a topic. It wasn't until I moved to the West Coast that I was able to write my book *The Reflowering of the Goddess* (Pergamon Press, 1990), in which I am proud to have a most moving and beautiful preface by Merlin Stone to introduce my research.

The story of what my department chairperson said was given here in order to contextualize the era in which Merlin's book appeared. At that time, we knew the book and what it argued with painstaking re-search and detailed documentation, but anyone you spoke to about it in a serious way looked at you with an expression as if to say, "You can't really believe all that, can you?" It was many decades until this culture shock began to sink into the consciousness of contemporary society, and perhaps even longer until it was accepted in academia.

I will never forget my experience at the first Great Goddess Re-emerging Conference in Santa Cruz, in 1978. I was teaching at a university on the East Coast, and this was a great occasion for me to learn more about the pioneering research that was unfolding in many disciplines. One of the highlights of that conference was Merlin Stone's presentation. It was there, I feel sure, that I first heard about changing the year of the conference (and all years before and after it) from 1978 to 9978, thereby adding at least eight thousand years to our calendar that preceded patriarchy about which we had the most information. It was mind-stretching to realize how many thousands of years had been abolished from our understanding of our true herstory (the term I used for the first time at the conference).

That conference was memorable in many other ways that also ex-ploded my paradigms—specifically of just what a conference was sup-posed to be, and what constituted research. In the middle of the con-ference, one woman became possessed by the Goddess. As an East Coast academic, this was truly the first time I had ever witnessed such an occurrence. What was happening? The woman was crying and keening. Z Budapest hurried over to "om" over her, and she told us that the woman was possessed by the Goddess. Z, who continues to be a major feminist activist, came to the U.S. from Hungary in 1959 and to California in 1970. In 1975, she became famous for winning an ap-peal of a conviction for illegal "fortune telling," when the California State Supreme Court vacated her guilty verdict, acknowledging Wicca as a bona fide religion.

Some members of the audience protested that the woman who was possessed was just acting it out to gain attention. But Z was firm in asserting that, often when one acts something out, the spirit of the role she is acting takes over. That, Z said, was what was happening in this case. For some local color of the Californian variety (also a first for me), young girls soon came blithely tripping down the aisles distributing flowers from their baskets along the way, as if we were at a wedding. Then we were led out to an amphitheater, where many spirited feminists were waiting perched in trees and drumming to accompany the rhythms of a ritual dance that other bare-breasted Goddess revelers participated in. All the while, Barbara Hammer, who by then was already known for her work as a filmmaker focusing on lesbian issues, flew around taking videos of the great gathering of energy in the name of the Goddess.

There was only one male at the Great Goddess Re-emerging Conference. It was Geoffrey Ashe, who had written about the Goddess in his book *The Virgin: Mary's Cult and the Re-emergence of the Goddess* (first published as *The Virgin* by Routledge & Paul, London, 1976). He invited any of us who were planning to travel to England to pay him a visit at Glastonbury Tor, where he lived. In 1978–79, as director of the Rutger's Junior Year in France program, I decided to pay a visit to the sacred Goddess sites in England, and I contacted Geoffrey. He seemed thrilled to take me around Glastonbury and share the stories with me. But at the end of our tour when we went inside, his expression grew somber, and I felt as if I were at a summit meeting. He took out his book on *The Virgin* and showed me the ample bibliography and the many pages of footnotes that were appended to the text.

"You see all these footnotes and bibliographical references, don't you?"

"Yes, I see them," I said.

Then he showed me a number of articles from the press in England. In each of them, he had underlined the critique of his work, the paragraphs where it was denounced as worthless for the lack of sufficient references and documentation. It was outrageous. He smiled wryly and simply said, "Note that if this is what they do to men, just imagine how they will crucify women who write on the Goddess." I felt that I had come to Glastonbury specifically to receive that warning and to view the proof that those who write on the Goddess are demonized even when they are male, but a much worse fate would be in store for women who lifted their voices in praise of Her.

When I returned to the East Coast, I was asked about the conference. It took a moment for me to relate to the word "conference." It was so unlike what I thought a conference was—and it was, obviously, because it was more than a conference. It engaged the mind, the body, the energy, and the imagination of all those who already related to the West Coast's expanded notions of what we should do when we have an important gathering. Inspired by Native American rituals and fueled by our imagination of what it was like in times when women had power and the priestesses would lead them in rituals, our contemporary feminist-matristic visionaries launched a new era in which we reclaimed thousands of years of pre-history as our very own herstory.

Thereafter, I could tell my students that not only did women have positions of prestige, but that at the center of it all was the acknowledgment that *God was a woman, a Goddess*, associated with the *Great Earth Mother.*

Merlin Stone was a sculptor, and you will see some of her creations for the first time in this book. It is also the case that Marija Gimbutas told me that had she not become an archeologist, she would have become a sculptor. It is important that I spend some time discussing Gimbutas, because both she and Merlin were visionaries, able to read the visual imagery of Goddess figurines that previously were believed to be the pornographic images of ancient cultures. Marija and Merlin understood that the corpulence of these figurines represented their fertility and their nurturing capacities. They also understood that the figurines revealed the sexual organs of women as gateways to pleasure, and that the Goddess religion did not have taboos on or repression of sexuality.

When Merlin Stone's book appeared on the scene, the conversation about Goddess imagery had largely to do with the Jungian concept of the archetype of the Goddess, which would arise from the unconscious into the dream world as a symbol. Finally, we had the historical/herstorical documentation—research done with great precision by Merlin Stone. That said, Marija Gimbutas also turned her substantial archeological analysis and personal knowledge of many languages and mythologies toward the Goddess, publishing a trilogy of large books. The trilogy began with *The Goddesses and Gods of Old Europe* (first published in Europe in 1974, and then with Linda Mount-Williams, University of California Press, 1982). Later came *The Language of the Goddess* (with Joseph Campbell, published by Harper & Row, 1989). The culmination was entitled *The Civilization of the Goddess* (with Joan Marler, published by University of California Press, 1991). What was once considered merely a figment of the imagination or the unconscious took on a historical and earthly, concrete, historical reality. No longer could those who spoke of the Goddess be accused of living in a fantasy world their imagination had conjured up.

One can critique Gimbutas's convictions from a logical point of view, but we have to realize that when she interprets her findings, be they archeological or natural, based on her life experiences in Lithuania, it is likely she saw those images with an energetic imprint that is unique to people raised in a culture with vestiges of Goddess religion. Gimbutas would have known, personally, worship practices such as kissing the earth every morning to thank the Great Earth Mother for the bounty She provides. I also understand that many feminist archeologists would have questioned, as they have, her conclusions. And, while believing in the veracity of the particular conclusions she drew from all this vast data, I know that perhaps I should have waited for more excavations and more proof before being convinced. But I also think that learning to understand how she drew her conclusions was an incredibly important educational experience. We, the feminist scholars who attended her presentations, came to feel that she was correct, and that this was a vision that she was brave enough to publish, for she also paid the price for her daring. Yet she put her entire life's energy into expressing her truth—one that the world was not yet ready for or prepared to hear. Her work expanded our minds and continues to influence work in the field and in women's studies as a model for thinking outside of the box.

That being said, I also think that the conclusions she drew in her trilogy of books transmit important information that is transformational, though it may not be able to be proved conclusively through material means or through logic alone. Her research methodologies and conclusions allow room for personal life experience to fuse with educational knowledge in order to impart much hope to humanity. Consider her major contributions: She restored to us at least thirty thousand years of herstory that we had been deprived of. She reminded us that there was a time when the world lived more peacefully and equitably, male and female together, and that this could have gone on for millennia. If, today, we could reclaim our ancestors' wisdom, we might yet live in more egalitarian and peaceful relationships. Additionally, Gimbutas gave us the examples, the mythos and ethos of an era in which humanity believed in the reality of the spirit world and worshipped a supreme creator, a divine creatress, known as the Great Mother. Lastly, during this pre-patriarchal period of thousands of years, people respected the earth and all of non-human nature. They venerated both the powers of the heavenly bodies and those of all living things and beings, believing they, too, had souls.

If it were just these conclusions that we could take away from the great volumes of facts and inner knowing that Marija Gimbutas has bequeathed to us, and if this could stand as an example of "how it was done" once by our ancestors, this alone would constitute an extraordinary contribution that Marija Gimbutas has made to our contemporary civilization. There was one volume that remained unfinished when Gimbutas died, and Miriam Robbins Dexter completed it. The book, entitled *The Living Goddess* (University of California Press, 2001), brings Gimbutas's remaining research to us as the gift of her posthumous legacy. And, though Gimbutas has been duly criticized by the specialists in her field, as Blaise Pascal once said, "The heart has its reasons that reason doesn't know." One might take this thought into consideration when coming down too strongly in opposition to someone's theory whose roots include unique memories and unusual life experiences.

As I said at the start, Merlin Stone was most important to me and of major importance to the movement, anchoring us in facts and scholarship. Even so, in this introduction to a book remembering Merlin and her work, I felt it was important to contextualize her moment by mentioning the names of others who either preceded her or wrote on these subjects during the period in which the Goddess movement began to take shape. With the publication of these books, the yearning for more knowledge of the pre-patriarchal herstory of women increased. Women's studies programs were founded, and the educational landscape was finally prepared to receive Merlin Stone's *When God Was a Woman,* with its more finely tuned critical eye and a more refined ear. Merlin had already encountered misinformed pronouncements about the superiority of women over men. Critics of the earlier books were all too willing to point out the misconstrued idea that Goddess-revering eras were necessarily matriarchies. The observation of the power and status of women in Goddess-revering cultures had much truth to it. But it was Merlin Stone who provided a critical advance—the analysis of the relationship between biology, the gender of the deity, and generalizations about the superiority of women. Merlin researched the Goddess with more accuracy and subtlety than others.

What strikes us, right from the start, about Merlin Stone's book is how honest she is about the lack of written material about these millennia. In her Introduction, she tells us how shocked she was to find this out. She takes us along with her on her quest to uncover more information by visiting the many libraries, museums, universities, and excavations in Europe and the Near East in order to piece the larger picture together for us. Even when encountering the vastness of the patriarchal destruction of the ancient religion and civilization of the Goddess, she is careful to include the discovery that vestiges of this religion continued to be honored and even practiced during the patriarchal conquest.

Merlin discloses the multiple means that were employed to rid the world of all traces of these practices over time. Her position is that of a women's studies scholar who notes that only male authors had created the narrative of this history, and that they revealed their biases through their use of language itself. Merlin has always stressed how extremely incorrect was their use of the term "fertility cult" to describe a "religion" that prevailed for millennia over the vast territories of Europe and the Near East. Her book is a call to women's studies scholars, present and future, to become pioneers along with her. And, from the perspective of today, where we now find hundreds of women's studies (feminist studies, gender studies, etc.) programs across the nation, we understand that her invitation was a clarion call to re-search and re-vise all the inherited androcentrically biased narratives of pre-history. Typical of the methodology of women's studies scholars, Merlin always shows us how a particular version of a myth or other narrative is based on a male perspective, and how it inscribes a patriarchal version of history into all of our education about the most ancient civilization and religion. She problematizes issues about which previous writers had made incorrect proclamations based on their preconceived convictions. Thus, she questions the relationship between the sex of the divine creator and the status of women in a particular society. She teaches us how one cannot assume that, just because an entire country worships a Goddess, their women are treated with respect or are accorded an elevated social status. Rather, she explains that it is not necessarily the sex of the divinity that implies a high status, but, on the contrary, it is mostly the strength of the female kinship system. When it is matrilineal, that leads to the deity being female.

Merlin's work exhibits a constant subtlety of thought, and she is often surprised by her own discoveries when they contradict what might have been assumed to be the case through intuition alone. Her methodology deftly shows the importance of both documentation and intuition, but she is always careful to distinguish between the two. She did make some speculative observations, as others have done, linking words and their roots from language to language, when in fact they might not be related at all. Thus, she speculates that the Hebrew Levites, the priestly class, might have been related to the Indo-Europeans where we find groups named Luwains, Luvains, and Luvites among the Indo-Europeans. But Merlin confesses that this might be a controversial speculation, and she invites others to take it into consideration. She does not proclaim it to be truth. She suggests that if we dare to make these speculations and then find the proof (and only then), that this will help us immensely to understand the practices of the different groups throughout time, and will shed light on why their practices were suppressed.

Merlin always recalls that the Hebrews continued to worship the goddesses Ashtoreth, Asherah, and Anath, baking cakes for the "Queen of Heaven" until all their idols had been destroyed and the last of the temples of the Goddess had been closed, circa fifth century BCE. Merlin's book is an excellent example of how one can deploy the imagination and yet qualify fantastic speculations by pointing out that they are not confirmed as true. She invites the reader to entertain her (or his) own speculations because they just might lead to revelations, as long as they are admitted to be simply proposals for further investigation.

Thus, I realized that we had a longer and more complex herstory to be uncovered. This also was the time when African Americans were learning about their origins and history. Women of all backgrounds and religions asked what our actual origins were, and what were women's contributions to civilization. We were asking how much information had actually been omitted from the history books, how much knowledge of our origins we had been deprived of, and how much of our prestige and power had been erased and silenced. We learned from Merlin Stone how immense that herstory was, and how great were the contributions to culture made by women, often under the aegis of the goddesses of their cultures. We learned how tremendous was the excision of these millennia long past, where women's status and power as priestesses and queens prevailed for centuries before patriarchy, but also that these millennia were associated with what seemed to have been pacific, non-warrior values, and that their citizens revered both spirit and nature.

It should be said that the list of names of those who have worked hard for the women's movement and Goddess studies is so long that there is the danger, if I tried to make such a list, that I would inadvertently leave out an important name. We also know that no one doing our good work is unimportant. Yet I have been present at events where colleagues of Gimbutas criticized her, even insulted her, in public. But the admirers and the students—the women who had taken her classes, both in the university and at home, and the women who were mentored by her—went on to continue this work both with her and after she died. Women would come out in great numbers to support her at her celebrations, knowing that those who opposed her would be present and would try to put her down—either out of a sense of competition, jealousy, or adherence to established academic versions leading them to the conviction that they were correct and she was wrong. Merlin Stone, herself, has said she encountered vehement and ongoing opposition to her work—even a death threat. Many of you know what it is like for a woman to write about the Goddess. As Geoffrey Ashe warned me so long ago, "If this is how they critique men who write about the Goddess, just wait until you see how they will treat women." Yet we work on, as we must, and thus, it is wonderful to have this new book—containing new writings by Merlin Stone and much information even we, who knew her, didn't know.

merlin stone
timeline

Merlin Stone, 1992.

Merlin Stone Timeline

1931   Born Marilyn Claire Jacobson on September 27th in Flatbush, Brooklyn, NY.

1945   Graduated from Public School #217, Brooklyn, NY.

1949   Graduated Erasmus Hall High School with Metallic Art Medal Award.

1949   Entered State University of New York, Buffalo.

1950   Married and took husband's last name, "Stone."

1952   Daughter Jenny born.

1955   Daughter Cynthia born.

1958   Conferred bachelor of science degree and teacher's certificate (art), with minor in journalism, from State University of New York, Buffalo.

1958–60   Art teacher at Kenmore Junior High School, Buffalo, NY.

1962   Assistant art professor, State University College, Buffalo. Albright Knox Annual Sculpture Award (also awarded in 1965).
              Interest in ancient religions begins to influence her artwork and thinking.

1963–64   Divorced and moved to a farmhouse in upstate New York, where she continued to sculpt and exhibit her work.

1965   Returned to Buffalo, NY, and continued work as a sculptor.
              Taught children's creative arts classes at Albright-Knox Art Gallery, Buffalo.
              Completed summer session at California College of Arts and Crafts in Oakland, CA.

1966   Assistant Professor of Sculpture, State University of New York, Buffalo.

1958–66	Exhibited and commissioned to create architectural public artworks.
1967	Awarded teaching scholarship to attend California College of Arts and Crafts. Moved to California (Oakland, Berkeley).
1968	Received master of fine arts degree from California College of Arts and Crafts (dissertation title: "Energy & Art").
1967–70	Artistic work during this period included kinetic sculpture, "environments," light-shows, "happenings," performance art, and collaborations between artists and engineers. Taught courses at University of California Berkeley Extension. Began research and writing about matriarchal Goddess-worshipping cultures.
1969	Experiments in Art and Technology (E.A.T.) Bay Area chapter coordinator.
1970	Devoted herself to research and writing from a feminist perspective about ancient religions and influence on feminist thought.
1972	Moved to London, where she continued to research and write. Conducted research at British Museum Library (London) and Ashmolean Museum Library (Oxford).
1972–73	Traveled widely to collect evidence and additional research material for her books: Lebanon—Baalbek, Beirut, Byblos; Greece—Athens, Delphi, Eleusis, Smyrna, Halicarnassus, Rhodes; Crete—Agios Nikolaos; Iraklion, Knossos, Phaistos, Agia Galini, Lato, Chania; Turkey—Ankara, Ephesus, Istanbul, Marmaris, Selcuk, Mersin; Cyprus—Kition, Nicosia, Paphos.

1974   *Spare Rib Magazine*, London, featured an article by
        Merlin titled "The Paradise Papers."
        Married again (kept last name "Stone") and moved to
        Quadra Island, British Columbia.
        Continued research and writing.

1975   Widowed after thirteen months of marriage.
        Returned to London, then departed via Heathrow,
        arriving June 28, 1975, in Miami Beach, Florida, to help
        her mother care for her father, who had Alzheimer's
        disease.

1976   First edition of *The Paradise Papers* published by Virago
        Press, England.
        Met Lenny Schncir in Miami Beach, and soon after
        moved into his New York City apartment.
        Dial Press obtained rights to *The Paradise Papers* and
        republished under new title, *When God Was a Woman.*

1979   Completed manuscript for *Ancient Mirrors of Womanhood*
        and decided to publish using her own alternative press,
        New Sibylline Books.

1981   Authored a monograph entitled *Three Thousand Years
        of Racism* (New Sibylline Books).

1983   Writing included in the *Encyclopedia of Religion.*

1984   Rights to *Ancient Mirrors of Womanhood* sold to Beacon
        Press, Boston.

1989   *The Goddess Remembered*, a film produced by the
        National Film Board of Canada, featured Merlin Stone,
        together with three other feminist pioneers.

1990   Interviewed for *New Dimensions Radio,* PBS
        programming, "Return of the Goddess."

1993   Honorary doctoral degree awarded by the California
        Institute of Integral Studies, San Francisco, CA.

1995   Completed writing of unpublished novel, *One Summer
        on the Way to Utopia* (aka *Dreams of Getting There*).

1976–2005 Presented at conferences, workshops, and classes throughout the United States and abroad.

2005 Declining health.

Lenny and Merlin moved to Daytona Beach, FL.

2008 Diagnosed with pseudobulbar palsy.

2011 Merlin passed away on February 23rd, in Daytona Beach, FL, expressing that she had accomplished everything that she wanted to achieve in this life.

my life with
merlin stone:
a memoir

The day after Lenny met Merlin,
September 21, 1976, Key Largo, Florida.

A Note About This Memoir

—*Carol F. Thomas*

Lenny Schneir has written a unique tribute to his partner of thirty-four years. It is part memoir, part love story, reminiscent in many ways of a variety of regional American literary genres. Lenny's story begins as a coming-of-age narrative, a kid growing up in Kew Gardens, New York City. Filled with anecdotes of typical fifties adventures of the young and the restless, the story relates a magical falling in love, romance, and the transformation of a diamond-in-the-rough gambler by a beautiful artist, scholar, writer, and feminist.

I am not alone in this judgment. Miriam Robbins Dexter, PhD, author of *Whence the Goddesses*, calls it "a beautiful work of love ... celebrating the life of Merlin Stone." Vicki Noble, feminist shamanic healer and author of *The Double Goddess*, says, "Lenny Schneir's tribute to Merlin Stone—her life, her person, her work—touched me to the core." And I feel compelled to quote Donna Henes, author of *The Queen of My Self*, who says: "Lenny's chronicle of [Merlin and] their life together was extremely touching. His adoring vision of Merlin enlarged my admiration and respect for her as a supremely principled person who truly walked her talk and lived her ideals. She was an exemplary role model. May we live up to her shining example."

But why do I feel I must preface Lenny's memoir with these words? Because, in fact, at least one prominent feminist declared, "Lenny, you just don't get it." She felt a book about Merlin should be authored entirely by women, and that Lenny, though Merlin's life partner for all those years, really was not the one to praise her. Clearly, I and others strongly disagree. I first met Lenny when I was giving a poetry reading at the Casements, a cultural center in Ormond Beach, Florida, near where we both live. I had just finished reading when a tall gentleman approached wearing a brilliantly colored tie-dyed dashiki and bandana. His demeanor was courtly and he was very complimentary of my reading. The poems I read that evening suggested a need for change in the deeply asymmetrical relationship in contemporary American culture and a critique of the patriarchal lexicon, which leaves out any trace of women's voices, sensibilities, or perspective.

After introducing himself, Lenny told me who he was—the loving partner of Merlin Stone for thirty-four years, the last three spent attending to her as she fought valiantly against a cruel disease that rendered her voiceless and helpless. Lenny asked me if I would help him create a memoir/tribute to his beloved partner. As he told me bits of his story, he could not have known that I was very familiar with Merlin Stone's landmark books, research, and scholarship in *When God Was a Woman* and *Ancient Mirrors of Womanhood*. Her books were crucial in the research for my teaching and writing, as well as that of my students at a number of colleges and universities.

When we met for a second time to discuss Lenny's project, I was deeply impressed with his breadth and depth of knowledge of very specific and different fields of expertise. He was well known in the world of collectors of memorabilia, and the author of *Gambling Collectibles: A Sure Winner*, which built his reputation among serious collectors, gamblers, and poker players. As he continued with his narrative, he also revealed the development of a growing appreciation of a wider world that included an admiration of the extraordinary sculptures of his partner and her fame as both artist and art historian, scholar and accomplished author. He also developed a deepened understanding of the voice and heightened sensibilities of the woman, both as artist and partner, a partner who would not suffer male chauvinists easily.

This memoir, which Lenny related to David Axelrod and to me, is genuinely in Lenny's own voice. We have worked hard to preserve his point of view and even his speech patterns. We did that because the more time we spent with Lenny, the more we saw him as more than just a man who adored and assisted his partner, the famous Merlin Stone. We came to feel that he was, in many ways, a conduit for her energy. At a benefit memorial celebration in honor of Merlin Stone presented by feminist pioneer Z Budapest in September 2011 in Clearwater, Florida, Lenny made a speech—the earliest version of his memoir—that was so heartfelt as to win over nearly every heart in attendance. The memoir you read here is one more of his gifts given with the intention of not just honoring Merlin, but of assuring that her work as a feminist honoring the Goddess will continue.

My Life with Merlin Stone:
A Memoir
by Lenny Schneir,
as told to David B. Axelrod with Carol F. Thomas

SHE WAS MOTIONLESS, in what I recognized as a full lotus position. I observed her at sunrise from a distance as the sky gradually lightened, bringing more details into focus. She had long, rust-colored hair that gently flowed over her shoulders and down to the middle of her back. She wore a Levi's jacket and, just like I did, bellbottom dungarees, even though it was still very warm in Florida. And there she sat—a vision in the quiet Miami Beach dawn.

As she stirred, I made a move of my own and went over to talk to her.

"Where have you been for the last fifteen minutes?" I asked her, curious about her long, quiet posture.

"You wouldn't believe it if I told you," she replied, and I truly wouldn't have understood.

"So what are you doing here?" I pursued.

"I meditate every morning."

She was receptive, even welcoming, of my advance. She rose to brush the sand off her jeans, put her open-toe sandals back on, and strode up closer to check me out. It was clear she was quite self-confident. I had an eerie feeling she was more the one who was sizing me up than vice versa. I introduced myself.

"Lenny, from New York."

"Merlin, born in Brooklyn."

"That's an unusual name," I said, wondering what kind of wizard she was. "Are you vacationing down here?"

"I would be in London now except I had to come here to help my mom," she said with a slightly British accent.

That was September 20, 1976, the moment I first saw and spoke to Merlin Stone. But before I go on about our first meeting, "Return with us now to those thrilling days of yesteryear." I was not the Lone Ranger, but I knew what a Lucky Strike was: "LSMFT."

Picture dancing Lucky Strike cigarettes as they intoned, "Lucky Strike means fine tobacco." That was in the 1950s. Some who look back say those were the good old days when there were real family values. Of course, we were also told how great cigarettes were for us—pleasurable, sexy, even healthy. We were shown the ideal family on shows such as *Father Knows Best* and *The Adventures of Ozzie and Harriet*, not to mention *I Love Lucy*, with Ricky Ricardo's endlessly scolding and even spanking of Lucy for her mischief. These were the ideal and iconic albeit unattainable families and portrayals of the roles of father, mother, and "above average" children. Not only did father know best, but the wives, and mothers within the family, were to be obedient and subservient helpmates. Oh, those were the good old days.

I was a teenager living in the '50s, when these were the sacred rules for many families. I lived with my mother and sister in the middle-class New York City neighborhood of Kew Gardens, Queens. My mother was called a housewife, attempting to live up to the ideal portrayal, which our culture mandated. But my father was often absent from our fifth-floor apartment. He was a shoe manufacturer. He and my mother seemed to have a tacit agreement that he did not have to abide by the stereotypical ideals of the American husband.

My father and I had such a distant relationship that I never called him "Dad." He liked to smoke and drink, gad about—travel, gamble, drive a fancy car. My father wanted to be a bon vivant, living the American dream, but he was completely disinterested in his family. He always worked hard, to the point of being driven. My mother complained to me about my father's lack of interest in her and the family. Even as she reluctantly acquiesced to the lifestyle he imposed, she continued to hope that he might cease his obvious "escapades." As a young male myself, I missed having a father figure, though his absence gave me the time and freedom to become my own man.

It hurt me to hear my mother complain. We loved each other and were close throughout our lives. Though I was just a kid, she trusted me with her thoughts.

"I'm a doormat," she would reveal sadly while seated at the kitchen table in her flower-print housedress. "I wish I had a happy marriage. I don't understand him."

"He takes care of us," I would say, trying to console her, but it was a weak try. I knew that in my father's eyes, money and status had tremendous importance. But for my mother, money had little meaning. She was searching for his love, so there really wasn't anything I could say to console her. My mother hoped he would change, but he never did. The result of my father's absence was that I was a juvenile delinquent in my own mind.

I worshipped James Dean in *Rebel Without a Cause*, Marlon Brando in *The Wild One*, and everything Elvis Presley. I lived in a *Blackboard Jungle* of my own creation, which brings me back to LSMFT—Lenny Schneir Means F-ing Trouble. That's what I told my friends it stood for. I was a twelve-year-old smoker, free spirit, and rebel, antisocial and ready for the gamble called life.

That, at least, was how I wanted to see myself. My mother actually changed the hospital record of my birth—from May 20, 1941, to April 20, 1941—so she could enroll me in school a year earlier. I was what my mother called "a handful." She didn't know what else to do with me. That set me on a course of competing with the older boys in my class—acting every bit the clown until I actually got a handle on what would impress them. Thereafter, even before my teens, I was the leader of a small pack of pranksters and street adventurers. We didn't do any major harm. We were more mischievous than malicious, though I certainly was a bully to many during that time. As I have grown older and wiser, I realize the harm I caused, for which I am truly sorry.

I learned early on how to manipulate my mother. I did what I wanted. I could escape the apartment whenever I pleased.

"Where are you going?" my mother would naturally ask.

"Down," I'd say, joking about our living on the fifth floor.

"You're too young. You shouldn't be going out," Mom would say, and then add ironically, "Look both ways, even on a one-way street."

And off I would go, first to the schoolyard, and then into the world of fun and games. My best friend, Nick, had four brothers, and on Friday evenings I'd go over to his house, where his parents would bring out some worn playing cards and a cigar box full of pennies. They would divide them equally and we would play poker. It was family togetherness, an eight-handed game—seven family members and me. At the end of each session, we all put our pennies back in the box. I almost always lost, but in doing so, I learned to love the game.

Another idea of a good time, around 1955, was to gather some friends and take the subway to the "city," where we would heckle the street preachers near the Camel sign in Times Square. They'd stand on their soapboxes, a Bible in one hand and an American flag on a stanchion at their side. They would shout their Gospel message to a crowd, and we would stand at the edge driving them crazy:

"The Bible says, 'Repent. You are all sinners.'"

"Takes one to know one!" we'd shout.

"God will judge you."

"Who says there's a God?" I'd scream, and my friends and the crowd would crack up. Later in life, I realized it wasn't a bad idea that I rejected God as a bearded old man in the sky, dressed in robes, looking down at all of us to judge our every move and dictating who goes to heaven or hell. Besides heckling the preachers, my gang and I loved the thrill of the penny arcade, skee-ball, shooting games, the peep shows, and naughty bookstores. At fourteen or fifteen, we thought we were manly men.

I had discovered Times Square as a pre-teen. First, I went there with my friend Monk, who was six years older. He had a route servicing vending machines in Queens and Manhattan, so we walked into some odd establishments. It was about that time I discovered Hubert's Flea Circus, a freak show in the basement of a penny arcade. It was ten cents to enter the place. There was a contortionist, a sword swallower, a tattooed lady, a six-hundred-pound woman, and Strongman Sailor Jim White, who could bend steel bars behind his neck.

Later, I ventured there on my own, fascinated by the action, the strangers and prostitutes. I always loved unusual types of people. I could learn from them. When I realized the excitement that was there, I organized expeditions with my followers—only the guys I picked. We'd ride the subway into the heart of Manhattan and dash in and out of any adult store or show that let us in, along with spending endless hours in the Sam Goody record store. I remember admiring a purple shirt, blue suede shoes, and orange pants in a 42nd Street store window. To me that kind of flash was what life was about. I wasn't even thinking "pimp." I don't think I knew what a pimp was. I was fourteen and wanted to grow up fast, looking teenage cool.

Of course we weren't manly men. We were just attempting to live out our fantasy. But fantasies have a way of vanishing, and I found myself heading toward the University of Denver, bringing all my old ways with me for what became an extremely unique and nontraditional education. The mile-high altitude of Denver agreed with me, two thousand miles away from all responsibilities.

My father made me an offer I couldn't refuse. He promised that if I went to college and didn't flunk out my freshman year, he'd buy me a new car. I applied to a lot of colleges, but only two accepted me. I chose the University of Denver—far away from everything I knew—because I could truly branch out on my own. Actually, I left Kew Gardens, at least in part, because my girlfriend of three years, Legs Levine, wanted to get married. She was sixteen and I was seventeen.

I joined a fraternity and carefully balanced my studies to find the point where I could get Cs and stay in school. Thereafter, college was every bit the adventure I craved—yes, wine, women and song, gambling and poker. Of all those things, school was mostly poker—my major was "poker finance." I grew up a generation before the more popular drugs became available, but there was still plenty of sex and rock and roll.

I tell you all this because I want to be completely honest about the miracle Merlin Stone performed in my life. Modern women, feminists, those who are aware of or worship the Goddess, would definitely have hated me through most of my youth. I was groomed on the prevailing notion that boys and men were "entitled." We could run where we wished and do what we wanted. My father did. His idea of raising me was to show up on Sunday to take the family out for dinner. Or he would hang around a day or so, when I was little, and teach me to ride a bike. When I got older, he'd take me to the track on Saturdays.

He was cool, handsome, and self-assured, and a fancy dresser—suit and tie. He was not so much mean to my mother as commanding. She did what he said. Why would I want anything other than that for myself and from women?

Are you getting a proper picture? I was trying to live up to the image of the typical, hot-to-trot American male. There wasn't a good-looking skirt I didn't admire or chase. There was no reason to regard a woman as anything other than someone I could have a good time with. I should mention that I grew up admiring the heroes of World War II and Korea. Audie Murphy was my idol—the most famous and arguably the most-decorated soldier of WWII. So it made sense to me that I would join the army after I graduated college. That meant six months in Fort Dix, New Jersey, training as an infantry man and machine gunner. In that venerable man's world, I used all my skills to avoid danger.

When I left Fort Dix, I still had to complete five and a half more years of reserve service based at the armory in Flushing, Queens, New York. I settled into something similar to the role of a Sergeant Bilko, eventually attaining the rank of E5, Sarge status. As a handsome young uniformed man, I saw women as entertainment, nothing to get serious about.

I don't want to paint myself as a total user. I was capable of love. I had at least a few romances. Still, marriage was never part of my equation—and especially not children, who I thought would be an anchor. Worse, they might be little Lennies. If a relationship got too serious on her part, I would escape like Houdini.

In the thirty-five years before I met Merlin, I managed to avoid any genuine commitments. I was surviving by using my wits. Because my army reserve duties were in Queens, I returned to my native Kew Gardens, where I tried working for my father in his shoe manufacturing business, but that didn't work out. To his credit, he had bought me that car—a 1960 Chevrolet Impala convertible—that my best friend called a "chick magnet." But I wasn't going to hack it working for my father, because he actually expected me to work. His teaching philosophy was "sink or swim," so I sank. Besides, my life was changing quickly. All my buddies had already left the neighborhood, drugs were exploding into the picture, and I wasn't the leader of the pack anymore.

I was living in Kew Gardens in what was called a "stewardess building," where we all lived three or four in an apartment—an express bus commute to both Kennedy and LaGuardia airports. It was a party building, and I began to use another of my early skills to my advantage. I had saved up some of the money my father sent me for college and the money I won at poker over the years. I began with a couple thousand dollars—a pretty good grubstake in 1962. Gambling went back to my earlier years. I was a penny pitcher, a baseball card flipper, and a winning poker player as a teenager when I gambled with my peers. Now I was playing poker with pilots.

I always enjoyed a good game—a gamble, a wager, a shot at easy money. And I had a knack for it, so I could make some decent simoleons from an early age. I played a skilled percentage game, always learning from the best, and was able to find action whenever and wherever I wanted. When I moved to New York City, I found that people craved a good poker game, and I became a regular at the clubs and private games. I moved into Manhattan in February 1968. Shortly after, I met a gentleman named Harry, who introduced me to the Mayfair Club and the poker scene. The Mayfair wasn't known for poker back then, but mostly backgammon, gin rummy, bridge, and even chess and Scrabble. Over the years, we changed that. Eventually, the best poker players in the city played at the Mayfair. I was making my living.

Years of drinking, smoking, and staying out all night finally caught up with my dad. He had a stroke in 1969, and his business was liquidated. He was only fifty-five and dramatically in decline. He wound up in the Miami Heart Institute, where they rehabilitated him. When he was able to move back to his New York apartment, in the classy old Manhattan area of Gramercy Park, a tall, statuesque Swedish woman moved in with him.

My mother, from whom he was formally separated by then, was all the more hurt, still believing it was her role to care for him. When he died, from a second stroke in 1973, my mother was by his side—not for love, but out of a sense of duty. My mother had been going to Miami Beach for several years already, adding geographical distance to the separation my father had imposed. It was late September in 1976 when I went to visit my mother. Of course, it could have been to escape the dreary northern weather, but this was atypically early for me to journey south.

I don't want to be too mystical as I tell my story. In fact, my intention has been to depict things in a way that would make me most undesirable to those who are likely to read this. I am not exaggerating, but rather trying to set the scene for the miracle that I believe came about in my meeting and loving Merlin Stone. The extent that she transformed me, redirected my life, raised my consciousness, and allowed me to be a participant and in some small way a facilitator in her world-changing work is a part of Merlin's mystique. My real purpose here is to see her legacy live and grow forever.

By the time my father died, at the age of fifty-nine, I had graduated college, completed military service, and landed on my feet. Mom always told me of her regrets that my father wasn't a real family man, so she must have been somewhat relieved after he passed away. Mom was the beneficiary of his life insurance. She was able to collect survivor benefits, and at last, she was free to do more of what she liked. She was no longer accountable to him.

I traveled south to see my mother and stayed with her in what is now funky-fashionable South Miami Beach. I put on my rock-and-roll T-shirt, hippie bellbottoms, and high-top Converse sneakers to just hang out. Sometimes I'd just get up early, find a bench, and watch the sunrise. It was on such a morning that I noticed a woman sitting cross-legged on the sand.

That, as I told you, was the first moment I met and spoke with Merlin Stone.

"What were you doing in London?" I asked her.

"Researching and writing, but I'm here now because my mother needed me."

"She's sick?" I inquired.

"Actually, it was my father. He had Alzheimer's for years and it got so bad my mother couldn't do it all herself, so I came to help."

"That was very noble of you. How's it going with him?"

"He passed away two months ago. I really adored him. He encouraged me when I was young. He believed in me. I sang to him and comforted him at the end."

"That was good. When my father died, he and my mother were separated."

"Sorry to hear that," she said. "Love is different than marriage. My mother is trying to cope on her own now. They were actually a loving couple after all those years."

"I'm here visiting my mother now. I'm staying in her place at the Triton, 29th and Collins," I informed her.

"Our mothers live in the same building. I live across the street in the Glades Hotel."

High school Lenny, 1958.

Hip Lenny, 1973.

"Our mothers probably know each other." I made small talk mostly about the weather—what else? I told her I was a poker player, hoping to impress her. She identified herself only as working the switchboard at the Glades.

We sat on a nearby bench and talked for a couple of hours until, finally, I asked, "Would you like to join me for dinner and a movie tonight?"

"A date?" she countered. "A real date?" And to my delight, she responded, "Yes. See you tonight," and she gave me instructions on how to find her.

What a treasure, I thought. *This beautiful, intelligent woman is staying right across the street. With luck, it might lead to a relationship.* Did I ever mistake how the situation would play out? How completely blind was I? Of course, I didn't recognize what a life-changing moment it was.

When I showed up at the hotel where she lived in what amounted to a storage room located next to the switchboard, I was dressed in my usual dungaree bellbottoms, T-shirt, and Converse sneakers, but she was gorgeous. She didn't have to do anything—no makeup; her skin was smooth and very white. She wore no eye shadow or eyebrow pencil, but her brown eyes were so alive. She did have on some light pink lipstick, no rouge or face powder. She was always that way, so natural. She looked perfect, dressed in that same jean jacket with a feminist symbol, and an "Earth is our Home" button. She was the opposite of a prima donna or princess—a real woman.

Before I went out with Merlin that night, I returned to my mother's apartment and told her and my Uncle Al, who lived nearby, about this woman. "Mom, I met a really interesting woman, and we are going to a movie and dinner tonight."

"Why don't you invite her here? I can cook you dinner."

"You don't have to cook."

"It's no bother. I like to cook. And this way I can meet her."

"Ma, I just met her. I don't even know much about her yet."

"Where does she live?"

"Across the street, and her mother lives here in the building."

"I'm going to Key Largo tomorrow," my Uncle Al piped in. "Ask your new friend if she wants to take a ride with us."

When we went to dinner, I asked Merlin, "Do you want to go to Key Largo tomorrow with me and my Uncle Al and his girlfriend?"

"Let's see how our date goes," she said.

After Chinese food, we went to see *Dog Day Afternoon*, the Al Pacino movie about two men who hold up a bank to get the money to help their friend have a sex change operation. She liked the movie enough that we watched it several more times during our life together—to remind ourselves of that first joyous evening. From the first time we saw it, she was always very empathetic toward a man feeling trapped in his body, wishing he were a woman.

I was still thinking like a male chauvinist pig. "Let's have a drink," I suggested, hoping she would get a bit tipsy. I'd loosen her up a bit. Men!

Merlin didn't drink, nor did I, and for thirty-four-plus years thereafter, we simply weren't drinkers. Merlin didn't need alcohol to loosen up. She was sexually liberated.

"What time tomorrow?" she asked me before I reluctantly left in the wee hours, happy to know we would see each other again that very same morning.

I was instantly aware that something special had happened. She was so strong and enthusiastic; I was spellbound. She was gentle and wise in the ways of love. I felt we were kindred spirits—soulmates.

I guess I'd never known what love was or could be—its infinite possibilities for friendship, tenderness, partnership, with so much more delight, humor, and the desire to be only with each other day and night. I could see that this woman was not just another "love 'em and leave 'em" for me. I was at the start of my learning curve, but I already understood there would be a lot for me to comprehend. What an ardent student I became. The transformation had indeed begun.

Merlin had been doing a lot of odd jobs. Money wasn't important to her, but she had to stay afloat. Working in the hotel was a way for her to absorb knowledge from the elders. She spent a lot of time in the lobby chatting with the old women, gleaning what she could from their stories and philosophies of life. The next day, I had to stand patiently waiting in the lobby while she conversed before we set off on our second date.

The trip with Uncle Al was a pleasant junket. He drove and Merlin and I sat in the back seat holding hands. The conversation was breezy. We were getting to know each other, playing the game "Who do you know and what do you like?"

"The Beatles? The Stones?"

"Me too," she said. "I like folk music."

"Bob Dylan is my favorite writer," I told her.

"I love the voices of Joan Baez, Joni Mitchell, and Judy Collins."

"Me too."

"Do you like sports?"

"The last time I played sports was volleyball in summer camp as a teenager."

"How about poker?"

"I don't gamble, but I like to try new things."

"So do I." Was I forcing the situation? Trying too hard to find commonalities?

"I'm a writer," she told me.

"Really? What do you write?"

"I wrote a book about ancient religion."

"What about ancient religion?" I asked, not particularly interested.

"It's called *The Paradise Papers*. It's about the greatest con game ever perpetuated on women."

"What was that?"

"Adam and Eve."

I had no idea what she was talking about. How could I know the book was the initial version of *When God Was a Woman*, the book that would influence the ways in which women think about themselves, men, one another, their religion, and the world? The beginning of our relationship came just as Merlin was working toward gender equality and a greater respect for humanity and the planet.

Meanwhile, we had one last day together before I was to return home. We spent it viewing art at the Bass Museum. We walked hand in hand around the area and exchanged ideas and personal points of view, learning more about each other. Even then, she didn't reveal that she was an artist—a gifted sculptress who had already built giant mixed-media and welded sculptures on commission from such companies as Union Carbide and the City of Buffalo. Who knew she had already been a professor at two universities, a pioneering feminist? She didn't tell me. She revealed herself only as she wanted me to know. As long as I knew her, she could still conjure up amazing surprises.

She was going to Boston to see her sister, Myrna, who had stored things for her. Then, Merlin was going to move to San Francisco to be close to her grown daughters.

"Merlin, on the way to Boston, come see me in New York." I was in love with her already. "You can share my place and space."

"I'll stop on the way," she said. "I'm curious to see how you live." And there she was, just three days later, ringing my bell at 184 6th Avenue in New York City.

She stayed two nights before she left for Boston.

"Stay with me here," I begged her. This wasn't normal for me. I wasn't trying to be manipulative. To myself, I was thinking, "I want this to work. Don't lose this chance. Make this miracle happen."

"I have my own plans," she answered, and off she went.

"Come back, come live with me," I pleaded with her on the phone when she got to Boston.

Finally, after days of my efforts, "I'm coming back," she agreed.

"I'm so happy, I don't know what to do."

"I trust you. You know exactly what you're doing," she said, and that, oh love, was Merlin's mantra throughout our entire relationship—something she said thousands of times during our relationship. What a gift that was. What more could anyone ask of a partner?

I had been hosting a poker game at my place once a week, and I could make a couple hundred bucks that way. I moved the poker table to my cousin's apartment next door, where the game continued weekly.

I had no clue who this woman was. I wanted to buy her a welcome present. I bought her a lacy Victorian hand fan, with tortoise-shell decorations—very feminine—thinking it would be to her liking. Later, when I gave it to her, she was too polite to say, "Strike one." But sometimes I did feel as if I could lose her if I stubbornly kept going in the wrong direction, making poor decisions, not learning, progressing, or absorbing fast enough.

So when she arrived, she informed me, "I'm a writer. I need to make this space a writer's room." That meant finding her the right furniture in a now-empty front room.

"I need an armoire."

The apartment had only one small closet filled with my own rags. She arrived with just a backpack, but she was going to have things sent to her. I took her to a used furniture store, where I expected to take charge and pick something out. Not. The vibes were, "I'll handle this. Back off."

She chose a large double-door wardrobe, which she immediately set out to restain. Who knew she could do such a thing? Apartment-dwelling New York City fellows like myself were anything but handy. It wasn't our strong suit.

"You'll ruin it," I told her.

"It will be easy," she reassured me, and headed out to the hardware store two blocks away.

"You'll get stain all over the parquet floor," I complained.

"Just watch me," she announced, setting up her tools after she returned with everything she needed. A day later, she had done it. She had stained the armoire dark and light, a perfect two-tone, so the doors came alive with details that looked like eyes, the grains contrasting dramatically. The floor was cleaner than when she started. From that first artistic improvement on, it was always that way. The die was cast.

"I need a table," she told me.

"I'll take you to a shop I know," I said, but luckily, by then, I was making progress. I could see my two cents' worth wasn't needed.

"I'll take this one," she told the shopkeeper. "Thirty-five bucks, delivered." *A good price negotiator, too,* I thought.

"Bookshelves," she told me. Her sister, daughters, relatives, and friends were quickly sending books and papers. I bought her some tall shelves at a drugstore that was going out of business and had them moved into the room Merlin was making her own. I added a rocking chair, an antique trunk, and an old shoe rack to make her feel more at home. All this was happening quickly—in just the first few weeks.

It was a transition I was comfortable with. "How come?" I might have asked myself, but furnishing the room together with Merlin was actually refurbishing my own interior emotional and intellectual self. I was learning intuitively what we could be for each other. Empty room, empty heart. She filled them both. We were together for two months, during which the relationship was blooming. I felt like I was the first male to give birth. When Merlin arrived, a new Lenny was born.

I was cutting back on poker nights, spending my time helping her get her life together in New York. Merlin wasn't one to watch television, and I, myself, only had an old fifteen-inch TV, which, like a lot of old hippies, I kept hidden. We were still getting a sense of each other's tastes and habits, so I invited her to play a game.

"Merlin, let's play Scrabble." I was good at the game.

"Okay, but first I want to read the rules."

They were printed on the inside of the box, so I handed her the box cover and she studied them for a while as I made a place for us to play on our bed.

Merlin went first and spelled "Gaia."

"What's that?" I asked her.

"It's a real word," she reassured me.

It only earned her ten points, so I didn't challenge it. Had I looked it up, I'd have learned it was the name of an early mother goddess, but proper names aren't allowed in Scrabble.

After three turns, it became clear that Merlin wasn't trying to win the game. I was already way ahead when her turn came and she played another word that looked like a name.

"Six," she said triumphantly.

"But Merlin," I observed, "the word isn't even attached to another word." I let it stand, but I was catching on.

"Ante." I spelled a poker word worth four points. I wasn't trying to win either. And I noticed a tiny glint in her eye.

"You don't have to keep score," she suggested.

We continued the game in similar fashion, having a lot of laughs. It was much more fun after that—with no pressure at all. And indeed, we ended the game with the strangest words spelled out across the board.

"What was that about?" I asked for clarification. "Why did we play like that?"

"There'll never be any competition between us. No game playing, no aggression, no keeping score, no winners or losers. Only cooperation."

A light clicked on for me. I thought it would be my chance to shine, but she refocused me completely using the Scrabble game. It was liberating. I didn't have to be better than her. Not much later, if not already by then, I knew it would be crazy for me to even try to compete with Merlin.

Everything fit. We were off and running, but it was hard to keep pace with Merlin. She was just smarter, stronger, and more energetic.

She certainly had better taste and ideas. Deal me in! "Next stop," as Merlin herself would often say, "paradise."

Our lives blended together easily. We'd eat all our meals out at the Vandam Diner across the street except for the twice-weekly pizza slices we shared. Neither of us cooked. I didn't even have a kitchen. Okay, I had a twenty-inch stove and a small fridge, but both were out in a small, unheated alcove at the back of my two rooms. All I had for food before I met her were a few cans of soup that I kept on top of the fridge. Merlin built shelves over the stove. She borrowed the tools from the lumberyard nearby. They loved her there because she could speak their language.

Gradually, she settled into the life she wanted to lead.

I loved her. I was so happy. She was not a burden of any kind. I didn't need to make any real adjustments. My days and nights were a delight with Merlin, although there were some challenges.

Merlin told me, "You should meditate." She did so often.

I tried, but "no can do," I told her. "I've already got an empty head," I'd say, trying to joke my way out of it. But the truth was, at that time, my mind was always racing.

She, on the other hand, was communicating with her Goddess. Much as she tried to help me all through our years, I could never find that meditative state, but her advice did have an effect on me, helping me to be a better observer. Not coincidently, it seemed like my results at the poker table were also on the upturn. I was earning much more in two nights a week than I made with more frequent sessions before Merlin came to live with me.

It was about two months into our relationship, in December 1976, when Merlin said, "I want you to meet my daughters." She was slowly letting me know about the life she had lived before we met. Her daughters were already establishing their own lives in San Francisco. Jenny, the oldest, was a printer, and later became a teacher and school administrator. Cynthia became a sous chef and a long-time fashion designer in Paris. Both found loving husbands, and each had two children. Merlin was always so delighted when her grandchildren came for a visit.

Did I mention yet that Merlin was ten years my senior? She never looked it. Most observers would have seen me as her older companion. I would have been shocked to know that she was forty-five when we met in Miami Beach. She was in such fabulous condition.

I'm not saying this from a male-chauvinist point of view. I just want to admire how much vitality she had—what strong energy. She was five six and one hundred twenty-two pounds when she moved in. Her stomach was flat, with well-defined abs. Her back was well muscled. Even her arms and grip were strong—the result of carrying a large, heavy backpack during her travels.

She told me more about Jenny and Cynthia to prepare me for our trip. She had married in 1950, at the age of nineteen. The groom was the father of their two daughters, born in 1952 and 1955. The marriage lasted until a divorce in 1964, after which Merlin moved to a farm in East Aurora, near Buffalo, New York. There, she worked in a large barn, sculpting and painting.

"I had to get out of it," she told me.

"I wasn't scared. I wasn't even worried," she said. She was still Marilyn Stone, not yet Merlin. She was a single mom who would have to make her own way. From what she told me, it seems like she left him to establish a more independent identity than that of a conventionally married woman.

She was already breaking boundaries for women in the arts with her sculpting. In fact, it was her early interest in women's figures as she studied sculptures in museums that alerted her to the possibility that women were far more important in ancient history than men acknowledged. She was creating new worlds for women.

"Leaving him made a feminist of me," she declared.

"I have no idea what that means," I confessed. That was early in the relationship, and she really never spoke about him again. But I know that their separation gave Merlin the chance to pursue her passions. By 1966–67, she was already writing for a women's newspaper in the Bay Area. (I've lost track of the name of it.)

One night, soon after she arrived to stay with me, I turned on a sitcom for a little entertainment. Throughout all our years, she never watched much TV, but I indulged at the time.

"Let's turn this off," she said, reaching for the remote while we lay in our bed watching the nightly news.

"What's wrong?" I asked.

"Didn't you notice what he just said?" she asked me.

"What?"

"That dumb blonde joke," she coached me.

"How many blondes does it take to change a lightbulb? I thought it was funny."

"That's the trouble with the way men act toward women," she continued. "Language is important. If you speak ill of people, you treat them badly."

This was all news to me. It wasn't something I would have thought about, but I was open to the idea.

"He insulted me," she said. "Sexist language."

"I guess I get it," I said, though I didn't grasp the importance of this early lesson at that moment. It was a slow process for me, and Merlin became my patient instructor. It wasn't as if she made a list of forbidden words, but for me there would be no more "babe" or "bitch." No more blonde jokes, that's for sure. Certainly no casual references to female parts of the body. Eventually, no sexist, no racist, no hateful words at all. And no references to God as "Our Father," "He," or "Him." From that moment on, I would become more and more aware of how people spoke—a practice we both adopted and promoted for the rest of our days together. Learning to be aware of how people use language even made me a better poker player.

Not long after that, I came back to the apartment and told Merlin about a poker friend of mine whose wife was an editor at Bantam Press. "I told him I would set up a meeting so she could meet you."

"I can't do it," she said.

"Why?" I asked her. "It's a great opportunity." Of course, the opportunity was, as much as anything, for me to impress my friend with this cool woman I was hooking up with.

"Don't you get it?

"Not exactly, Merlin. Don't you want to help me?"

"You're just using me to show off." Bingo! She had already drawn me out. She sensed immediately it was as much about me—probably more—than about her.

"So, you don't want me to help?"

"Not that way. I need time for myself. I'm writing my book. We'll do those things when the time is right."

I started to raise my voice, "I'm not being selfish. This is a good idea."

"You're bringing me into something I don't want to do," she said calmly. I don't remember Merlin ever losing her temper with me or raising her voice. Then, and throughout our relationship, she never expressed anger, and still won every disagreement.

I went into the other room, fuming, and there I let myself think a moment. "I'm happy with Merlin. She's setting up her room. We're getting along fabulously. She's busy with her writing project. It's not that big a deal, this meeting." I took a deep breath and went back into her room.

"I'm sorry," I was surprised to hear myself say. *Why am I apologizing?* I thought. But this required an apology. The better part of me, the part Merlin was tapping into, was already seeing more clearly. I didn't need to seek status—particularly if it meant trying to push Merlin to do what she didn't want to do. I knew that I loved her. It occurred to me what it was.

"Merlin, you know what?"

"What?"

"I'm sorry it was me, me, me. I made a mistake."

"Don't worry about it. It's over."

She just let it go, and always did. I actually never found a reason to raise my voice again in all the years of our relationship.

It was fairly early on in our days together that one of Merlin's friends asked her what kind of fellow she was living with. Merlin laughed and replied, "Well, he protects me, he takes care of me, he makes me laugh, and he brings home the money. I feel comfortable and at home with him. What more could a woman ask for?" she told her friend. I was so happy Merlin felt at home. Actually, I didn't have much of a résumé and I wasn't a good wage earner at the time. I wanted to be her benefactor, but mine was an erratic lifestyle. She was the one who became "Lady Luck" for me.

When we went to visit them, her daughters and I hit it off. I liked them. They were easy to get along with. Merlin had done her job well. The first trip to San Francisco, at Christmastime in 1976, was interesting for us as a couple. I was cold, bothered by the stiff wind and dampness. Merlin always had such good energy, sleeping on top of the quilt that I pulled up to my chin. She laughed at my chill. She went to the University of Buffalo, a state school, not just because she was frugal and could save her folks some money, but because she was a "Buffalo Gal" and she loved cold weather.

She took me to Lombard, known as the most crooked street in San Francisco. We rode the cable cars and went to every book and antique store we could find. She knew the city well, explaining that she had lived first in Oakland and then in Berkeley with her daughters, from 1966 to 1972, so she was close enough to really get to know San Francisco. She had a great sense of direction. She loved her maps. Wherever we went, we would buy maps and she would spread them out on her lap. With this remarkable, intrepid woman by my side, I would never be lost.

This was the woman who set out, in 1972, to research her landmark books. She went unaccompanied to Lebanon, Greece, Turkey, Cyprus, Crete, and other countries. She slept in caves, often hitchhiking or traveling by bus to libraries, museums, and archeological sites, gathering bits and scraps of information, most of which had been destroyed or hidden away. She did all this with little money and no direct knowledge of the culture or languages. She was among men whose viewpoints were then, and remain, hostile to women.

Merlin guided us both wherever we needed to go. Her good energy and enthusiasm set the tone for the many trips we took together.

But it didn't start all that smoothly. I still needed coaching. On one early occasion, I suggested we go to Pennsylvania Dutch Country, where she could enjoy observing their countercultural lifestyle. After a two-hour ride, we pulled into a rest stop. When it was time to get back on the road, she refused.

"I'm not getting in that car with you," she declared.

"What's the problem, Merlin?" I asked, totally clueless.

"I told you to slow down. You're a speeder and you drive recklessly."

"Why drive slow?" I asked. I was driving the way I always drove, like a racecar driver at the Speedway.

"If you want me to get in the car," she informed me, "you'll have to promise not to speed. No weaving. No tailgating."

Who the fuck are you, the police? I thought, but there was no way I would have said it. I loved her, though she was not yet smitten with me. This was going to take some advanced strategy. Meanwhile, she was walking away.

"Wait up!" I called, catching up to her and touching her elbow. "Okay, Merlin, if that's all it takes—no speeding, no tailgating, and no basket weaving," I joked to lighten the moment.

She got in the car. You can bet the ranch I kept my word. A little piece of me was doing a slow burn, but what she said next fixed that fairly quickly.

"Be a careful driver. I've got places to go, and so do you." It was amazing how much her compliments meant to me. From then on, she never missed an opportunity to praise my driving, always reminding me how I made her feel safe and secure.

Between Merlin teaching me better habits and her having extraordinarily good luck, I can't remember her ever giving me bad advice.

It was only about three months into our relationship when I told Merlin openly, clearly, "I am in love with you. Do you love me?"

"Yes," she said.

"You know, Merlin, I'm in the *Guinness Book of World Records.*"

"For what?" she played along.

"For falling in love with you instantly. How long did it take you to fall in love with me?"

"It took me a little longer to unpack my toothbrush."

She had showed up with little more than a battered mountain backpack. If she had needed to leave, it wouldn't have taken her long. She was the Ruby Tuesday of the Rolling Stones when I met her, but not because she was irresponsible. Rather, she was open to taking any turn in the road of life she wanted. She had always lived that way.

When Merlin and I lived in New York City, we'd pick places to travel, often just short trips with a rental car. City folks didn't have to own cars. We would take the subway to the Port Authority Bus Terminal and take a bus to Kingston, New York. We'd have a meal at the diner and make a call to Enterprise Rent-a-Car. They'd pick us up. And, as habit had it, I'd wind up at the wheel, headed toward Phoenicia, New York, where we'd rent a cabin. Phoenicia seemed suitable because it was, after all, the name of an ancient civilization and Merlin, at the time, was fully engaged in writing her next book, *Ancient Mirrors of Womanhood.*

"I feel like I'm on my honeymoon," I told her when we would go to the cabin in Phoenicia. We must have rented that cabin at least a hundred times in our thirty-four years together. Merlin, herself, began to call it our "honeymoon suite," and each time we retreated there, it was our honeymoon all over again. The love and tenderness, the joy and passion we found with each other over the years not only never waned, but it deepened and enriched both of our lives. We were happiest when we were alone together.

Over the years, a person's greatness can eclipse their real humanity. Merlin always believed that one good indication of intelligence was a sense of humor. She loved to laugh, so I always tried to be funny. She was serious when necessary, but between us, we could get silly. Of course, it was all I could do to try to keep up with her linguistically, but we enjoyed exchanging our unique lexicons.

In Phoenicia, we'd lean over the railing of a bridge, a short walk from our cabin, to watch as people in huge truck innertubes made into platform rafts floated down the Esopus River. They'd bounce off the rocks and fall out of their little crafts, and we'd laugh.

"Man overboard!" I'd shout, even if it was a woman.

"Shall we throw them one of our Life Savers?" she'd ask, reaching for a roll of the candy in her shoulder bag.

"Does that look like fun to you?"

"We'll jump off that bridge when we get to it."

"It's a bridge over troubled waters for me. I'm not jumping in."

"They are pretty good-looking for tubers."

"You're an expert linguini-ist," I'd tell her, praising her cleverness with words.

We rejoiced in the sunshine, the screams and laughter of the adventurers on the river, our own sense of mirth, and our love for each other. Merlin always said, "Do what's fun and let it energize and excite you, as long as it doesn't hurt you or anyone else." With her, that was the easiest thing I ever did.

For the next two years after we got back from our visit to see her daughters in San Francisco, Merlin was writing *Ancient Mirrors of Womanhood*. I surprised her with the new technological tool of her time: an Apple II Mac computer. *When God Was a Woman* and *Ancient Mirrors of Womanhood* started as notes she took while she traveled—written and carried in her backpack as she researched. Then, she transferred her notes meticulously on a portable typewriter back in London. Merlin infused tremendous energy into the movement for women and men alike, not with conventional methods but with a typewriter. The result, ultimately, has been a victory for all people in search of gender peace and equality.

In our apartment, where she had carved out the front of our two rooms as her own place, she sat at a long, old wooden claw-footed table—not a desk, but a wide space to spread out on, books and all.

The room was lit by a chandelier I had reclaimed from a dumpster. It was crystal, with marble-sized balls on strings, positioned exactly over her table. She had a heavy, old wooden desk chair with arms to help her rest while taking a healing breath. She worked there for hours at a time. When Merlin moved in, she opened the shutters I had kept closed. I lived on the parlor floor and didn't want folks looking in. My friends named my apartment "the morgue" when I lived there alone.

Merlin opened those shutters to the street, literally bringing warmth and sunshine into our lives. She watched the world walking and driving by as she wrote, immersed in her routine. Awake at perhaps 7:00 am, she would make herself a cup of black coffee with sugar, light up a cigarillo, sit down by 7:30, and work for hours.

Often, if I had been playing poker or buying and selling collectibles, I would come home at very odd hours and find her working on the word processor with ideas she had for her books and articles. I'd wake up to her saying, "Let's hit the Vandam," and we'd go out for an hour of lunch or dinner. My being employed away from home gave her an undisturbed place to work. We'd return from our meals and she would joyously go back to her writing. Later, to my delight, she might just put her head on my shoulder. But best of all, when she was finished writing, we'd have only each other.

We would walk three blocks to our favorite haunt, Washington Square Park, and sit near the chess tables where I knew many of the players. When we strolled over to the people playing Scrabble, Merlin was well known there. My friend Josh, one of the best Scrabble competitors in the city, worked at the Strand Book Store. He knew who Merlin was and spread the word.

"Look, that's Merlin Stone," he'd whisper to the other players as she approached. "She's the author of *When God Was a Woman*."

Merlin didn't want to be a celebrity, but people in the neighborhood learned who she was and they would speak to her. She'd be on the bench in front of our house, and two women would regularly invade her space with their presence along with two cups of coffee so they could sit and talk with her. Even the old Italian women in the neighborhood, sitting on their bench as we walked by, would poke each other and say, "That's her."

Merlin and I often went to many other locations, usually by bus or subway—Central Park, Battery Park, South Street Seaport, the financial center, the Hudson River piers, and eventually almost every NYC park. We'd always hold hands. I was holding on to her for dear life.

We walked all over lower Manhattan. We visited museums where she was completely fluent about the artists, the art, the antiquities. She knew every style because she taught art history. She knew the stories at every special museum: the National Museum of the American Indian, the American Museum of Natural History, the Guggenheim Museum, the Museum of Modern Art, the Museum of Jewish Heritage, and so many more. We probably hit them all, and she could have been their tour guide. An extraordinary memory alone does not explain what Merlin knew.

We watched people. I dressed in tie-dyed clothes or fancy Western shirts—still do—and folks noticed. As they approached us, Merlin would lean toward me and say, "Here comes another compliment." Sure enough, someone would say, "Hey man, I love your outfit." Some Merlin had made for me, sewing everything with a needle and thread. We were a groovy couple.

Merlin did not need to dress up to be gorgeous. She actually seemed to disguise her natural beauty. She wore Levi's jeans tucked into knee-high, low-heeled boots—sometimes low-cut Converse sneakers—for the first fifteen years we were together. She usually wore shirts she had made herself, along with a flat-topped, brown suede hat and tinted glasses. In the winter, she wore her peacoat.

A story about the peacoat! She came to New York to live with me on October 1, 1976, with just her mountain backpack. She had no coat and the weather was getting cold. Imagine, she was that far along in her life and all she had or wanted at that moment fit into her backpack. She said, "I need a coat."

"We can go uptown," I suggested, thinking something fashionable.

"I'm thinking peacoat."

Bloomingdale's was selling reproductions for a fancy price as a new fashion trend.

"Do you know where there's an army-navy store with used items?" she asked.

I knew one close to Canal Street. The peacoat she bought that day for eight bucks lasted for more than twenty years. She never desired or needed fancy things. She would save the shards of soap and make them into a larger bar and wash her clothes in the tub. In her travels, she learned how to wash her clothes in rivers, streams, creeks, or even puddles. She shopped for the least expensive items, purchased at the stores on Broadway, Canal, or Orchard Street where they had bargain bins out on the sidewalk. It wasn't because she was cheap as much as she didn't need to prove anything. She was a minimalist. The less I spent, the more she loved me.

"A true believer needs nothing and has everything," she told me. She simply bought only what she needed to survive. Merlin was a waste-not-want-not person. In fact, it was only days later that I told her, "I'm going to Angelo's for a haircut."

"You don't have to go to Angelo. I'll cut your hair."

"You know how to cut hair?" I asked.

"Of course, I know."

"Okay," I told her, "I'm a gambler. I'll take a chance."

"Let's go outside to our bench," she instructed me, picking up scissors, a hand mirror, and a plastic bag. She already had declared a city bench to be ours in Father Fagan Park right in front of our apartment. There, she sat me down and asked, "How do you want it?

"Keep it long as possible, but neat. Trim behind the ears and shape the beard."

She took a snip. She held on to the hair and put it in the plastic bag so she didn't create any litter. Snip. Snip some more. She took her time. The process took at least thirty minutes. Merlin never rushed anything. When she finished, she showed me her work in the mirror.

"Fantastic," I said, and I meant it. "How did you do that?"

"I'm a sculptor," she revealed. Not only was that true, it was a major understatement. That was an important accomplishment I had never heard about until then. She didn't brag. She had nothing to prove to me.

In warmer weather, we'd go out together and, from the way she dressed, you wouldn't have known she was the influential and renowned author I was getting to know. She often wore tights, moccasins, and a black top she had made for herself with straps that were loose and comfortable. In the mornings, I loved to watch her get out of bed and get ready for work. Every move she made was a visual symphony to me.

"I'm on a schedule," she would say. "See you later. Sweet dreams." Just holding her hand, kissing her, touching her skin, hugging her, absorbing her words, and looking into those expressive, brown eyes was paradise.

Early in 1976, Merlin completed *The Paradise Papers: The Suppression of Women's Rites*. The publisher was Virago Press, in association with Quartet Books in London.

"They found me," she loved to say. "Things are constantly being dumped in my lap." And, indeed, she attracted innovative ideas and creative people, always working for a better planet. She was guided, I witnessed, by her Goddess. When I met her in September 1976, the book was selling well for what it was—a mid-level publisher in England, circulating what was, they believed, a "women's tract."

Shortly after Merlin moved in, she gave me a copy of her book. I could barely read it. It was much more than I could handle given the habitual anti-academic life I had cultivated. I just wasn't ready for that type of information. I was the kid who heckled street preachers. I didn't believe in God, much less a Goddess. But others could see the treasure for what it was. The Virago edition of *The Paradise Papers* appeared in March 1976, which was just six months before we met. In December 1976, Dial Press contracted to republish the book as a hardback with its new, celebrated title, *When God Was a Woman*. The title came from lines in the opening chapter of the book: "At the very dawn of religion, God was a woman. Do you remember?"

In early 1978, Harcourt Brace & Co. published it as a soft-cover edition, which immediately began appearing on bestseller lists. *When God Was a Woman* had begun to change the world.

Merlin increased her energy, giving lectures and visiting bookstores. When she came home from her initial publisher's book tour, she said, "I can do this better myself."

Thereafter, she went to women's bookstores and women's studies groups—even before there were many women's studies programs. Being Merlin Stone, she had developed an extensive network of contacts within the women's movement. She was so proud and amazed at the progress of *When God Was a Woman*. Prior to her work, women's

studies courses consisted primarily of the history of the nineteenth-
and early twentieth-century suffrage movement. Merlin's seminal
publication helped inspire a shift from political issues to include spiritual feminism. The role of religion in establishing and maintaining
patriarchy became a part of women's studies courses.

I watched Merlin sit on the edge of our bed and dial her mother
with the good news. The conversation I overheard was truly a moving
moment between Merlin and her mother, as it revealed the difference
between the older generations of women. There had been a true shift
in women's expectations, perceptions, and values.

"Mom, the book I wrote has come out in the U.S. They even gave it
a better title, *When God Was a Woman*."

"How much did they pay you?" her mother asked.

"It's about much more than the money, Mom."

"But they paid you, didn't they?"

I watched as her whole demeanor changed when she realized that
her mother, like so many women of that generation, didn't understand
the importance of Merlin's feminist work. I could tell that her mother's
response to the news hurt Merlin, and she brought it up several times
later in our lives. She felt that, as much as she and her mother loved each
other, her mother was just from a generation of women who found it
hard to understand what Merlin was doing.

Her father supported her early interest in art. She adored him. She
started to sculpt when she was eight or nine. Her brother recalled that
she had received the first sculpture award issued by her high school,
Erasmus Hall. It had the largest student body of any high school in the
country, and thereafter, they always gave an annual sculpture award.

Merlin redoubled her efforts toward completing her new book.
She spent over two years on its composition. *Ancient Mirrors of Womanhood* was published in 1979.

"I'm going to self-publish," she informed me. "I found a printer in
Wisconsin. Cynthia is doing the artwork. It will cost a buck a book for
3,000 copies." New Sibylline Books was born.

"When do you need the money?" I asked her, literally jumping up
to go get some cash. Would I ever hesitate? I was so happy to contrib-

ute. In fact, this was the beginning of my spending much more quality time with her—running errands to the post office and back and buying shipping supplies. I was helping to set up her business. This was a new calling for me.

It took only a couple of months for her to produce the actual physical book. She did everything thereafter—the layout, front and back cover design, fliers, mailers, publicity, bookmarks to hand out. The orders for the book came almost immediately. Merlin, directed by her Goddess, as always, knew exactly what to do. This was a pre-digital world, so she kept records in handwritten notebooks and files. She packed and addressed boxes. Fifteen thousand copies sold in just five years, all sent from our two-room apartment. Merlin was her own lawyer, reading and negotiating publishing contracts. She was her own manager and agent, distributing her new book even as she was still traveling and lecturing to introduce *When God Was a Woman* to an eager audience.

In 1984, Beacon Press, located in Boston, was alerted to the success. They characterized the initial sales as just testing what they called the "hardcore market." That meant—and they were quite right—that when they republished it with their mass marketing, it would find the hundreds of thousands of women internationally who needed to know what Merlin was writing. *When God Was a Woman*, at the time of this writing, has sold an estimated one million copies and has been translated into four languages.

"How did you do it?" I often asked. I actually asked her this hundreds of times through the years. Her quest was astounding to me—beyond my love, comprehension, and admiration for her.

"I had help," she would state clearly, and then she would add, "I was guided."

"Who guided you?" I would ask incredulously.

"It isn't like one person or another," she would try to explain. Merlin had no specific name or image for her Goddess. "I feel there is something inside me. It's an inner understanding."

"What do you understand?"

"It's a voice. It's like a female energy in the universe."

"Can you tell me what she says for you to do?" I simply didn't understand.

"As long as I'm willing, then the direction She guides me is the correct path that I should travel. It feels like I'm being gently pushed or pulled into situations that need to happen."

"Do you feel like you are being told to do these things?" I would ask, concerned that she might be trapped by some kind of compulsion.

"It feels natural. The Goddess wants it done."

I wish I had been able to comprehend what she was saying at the time. I know it isn't only "a woman's thing." And as much as I believe it's true that women see the world in a different way, often more clearly than the way men see things, I know Merlin had a gift. She could hear, intuit, and actualize the energy of her creator.

Once, I told her, "You remind me of two fictional characters: Sherlock Holmes and Johnny Appleseed."

"I like that: Shirley Holmes and Joanna Appleseed."

She was the consummate detective because she had that intuitive power to see things others didn't see. At first, it actually was scary for me.

Of course, some little devil in me would periodically find a way to misapprehend or try to misuse her gifts. Merlin had no interest in horse racing, but one day she watched the Kentucky Derby with me.

"Who's going to win?" I asked her.

"Why are you asking me?"

"Here's your chance. You can see the future," I coached her.

"It doesn't work that way. I can't tell the future. I can only tell my own future."

"That's it?" I said, genuinely disappointed.

"Seattle Slew," she proclaimed.

The race went off with all the pomp and ceremony. Her horse won.

"Wait a New York minute! You said you couldn't see the future. How did you pick the winner?"

"I liked the way the horse wiggled his ass as he walked to the starting gate."

But Merlin did hear the Goddess, and through Merlin's words, human/womankind heard the Goddess as well. Living in her presence, I also heard whispers from the Goddess. It was all the more wonderful because Merlin was the one whispering to me. It took a long time, but I became an ardent feminist and believer in the Goddess. Merlin sculpted my life for the better in so many ways.

"What did you want to be when you were a kid?" Merlin asked me.

"What did you want to be when you were a girl?" I asked, trying to turn it around. I probably didn't know it, but I was embarrassed to tell her my youthful dreams.

"A ballet instructor," she answered quite happily. She was incredibly flexible. She could kick her leg way over her head. She could stretch, sitting on the floor, and was able to put her hands way beyond her feet. Standing, she could touch her elbows to the floor without bending her knees. Her superb physical condition continued well into her older age, until accidents and illness took their toll.

"What did you want to be?" she'd ask me again. She wasn't going to let me off the hook.

"I loved playing cards." Naturally, I was playing well and still learning my craft. "And I loved to collect stuff."

"What did you collect?"

"Comic books, coins, stamps, baseball cards, non-sport cards, Dixie Cup lids, bottle caps, rock and roll records, magazines, and much more. I started selling comic books when I was seven years old in Brooklyn. I'd find them in the garbage, brush them off, set up a couple orange crates with a board, and sell my treasures. My mother would watch me from our apartment. I had no overhead. How could I lose?"

"You were very clever."

"I suppose."

"And you were good at what you did?"

"After my entrepreneurial attempts with the comic book stand at the age of seven, we moved to Kew Gardens. I used to go to the incinerator room on each floor of our apartment house and go through the magazines, comic books, Dixie lids, baseball cards, and other ephemera people left for the janitor to dispose of. After a while, the building super saw what I was doing and let me go into the main incinerator room to look through everything at once. It felt good to find treasures, but I wasn't making any money at it. I could trade with friends if I found something desirable."

"How did you feel when you did that?"

"I felt great. I made friends, I had a few pennies in my pocket, and I saved the best comic books for myself."

"So do that, collect. Start collecting playing cards and you will become a leading collector."

Another prediction she got right. She never missed. And with that whisper from the Goddess, I started my education as a professional collector. First it was playing cards, which went with my nightly vocation. Then it was, more broadly, gambling collectibles.

I became partners with Gene Hochman, a true expert and the author of *The Encyclopedia of American Playing Cards*. We did shows and bought collections. Together, we started a business called "Full House." He became my personal tutor.

I'd meet men in the collectibles field who would tell me about their specialties, always phrased in male or patriarchal terms.

"Mankind has created these treasures," an expert would say.

"A statement like that makes women invisible," I would declare.

"You don't know what you're talking about," I'd hear.

"It's sexism," I would persist. "Women have to have an equal place."

"Look at this deck," the same man would say, reaching for a deck depicting nude women.

Clearly, men, even in the late '70s, still didn't get it, but I was growing. I was able to build collections of not just playing cards but antique gambling items of the broadest scope. I found areas that weren't being collected and made them my own specialty, acquiring the very best items before others saw the value in them. I had a keen eye. Eventually, my childhood interests made me as much money as any profession I could have pursued in the business world.

When I went to play poker, I obviously didn't always come home a winner.

"How did you do?" Merlin never failed to ask. She wasn't checking up. She was interested.

"I lost $5,800."

"Let's go out and celebrate."

"Merlin, I said I lost $5,800. What's to celebrate?"

"We love each other."

Wow, what a lesson! Whoever had a more supportive partner? And with that loving boost of confidence, reassurance, and knowledge, I had the strength to persist. I would go back to the tables and have a good run. Merlin also had far better recall for details than I ever did. She accompanied me on hundreds of excursions to antique fairs, exhibitions, collectors' homes, conventions, and book shows, which she loved for reasons of her own. Merlin reminded me, years later, of events I had forgotten. She showed nothing but support and encouragement for whatever I chose to do.

It was a true combination of what Merlin said and what I, myself, began to perceive. Picture me sitting with seven men—sports bettors, nightclub owners, lawyers, businessmen, and those trying to give you the business—all kinds of professional hustlers. Every one of them was there to make some money the easy way. We were in the basement of a single-family house that my friend Sam owned. It was near West 10th and Hudson, where you had to go through a wrought-iron gate, past a camera. Sam would buzz each of us in. We'd go down into the basement, greeting each other.

"Hey, what's up, Lenny?"

"I hope I break even tonight. I need the money."

"What's the line on the Rangers?"

"What do I know about hockey?"

Some of these fellows bet games all over the board. They were all very intelligent, very aggressive, and basically at different poker levels, but they were all winners in their chosen professional fields.

We'd sit in this bare concrete-floor basement, which was unfurnished except for the antique, octagonal oak poker table and some old armchairs with cushioned bottoms that were comfortable enough that you could sit in them all night, even into part of the next day.

There was a long, bright fluorescent light fixture hanging above the table.

Ideally, you'd start off strong, winning early. Poker is a very emotional game, and it takes some time for people to tilt. You need to identify the players who become the underdogs. After a few hours, you'd see them unravel. Six hours in, they would be transformed, desperate, playing like trapped, panicked animals trying to get even.

There I was, seated as usual at the table, feeling confident. I felt like I was a favorite to win, I rated to win. I knew the game better than the others. A good poker player knows the percentages. It's a creative numbers game. Every decision requires a strategy. But if you play by a strict set of rules—if you are too predictable, so-called playing by the book—that is not a winning style. It's not good because other players will pick up the pattern and read you. Then they can beat you at your own game, or completely avoid you.

That particular evening, I watched how Tubby, an overweight fellow at the table, would shift in his seat if he had good cards. Almost everyone does that, but an overweight player is more likely to seek a comfortable posture to go along with the anticipated pleasure.

Then there was Nick, who smoked. When he started with good tickets, he'd always light up a cigarette. That was his super comfortable position because he was set to pounce. I rarely saw a poker player light up and then fold. It was a reliable giveaway of their hands. (It's a pity they banned smoking later in the clubs where I played.)

I listened to their conversation as the cards were dealt.

"You know, I actually had a tryout for the Cubs twenty years ago," said Lynch.

"Well, I played minor league ball," said One-Upper, "and if I hadn't gotten injured, I'd have been moved up to the Brooklyn Dodgers."

"I used to drink all night when I was in college, but I was always on the honor roll."

"I drank all night and rolled with two women," One-Upper bragged again. It was senseless, constant banter, and I would invent situations to make fun of them.

"Yeah, and I once did five hundred pushups in five minutes, and knocked out Joe Louis in the first."

"The older we get, the faster we ran," I yawned. But suddenly, it was more than just one-up and banter. I looked around at the other seven men and thought, *Who are these guys? They all have such weaknesses. The conversations, body language, the way they toss their chips into the center of the table—what a bunch of narcissistic, macho men.* With Merlin's help, I had them figured out.

Then there was Peter, the Wall Street whiz whom I had a very strong read on, though he wasn't quite as regular in our circle. I could see beyond the usual behaviors that revealed he was bluffing. He tossed his chips in like a real bully—clack, scatter, smash. "Take that!" he might as well have said. But there was Peter, with doubt in his eyes.

He had just performed his regular routine, bragging about his numerous sexual conquests, again attempting to prove that he was the consummate ladies' man.

"They loved my body," he boasted.

"There it is," I thought. "His whole life is a bluff." What he was trying to tell me was he wanted me to back off, get out of his way. He didn't have the cards—no grasp at all of what the game was about. His masculinity was all bluff. The hand he was dealt in life was a bluff.

I warmed with my newfound perception. I called his last bet. My weak hand beat his nothing. It was almost embarrassing when I turned my cards over and showed the table that I'd won. All the players were astounded. There I was with a dead read on the guy. The other players would go all night and never have a perception like that. But I was learning from a real master—a mistress, in fact, a Goddess, my mysterious Lady Luck.

From there I started to pick up clues in the language they used—not just macho bragging, but all the language, all the words, their self-defeating lexicon.

"I'm not getting along with my wife," Ratso would sigh. He would confess he was in distress. Most poker players wish they could lock up their personal lives, but they leave themselves open for continuous failure. They simply don't know how to securely lock or unlock their own door. I knew Ratso was going to play far too aggressively to compensate for his failing marriage. I could anticipate how players would play based on not just superficial words and gestures. I was more sensitive to every happening in the room. It was Merlin at work. To begin with, I wasn't having the problems some of these poor guys were having. I was empowered by her. I had always been into numbers, but what I had missed was that things don't always have to add up. Merlin, herself, didn't add up. She showed me how to get closer to my own intuition and my own gut feeling. It's a trust equation.

With Merlin, I was a winner. She was making me feel more and more secure. She would frequently tell me, "I trust you. You know what you are doing." I was just more aware of where I was and what was happening around me at each moment—not just at the poker table, not just in my growing collectibles business, but in every aspect of my life. What a miracle. Thank you, Merlin. I love you.

~

Merlin was born Marilyn Jacobson. Her first married name was Stone. She was, by the way, married three times. Her second marriage was to Doug, an artist/art teacher, while she lived in East Aurora, New York. Merlin didn't speak much about him. The marriage, as I understand, was of so short a duration that it was annulled. Her third husband, Warren, was someone she loved and married in London. Then they moved to Quadra Island off the eastern coast of Vancouver, British Columbia. They hadn't been together long when he disappeared after he went into the mountains either to hunt or hike. They never found his body.

"None of that is important in our lives," she would tell me. "I have no regrets. I have no anger."

"None?" I would ask, often incredulously.

"None," she would assert. "I did what I wanted. I do what's in my heart."

I did ask her, "So how did you get the name 'Merlin'?"

"I was living in Berkeley with my two young daughters. That was the time, about 1966, when I moved with the girls to that area. They were in their early teens. I was making clothes—T-shaped dresses with wide sleeves, which were more like something from King Arthur. The girls called them 'Merlin dresses,'" she explained.

"That was it? You were Merlin."

"The name stuck," she said. "They renamed me."

It was 1969, and people were still living out the Summer of Love. I can just picture it. She was the coordinator of the Bay Area chapter of Experiments in Art and Technology, an arts program in the area. Merlin was an instructor in 1969 at the University of California, Berkeley Extension, teaching courses entitled "Art as Ecological Awareness" and "Energy Art: New Media of Art and Technology." She was making complex flashing-light kinetic brain-wave-controlled sculptures. She was a moneymaker, a doer, a major force, a feminist genius raising two daughters.

"You did a terrific job with those girls," I would tell her.

"They raised themselves," she would humbly reply.

She was a miracle to behold, truly a magician. Merlin was Merlin from very early on—an amazingly strong and independent woman—but I do like to think that I was an important contributor to her life. Certainly, her author's career and Goddess activities flourished during our relationship, which raises an interesting question. I have been criticized for painting Merlin as a saint, flawless in so many aspects. Still, I'd like to think our long and stable relationship provided a place for her to do her work. In the same way I don't remember her faults—suggesting she had none—I don't lay any specific claims to her successes. Still, I know my being there for her was mutually beneficial.

As for my own personal development, she didn't make demands, but the detective in her found my missing pieces and put them together. The artist in her was sculpting me. Perhaps that was also something the Goddess wanted. After all, I didn't plan to become an ardent feminist or a worshipper of the Goddess, but that's what happened.

I went with her once to Toronto for a lecture she was giving, I think probably for *Goddess Remembered*, a 1989 documentary that included Merlin. It was directed by Donna Read for the National Film Board of Canada. Merlin wanted to introduce me to her colleagues. We took the train and stayed in a fancy hotel, the Royal York, and at the conference, they treated her like a star.

Merlin was so organized. Everything that happened was orderly, peaceful, and easy, not rushed. Things just fit into place. I remember watching her walk into a room. Other feminists immediately wanted to talk to her. She hated the spotlight. She didn't want adulation, but it came to her truly naturally. They would approach her almost furtively.

"You changed my life," a woman would tell her.

"You changed your own life," Merlin would repeat back. "You did it for yourself." Merlin didn't need to be thanked in such a dramatic way.

"I'm free now. No more doing what some man tells me to do," a woman would proudly state.

"That's right," Merlin would reply. "Exactly. You are capable of creating any world you want."

And it wasn't preaching or proselytizing. Letters thanking Merlin arrived with frequency.

"Dear Merlin, I am writing to thank you for what you did for me. I actually got my PhD from Yale in religious studies. Can you believe that in all my academic training, I never heard of the Goddess until I read your book?"

"Dear Merlin, you transformed me."

"Dear Merlin, you saved my life."

Merlin would bring me those letters—a trunk full of them saved over the years—and we'd read them. It opened my own eyes to what was happening. She was, of course, getting more and more accolades, but more significantly, the women's spirituality movement was growing huge. It was branching off into Witchcraft, nature cults, Goddess worshippers, Wicca, and all manner of Goddess persuasions. There was, of course, the more public feminist movement that women like Gloria Steinem championed. Certainly, with the publication of *When*

God Was a Woman in 1976, Merlin resurrected the Goddess and introduced her for the first time from a feminist perspective. In spite of her growing reputation, Merlin preferred to maintain a very private, secluded lifestyle.

Not that she didn't relish little moments when it really seemed like she was directly in league with the Goddess. After all, if you have a spiritual communication, why not use it? Typically, I might ask her to go with me on some trip, but we avoided rituals like weddings. However, I had a close friend from my childhood in Kew Gardens who asked me to attend his wedding, and Merlin did agree to accompany me. In gratitude, my buddy arranged for a friend of his to drive us back and forth to Philadelphia for the celebration.

On the way back home to New York City, the car sputtered and broke down.

My buddy's friend got out and began kicking the car and pounding it with his fists, screaming, "I paid a fortune for this piece of crap!" He was flipping out.

"He's howling at the moon," Merlin said calmly, as we watched him from the back seat.

We looked at each other and just knew it was time to find our own way.

"We're on a deserted road," I told Merlin. It was before cell phones. "What's our best move?"

She took a good grip of my hand, opened the car door, and pulled me out her side of the car.

Just as I stepped out, before I could so much as look for any help, a Checker Cab appeared seemingly out of nowhere. The cabby's passenger-side window was open and the driver said, "Get in."

As we pulled away, I was stunned, my heart pounding. Merlin looked completely serene, her eyes closed, as if she knew all along we would be just fine.

Still, no one was more blown away by what was happening in her life than Merlin. She truly didn't expect or want the spotlight. She worked tirelessly for so many years to help millions of women see themselves as empowered, autonomous, and equal. But she didn't dress like, look like, or want to be someone famous. Sure, it's special to be the messenger of the Goddess, but it's also tremendously demanding, though it was a role she gladly accepted.

Around 1991 or 1992, she became exhausted from her monumental efforts, including her travels to exotic places and her teaching, lecturing, and workshops. It wasn't something we talked about, but the movement—the things she wanted to happen—were happening even beyond her wildest dreams. The Goddess in her many forms had taken on a life of her own. The phone was ringing frequently, but Merlin decided to just turn the ringer off and let her answering machine pick up. At the end of the day, she would return the calls she selected. She kept in touch with her closest associates, but she began to withdraw from public life.

One day, I was with my best friend Jerry, who I hung out with for many years. This was a fellow who would jokingly say, "Lenny, what is she doing with a guy like you?"

"Why are you asking?"

"Well, it isn't for money. It can't be your looks, that's for sure, and certainly not your mind."

"She's changing me," I'd say. "It's serendipity." Sometimes, even I wondered.

"What's it like to live with Merlin?"

"I'm living with Wonder Woman, but she never goes back to her secret identity."

One time, Jerry walked into a Barnes & Noble bookstore and found Merlin's books all over a promotional table. When he arrived at our place, he was very excited and asked us to go see the display at the store. Merlin didn't need to. We didn't go.

Another time, *When God Was a Woman* was being read over WBAI, the New York City public radio station. They were presenting a chapter at a time. They were on, let's say, chapter five. John Lennon called the station and asked Linda Perry, the program director, for a signed copy of the book. Merlin got the message and signed a copy "To Yoko and John." That book was then delivered to them by Linda. A housekeeper for the two told Merlin—when Merlin met her, coincidentally, many years later—that John and Yoko kept Merlin's book by their bedside and read passages to each other.

Merlin could have delivered the book to them herself. They wanted to meet her. She wasn't star-struck. I would have given anything to meet them. She declined.

By 1994, I was ready to change my lifestyle so Merlin and I could spend more time together. It was a mutual thing. We were both more and more content to just share our days. I prepared my playing cards and gambling collectibles to be sold at auction.

Just five years after Merlin told me to follow my passion, I had such an extensive collection of playing cards and gambling memorabilia that I was given a show at the prestigious OK Harris art gallery on West Broadway in Manhattan. The show, in 1981, led to a long feature article by Rita Reif, "Antiques: Take a Gamble on Playing Cards," in the *New York Times* (Sunday, July 5, 1981). After reading the *Times*, a man called to offer a nineteenth-century Faro gambling box with six hundred ivory chips previously used in the Narragansett Casino in Rhode Island. Merlin was with me when I paid $400 for it, and in my 1994 auction it sold for $23,100. I had another exhibition at OK Harris in 2001, entitled "The Art of the Billfold," another collecting passion I pursued. Merlin set me free, inspired me. It was a joy for me, and she was the willing witness and instigator of any and every success I ever had.

But it was time to make some readjustments. Noel Barrett, who later would appear on *Antiques Roadshow*, arranged my auction on May 20, 1994. Merlin had encouraged me to write *Gambling Collectibles: A Sure Winner,* a year earlier. I gave her all the information, which she put into great order as she wrote. We spent eleven months together daily, with her working on a subject that really wasn't of primary interest to her. That was a true act of love—having her amazing abilities directed toward a project I wanted to do. I mailed the book on a Monday, and Merlin told me, "Now you can relax. It will take a while to hear."

Wednesday, that same week, I got a call from Schiffer Publishing, the folks I wanted to publish my book. They accepted it immediately. When it was published, the dedication read:

To Merlin,
who always helps to make my dreams come true,
and to my mother,
for teaching me the difference between right and wrong.

I continued to assemble small, specialized collections of wallets, rulers, billiard memorabilia, matchbox holders, calendars, Dixie lids, and items in other areas where I became, once again, a leading collector and dealer. My credibility was all the more enhanced by the gift of the book Merlin had constructed for me. The release of *Gambling Collectibles* coincided nicely with the auction, generating more interest in the collection. When the auction itself took place, it raised enough for us so that we could retire even more comfortably.

Merlin told me, "I'm a collector, too."

"Really?" I asked her. "What do you collect?"

"Wisdom and knowledge."

"So how did you wind up with me?" I mused.

"You were chosen," she informed me.

I was fifty-three and Merlin was sixty-three. For quite a while, I had known that I wanted to believe and think like Merlin. I worshipped her. She had sculpted me into everything I wanted to be. I needed her energy to succeed, and she gave it to me generously, naturally, fully. All that made it so much easier for us to make our transition.

Starting in 1994, Merlin and I settled into a lifestyle where we did everything together. We were frugal, but we treated ourselves to what we loved. We'd return to Phoenicia or take little side trips to museums or antique events in different cities, to places where Merlin and I could enjoy ourselves. We even went to the Baseball Hall of Fame in Cooperstown, New York. Oddly, she rarely asked to go to feminist or Goddess-related events. She loved dance and was more inclined to go to dance festivals—African dance, Celtic dance, all types of dance. We showed up at a square dance one time and, believe it or not, she actually was able to call the dance. Even after being together for twenty years, I never knew she could do such a thing. She couldn't sing a note, but she knew the steps and they let her call an entire number. Those types of surprises happened all the time.

We even went to a Mets game—the only baseball game she ever attended. There is actually a short story that goes with that occasion. At the Vandam Diner, where we almost always ate, there was a fellow I saw frequently. I learned he was once the mascot, Mr. Met. He lost his job because he was a drinker. We invited him over to sit with us, and he and Merlin became friends. Merlin encouraged him, raised his self-esteem, told him not to blame himself. Eventually, he told her she made him feel so much better that he stopped drinking. In gratitude, he took us to the game. It was just one more example of how Merlin was able to empower men and women alike.

Sometimes, I think back to my childhood idols: cowboys, war heroes, and even Elvis Presley, who may have left the building, but his mystique certainly lives on. He was the quintessential entertainer. Merlin was more than that for me and for a world of others. She was an "igniter."

I only saw Merlin speak once at a professional event, at a Manhattan high school assembly hall. I sat and listened to her entire lecture. There she was, dressed as always in her later years in her black tights and black skirt. She was wearing a shirt she had made herself, a black velvet one that exposed her shoulders, loosely fitting over her still impressive figure.

Her hair, by then, was pure white but still combed long below her shoulders, draped down to the middle of her back. She never went to a beauty parlor until she was seventy and then only for the pleasure of having her hair shampooed and conditioned. She did love long-hanging earrings, one of the few luxuries she indulged in—that, and two thin gold chains she loved, which I proudly had bought her. But she was never vain. If anything, it was as if she was hiding her beauty. Sometimes it seemed as though she wanted to be completely incognito, but I felt very privileged to be with, see, and experience her startling beauty every day. I never got tired of watching her sensual dancer's body.

She spoke with quiet confidence and with a slightly British accent she had acquired in the several years she lived in London before I met her. It wasn't like she was pretending. It was just an interesting, unexpected way of speaking that she had. And I was mesmerized, as usual.

Merlin never cursed. She was never obscene, though she could joke, and Merlin never raised her voice to me.

This is very significant, not just because I was brought up the way "men" were supposed to be—assertive over a passive woman—but because it was the best way for a teacher to teach. Growth, in a relationship, isn't coerced. Merlin never, ever spoke negatively about anything I cared about. Everything I wanted to do, she calmly encouraged me to pursue.

"I like the way you look and dress," she'd tell me. "I trust you, Lenny. You know exactly what you are doing."

"You are the only woman for me," I'd tell her, though she knew that about me. Earlier in the relationship, however, Merlin would point out that I was "looking at other women." But let's face it, back then, I was still inclined to look at other women.

We were sitting on a bench in front of our apartment, in the middle of a conversation, when she simply stood up and walked into our apartment.

I immediately knew what happened, because I had done this before. We were at the point where, if this wasn't corrected, Merlin would leave me. A woman had walked by in a short skirt and my eyes had wandered to her and followed her down the street. Guilty as charged. I went into the house.

"Merlin, I know what happened. I'm sorry. It's inbred. I know that isn't a real excuse, but I'm working on it."

"Work a little harder," she said. And that was it. I got the message. I stopped, though I'm sorry to say, the hardest thing for a man to do is to stop leering.

Merlin didn't scream at me. She made what I needed to know clear. I loved her all the more and learned all the more effectively because of her gentle way. I became steadfastly faithful, and life could not have been any better. And because Merlin was so unique, I knew I was never going to look at another woman. It was more than being scared. I was cured.

The leering lesson was a vaccine, and that's how vaccines work—they enter your system and build your strength and immunity. I shouldn't even have to say it, and yet I am ever so happy to state that straying from Merlin never occurred to me. She became my one and only.

The changes I made were either the easiest things I could do and/ or they were extremely beneficial for me. It appeared to me that Merlin was always right. She certainly always said the right words to me. When she spoke, she said what I wanted to hear. Imagine living with someone who was always right. For that matter, she was never late. She just had it all together.

Time had a greater significance for Merlin. For starters, she liked to point out that, because the Goddess had been invisible for at least eight thousand years, we ought to add that many years to our present calendar. She published an article entitled "Repairing the Time Warp," saying we actually lived in 9978 instead of 1978. Merlin mastered time, never rushing, always calm within her confident self.

"How many times have we ever been late?" I'd ask her.

"Never," she'd say, indulging me.

"How about having to rush?" I'd ask, fishing for a compliment.

"We've never had to rush," she'd reinforce for me.

"You're stuck with me," I'd say.

"We're stuck to each other," she'd lovingly assure me.

"Are we teammates, co-captains?" I'd ask her. I wanted to be partners with a one-woman gang.

"Always and forever."

Oh my Goddess, what more could a fellow need to hear? I was completely open to everything else she wanted to teach me.

Most people thought we were married. We were together thirty-four years and five months. She was every bit my wife to me. I asked her if she wanted to do the ceremony. She didn't want to. I would have been happy to get married. Imagine that—me, the guy I described at the outset, wanting, needing, hoping to marry Merlin. We truly didn't need to. As far as I'm concerned, the Goddess not only married us, She was my best man.

Maybe it was because Merlin had tried marriage before and didn't need to do it again. She said in a poem of hers that she was "appearing and withdrawing as the mood suited me." As I mentioned earlier, neither of us liked social affairs—weddings, funerals, or other conventional rituals. We had a pact that we might go separately to a social function, if prevailed upon, and to spare one or the other of us having to go. So why would we expect to have some ceremony of our own? Almost all our Thanksgivings, Christmases, New Years, and other holidays were spent simply in each other's company.

Merlin taught me what was important in so many ways. Imagine rejecting celebrity and, with that, a certain measure of wealth. She didn't want our lifestyle to change. Instead, we lived the way we wanted. In fact, I willingly and happily accepted my role as her "consort." That word has gained a bad reputation, but in the dictionary one finds three definitions: "A husband or wife; a companion or partner; a vessel accompanying another in travel."

All of those work for me. I was particularly ecstatic to be an accompanying vessel.

One time, to vary our activities, we decided to drive across the country to find some charming, abandoned ghost towns. Merlin agreed, but only if we took the back roads. No charging down the interstate for her. Instead, there was Merlin with a map on her lap in some thirty-five-miles-per-hour zone. We would pick out odd locations to visit and spend whatever time we wanted there. The trip took more than three weeks, and we were thrilled with our cross-country adventure. By prior arrangement, Merlin always chose our lodgings.

She picked out some pretty strange, Bates-like, cheap motels. But you can't believe how good a night's sleep you can have in a little mom-and-pop motel, with a window open to hear spring peepers chirping in a nearby pond. Oh, to heck with the peepers! There was Merlin next to me with her head on my shoulder as we fell asleep.

In Kansas, we stopped for a break, and I saw a leather jacket in a thrift store. Hey, six bucks. But I didn't buy it. We drove on, perhaps for another hundred miles, and Merlin could see I was mumbling.

"What's up with you?" she asked.

"I saw this beautiful leather jacket I liked, but I didn't buy it."

"Well, don't worry. We can get it when we drive back to New York."

"There's no way I will ever remember where the store is," I complained.

"Trust me," she asserted. "We'll find it. You'll buy it."

While driving back after weeks on the road and visiting her daughters in California, sure enough, Merlin instructed me to "turn here."

"There's the store you wanted," she said. "Go buy the jacket."

I still have that jacket in our closet. It reminds me of how Merlin was my original GPS system—the perfect voice telling me where to turn, the perfect guide giving me direction. She was my North Star. After she showed me the way, I was never lost again.

~

I never saw Merlin cry. Could it be? So much life and history we witnessed and shared. Merlin didn't cry. I don't know why. She also never complained. Why was that? She fell down in an Italian restaurant, on Prince Street, near our apartment. That was her first accident. She fell and couldn't get up. That occurred in 1995.

In retrospect, that incident was probably the first sign of something sinister starting to overtake her. We had to call for an ambulance. She had broken her hip. It took her almost a year to recuperate. She didn't cry. She didn't complain.

Not long after her recovery, we were out with another couple and we hailed a cab. I got in next to the taxi driver. Merlin was stepping into the cab, and the driver actually started to drive off, partly dragging her so that she reinjured her hip. The incident had serious consequences. Not only were we not going out to speed-walk any more—something we had playfully pretended to do during our frequent walks—but all her physical activities slowed. While these circumstances were difficult, Merlin remained amazingly resilient, stoic, and optimistic.

The next fall happened in our apartment in 2000. The wires for my computer had never been tucked under the carpet or taped down.

They had been there for years. She had never tripped on them before. I felt so guilty. She tripped and fell against my desk. She didn't want to go to the hospital. Her arm and shoulder were swollen, black and blue the next day. We finally called for an ambulance. She had broken her arm and shoulder—four breaks in all. They said at the hospital that she needed surgery to fix things. Imagine, she didn't even complain when the results of the surgery were not successful, leaving her arm partly immobilized for the rest of her life.

That was her right shoulder, and she was a righty. I had to help her with some of her daily functions. We were a team. We would recover from all this. We even decided to take a trip to Florida to get away a bit and avoid a New York winter. We were happy snowbirds flying away from the problem of the broken boiler in the apartment we shared. That damned boiler broke almost every winter. I had lived in that same place for thirty-eight years, the last thirty of which were with Merlin. The two-room apartment was just fine for us, but was increasingly a problem in the winter.

So, it was off to Florida, where we traveled extensively, implicitly looking for a place where we might eventually retire. We put in hundreds of miles cruising up and down the state. We wound up, that first time, at a Miami Beach condo that a cousin let us use. But we didn't like the lifestyle in South Florida—noisy, crowded, expensive, and too hard to navigate, park, and find services. Eventually, we rented in Daytona Beach, during the winters of 2001 to 2005. Then we moved there as permanent residents because we had learned to love the beach area. And there, in 2006, Merlin suffered another fall. This time she broke her knee.

It didn't require surgery, but she needed a wheelchair. Again, she endured all the discomforts without complaint. Her falls were draining her mobility and energy. And for the first time in her life, she looked older than she was. Just as her knee was healing, she fell again. I was, by then, holding on to her as much as I could. Who wouldn't want to hold on to Merlin, weakened as she was, but always so beautiful, so full of good and loving energy? A broken pelvis put her back into the wheelchair again.

Merlin was in need of help. I did what was needed the first year. We could even put the wheelchair in the car and take long rides we both enjoyed—watching a sunset, the bridges opening over the Halifax River, or dolphins playing in the channel, sharing a chocolate milkshake, enjoying new neighborhoods. It was a joy to be there for her and with her. We still had our quality of life.

It was after the various falls and the long recuperative periods that a general practitioner said Merlin should see a neurologist. The falls were a sign of something more serious. I didn't think we were in denial, but why this sudden seriousness? I was a romantic and never took into consideration that this could happen to Merlin. She was getting regular therapy for her injuries, and no other doctor had suggested a neurologist. When I noticed her more rapid decline, I thought we were just aging. I didn't think it was anything more than that— nothing neurological. We went for so many tests. Western medicine seems happy to provide some terrible diagnosis. But, of course, I was in a state of devastation and despair when I heard the news. The doctor told us she had pseudobulbar palsy.

Of course, the doctor didn't tell us much—or at least not enough. We had to go online to read the details. Healthline.com, one of those generic medical websites, spelled it out:

> Patients with pseudobulbar palsy have progressive difficulty with activities that require the use of muscles in the head and neck that are controlled by particular cranial nerves. The first noticeable symptom is often slurred speech. Over time, speech, chewing, and swallowing become progressively more difficult, eventually becoming impossible.

"The prognosis," they declared, "was quite poor."

After using an experimental drug for six months, the doctor said, "There is no known cause, no known cure. She will lose her ability to speak, and the disease will kill her."

"How long does she have?" I asked him, with tears flowing down my cheeks. "There is no timetable," he replied. "Take her home and make her comfortable." The glib indifference with which the doctor delivered the news led me to feel a sense of complete hopelessness.

There are lots of things in life that can scare someone, but Merlin was not one to be scared. It harkens back, almost comically, to what I call the "*Psycho* story." We were sitting in our apartment when she first moved in, and I said to her, "Merlin, one of the great movies of all time, *Psycho*, is on. Do you want to watch it?"

"No," Merlin said emphatically, "I don't like to be scared."

"You'll like it. It's interesting. Who doesn't like a good horror movie?"

"Me," she said. "I've seen too many horrors. I've traveled to places where women are stoned to death."

"This isn't real. It's just a movie."

"I don't need to pretend stuff. The reality is horrible enough," she explained.

It was clear, then, that Merlin was not a person who treated life trivially, though, in fact, she seemed to be getting her information from other than the conventional sources—not from print, TV, or other mass media. She didn't need to read or hear the news. She got her news from a deeper source. I took her explanation so seriously that I turned it into a code word, a running joke of a kind. Any time the movie was being shown, I'd tell her, "*Psycho* is on."

"It's not real life," she'd say, "so let's skip it."

If some terrible event was reported in the news, it was a *Psycho* moment. When Merlin was diagnosed, that was a *Psycho* moment, though this time, we only said it with our eyes.

She was fully coherent. She was very specific. "I don't want to go to a nursing home." Merlin was profoundly aware of her condition, knowing intuitively, physically, and emotionally that her life on Earth was finite.

"I just want to stay home with you," she said.

"Of course," I said. "No nursing home. Never."

Oh love, what a gift Merlin always gave me. What a gift to be home with Merlin. But I realized I needed more help.

I hired two women, Shirley and Dorothy, to take care of Merlin seven days a week. They did everything for her during her last two years—all the necessary and personal things. They were there from 8:00 am to 5:00 pm. I took care of her the other fifteen hours a day.

I held her hand. I read to her and was attentive to all of her needs. It gave me joy just to be there for her. Nearer the end, when she couldn't speak at all, we still communicated by her squeezing my hand. She could still move letters around on a magnetic slate I bought for her. I made a list of things she needed, and I would put her hand on mine and move my hand down the list, slowly, and she would indicate by blinking or squeezing my hand where I should stop so I knew what she wanted.

A friend of mine recommended VITAS, a nondenominational hospice care provider. They sent a medical doctor to screen us, and in the last week, they provided twenty-four-hour nursing care, though I continued to employ Shirley and Dorothy because they were such loyal helpers for Merlin. VITAS also asked if they could send a clinical practice chaplain, and though neither of us were ever practitioners of any traditional faith, I said "yes."

A middle-aged woman I will call Elizabeth arrived, dressed neatly and simply. "Maybe I can help to reduce the sting of death."

"I need help," I told her. Of course, I wanted Merlin to have comfort, but I confessed, "I don't want to live."

Though VITAS did not send a chaplain for specific religious purposes, Elizabeth was Christian, but she never asked us if we wanted to pray. She was, in the best sense of the word, a professional "listener." But she did tell us, "Merlin, you will be with your Father in heaven."

I took her aside that same day, and I showed her Merlin's books and papers. Elizabeth had never even heard of *When God Was a Woman*, but she was receptive so I gave her a copy.

The next day when she came for her daily visit, she said, "I read some of the book and it's fascinating. It will change what I do."

After talking with me for a few more days, she actually said, "Merlin represents a new concept. She is not just telling us things we have forgotten, she has started a new religion."

"I'm so glad you like the book."

"It's more than that. It's important to me. Even you, Lenny, are a big part of it."

"I don't understand," I insisted.

"If Merlin is revealing truths, you are an original disciple. You are going to spread the word."

With that comment alone, she gave me a way to cope. As consumed as I was by the moment, I had the hope that I would be able to carry on Merlin's work. To see how this woman, Elizabeth, in just a few short days of knowing us, validated what Merlin herself envisioned—that the Goddess religion was the savior and the saver of the planet—I realized how important it would be for me to keep spreading the word. There we were, clearly in Merlin's last hours on Earth, and she was still awakening people and changing their lives.

Her daughters came as soon as I called them. Jenny flew in from California and Cynthia from Paris. As painful as the circumstances were, Merlin's eyes still clearly showed her joy in their being with her. They were always the love of her life. They sat with her, talked to her, gave all the comfort that loving daughters could possibly bestow. No mother and daughters could have been closer, and it was hard for me to watch how they were already grieving for their mother.

Even in her last days, Merlin and I had an unbreakable bond. She never lost her ability to understand. The process of her dying took only days more after her daughters arrived.

It had been weeks and weeks that she hadn't spoken, but I sat with her in the last days, and I, for sure, was crying.

"I love you," I said.

"I love you, too," she echoed.

Her caregiver, Dorothy, was with me at that moment, and we were both quite startled. Those words were the last Merlin ever uttered. Two weeks later, she died at 4:52 am on February 23, 2011, in our home in Daytona Beach.

Merlin, love of my life, I only live for you. Your written words changed the world. The words you spoke to me transformed my heart.

poems by
lenny schneir

*Lenny and Merlin in front of their apartment
at 184 6th Avenue, New York City, 1999.*

A Note about My Poems

*T*HESE ARE NOT JUST POEMS. They are a short story that is still being told. How did she do it? How did Merlin manage to research and write her books? Merlin had no blueprints to follow, no shoulders to stand on, no roadmap, no compass. She'd never been to any of those places before. She didn't speak the languages. No computer, no word processor, no technology, very little money. She hitchhiked in Lebanon, Greece, Turkey, Crete, and Cypress. She used buses and trains, slept outside, slept in caves, found scattered clues often separated by hundreds of miles. Most of the evidence had been destroyed. Was she carrying a typewriter or taking notes? Hundreds of pages of notes?

Either way, it sounds close to impossible, yet Merlin gathered enough information for *When God Was a Woman* and *Ancient Mirrors of Womanhood* and wrote them in two distinctly different styles: prose and poetry. How did she do it? I was in awe of her strength and courage. I learned from her, and these poems are a small indication of that. In fact, I worshipped her!

—Lenny Schneir

Meeting Merlin

I thought I was a free spirit,
then I met Merlin.
I thought I was a nonconformist,
then I met Merlin.
I thought I was creative,
then I met Merlin.
I thought I was a rebel,
then I met Merlin.
I thought I was smart.
You get the idea.

Get Stoned

Get stoned on Merlin.
On what?

Words, wisdom, poetry and love
in order to feel her presence.
Levitate your mind and body,
reach for your own potential.

Get stoned on Merlin.
On what?

Friendship, loyalty, trust and love.
She is with you always,
returned the Goddess to you,
trusting you to carry Her torch.

Get stoned on Merlin.
On what?

Peace, tolerance, understanding and love,
enlightenment, endarkenment, day and night
time, space, calendars and life,
truth, morality, equality and facts.

Get stoned on Merlin.
On what?

Taste, style, vocabulary and language
energy, gusto, bravery and courage,
knowledge, learning, scholarship and knowing.
Trust the Goddess to guide you.

Leave Me Alone

Leave me alone with Merlin.
Leave me alone with my poetry.
I will bury myself with knowledge and wisdom.
Your words transformed me.
It is you and me as always,
but you are not here.
You are inside and I
carry you like you carried me.
You were the doctor,
I was your patient.
You cured me.
You were the teacher,
I was your student.
You educated me.
You were the artist,
I was your canvas.
With strokes of your brush,
I was born.
You were the detective,
I had no clue.
You were the lighthouse,
I was lost at sea.
You were the lending library,
I read your books.
You were the calendar,
it was my time.
You were the universe,
I shared your space.
You were the Goddess who moved me.
I am happiest alone with you.
Dearest Merlin, I will always love you.

My Lady Luck

Don't want to win the lottery
Or play the 3-shell game
Or hit the jackpot
To live on Easy Street.
All I want is Merlin.

Don't want, according to Hoyle,
To spin the wheel,
To make easy money
With an ace in the hole.
All I want is Merlin.

Don't want to be the king of hearts
Or go straight
Or hold four queens
Or draw new cards.
All I want is Merlin.

Don't want a big bankroll
To buy blue chips.
Don't want to be a wild card
Or a royal flush.

All I want is my Lady Luck.

Where Do You Live

I live in the eternal Grief Hotel.
The hotel has many guests
But they are invisible.
I do not want to mourn alone.
You can't leave.
There is no check-out time;
Lots of baggage but no luggage.
Where is the bellhop?
I live on a high floor
With no view and no fire escape.
There are no restaurants or restrooms,
No pool or beach,
But there is an ocean—
The grief ocean;
It floods the hotel.
There is no day
There is no night, no date
No month, no year
No time.
Every moment is the same—
No weather.
Not cold, not hot,
No rain, no snow,
No sun, no wind,
No rooms, no furniture,
No room service, no doors,
No windows, no halls.
No past, present or future.
No exit.
No way out.

merlin in her
own words

Merlin on "our bench," 6th Avenue,
between Prince and Spring streets, NYC, 1996.

Merlin in Her Own Words:

EXCERPTS FROM TALKS AND ARTICLES

Selected by Lenny Schneir

*I*HAVE ALL BUT memorized much of what Merlin wrote. Some passages stand out for me, and I have kept them in a journal of my own, considering them the core of Merlin's research, teachings, and accomplishments. Those passages are compiled here as a reminder of what she did and with the hope that those reading them will go further, using the more complete citations at the end of this book, to more fully read Merlin's work. The first quote appeared on the first page of her book *The Paradise Papers: The Suppression of Women's Rites* and gave rise to the new title, *When God Was a Woman*, when the publisher, Dial Press, reissued it in 1976.

—*Lenny Schneir*

"In the beginning, people prayed to the Creatress of Life, the Mistress of Heaven. At the very dawn of religion, God was a woman. Do you remember?"

—*When God Was a Woman*

"The Goddess is not just the female version of God. She represents a different concept. While the Judeo-Christian God is transcendent, the Goddess is located 'within each individual and all things in nature.'"

—*Time Magazine* (May 6, 1991)

"Women are beginning to feel strong and trust their perceptions. We know we don't like war. We don't support the destruction and pollution of the planet. We don't understand why someone has to dominate. It's an incredible new way to look at the world, and it may be one way to stop the destruction of the planet.

"Men are realizing... it makes much more sense for men and women to talk to one another like fellow human beings.... The myths and legends of the female deity offer a very different picture of womanhood than those of the male-oriented religions of today. The Goddess is back."

—*Houston Chronicle* (February 17, 1990)

"Faced with the all too real threats of poisonous pollution of land, sea, and air, and the complete extinction of many species of life on Earth, perhaps even our own, we might do well to examine the rituals, parables, and symbolism of spiritual beliefs that included regarding various aspects of nature as sacred—thus inviolable."

—*Conference on Gaia Consciousness, California Institute of Integral Studies* (April 6–10, 1988)

"Many women now accept Goddess worship as a religion.... It is very spiritually strengthening to feel that women have been made in the image of the Goddess. It is important to realize it was a religion, not a cult. We have given it the taint of paganism. Paganism is a term coined to put down early religions."

—*San Francisco Chronicle* (April 7, 1978)

"Calling a woman 'sweetie' or 'doll' isn't affectionate, it's sly and derogatory. It implies a status gap that immediately places the relationship on a one-up basis instead of one-to-one. The earliest law, government, medicine, agriculture, architecture, metallurgy, wheeled vehicles, ceramics, textiles and written language were initially developed in societies that worshipped the Goddess.

"Everyone, both genders, must strive together for an equalarchy ... The ultimate robbery with violence [is] rape."
—*The Globe and Mail, United Kingdom* (December 27, 1991)

"Now, it is time to think of the Supreme Being as both mother and father. It is kind of like having a broken home, to think of God exclusively as male or female. ... The image of Eve as temptress and evil pervades our society today. Only with the arrival of the male gods were women expected to have no sexual contact prior to marriage, and to be reserved sexually for one man in marriage."
—*Cleveland Plain Dealer* (January 22, 1977)

"Most modern religions—particularly Judaism, Christianity and Islam —believe in a masculine supreme being. Along with that belief has come the suppression of women and the development of theologies declaring women to be naturally inferior. ... The Adam and Eve 'myth' was created to give theological foundation to the suppression of women. To me God is a supreme life force. Therefore, God must be both mother and father. A supreme being would have to be both male and female to be creator. ... the world is entering a 'new religious era' in which all persons will be equal humans."
—*Pittsburgh Press* (January 1977)

"As the shockwaves of the new feminist movement began to swirl around me in Berkeley, California, in late 1969, I realized how little even my most educated friends knew about the actual history of ancient Goddess reverence, and how important I believed it was for women to know about this history as a major factor in our feminist analysis.

"Few people realize that the heathens so feared in the Bible were praying to a woman, and that 'pagan idols' generally had breasts. For years, something has magnetically lured me into exploring the legends, the temple sites, the statues and the ancient rituals of the female deities, drawing me back in time to an age when the Goddess was omnipotent, and women acted as Her clergy, controlling the form and rites of religion. ... I do hold the hope ... that a contemporary consciousness of the once-widespread veneration of the female deity, as the wise Creatress of the Universe and all life and civilization, may be used to cut through the many oppressive and falsely founded patriarchal images, stereotypes, customs and laws that were developed as direct reactions to Goddess worship by the leaders of the later male-worshipping religions.

"Even after the publication of the book, I still preferred to present myself and my work solely as academic and feminist. After a great deal of inner struggle, I had finally acknowledged, although only to myself, the help and guidance I had so mysteriously received throughout the entire process. I had even come to wonder over the years if I was being used as a messenger for Her, by Her, simply because I was willing. This, I felt, must remain as my private knowledge.

"Perhaps, someday, I will feel free enough to tell the entire long strange story of the years of receiving Her guidance that, amidst much other knowledge, not only told me what to write but which libraries and museums, which books and journals, contained the documented evidence to support this knowledge, at times even the page numbers.

"For now, there is no doubt in my mind or heart that the Goddess is asking more and more of us to let others know about Her. I believe it is because the planet is in danger and She is asking us for help by our spreading knowledge of the ancient attitudes toward women's wisdom about the sanctity of Earth and life. I am writing this on my fifty-eighth birthday, and as I write, I realize that Goddess energies and counsel have now guided my life for almost thirty years. Birthdays often cause us to look back over our lives, and looking back over mine, I see that, from the stubborn skeptic I once was, I have learned to totally trust the path along which She leads me."

—*Woman of Power: A Magazine of Feminism, Spirituality, and Politics* (Issue 15, October 1989)

"All of life is flux, change, process, continual creation. When we think of Goddess, it is as The Source, the Primal Fountain of Energy that continually creates, continually manifests itself ever anew in the universe. Each of us is a unique channel of that energy, and in that sense we are continually creating the world. Once we truly understand our own role as creator, we realize both our individual and collective importance in shaping change and evolution.

"When we have made that inner contact, we are in direct touch with Goddess guidance, and we can hear, see and feel Her energy flow through us as we learn to trust and follow that guidance. May you always swim in the fountain of Her energy as She flows in and through you."

—*Green Egg* (Vol. XXI, No. 81, Beltane 1988)

"Mine was the first book to be written that gathered the material together and presented it from a feminist point of view. My investigation of the worship of a female deity really was motivated to a great extent by the image of women presented by Judaism and Christianity … The woman known as Eve. … The women's movement has done so much to release feminine power into the world. The addition of women's spirituality as they regain their heritage gives the movement new dimension. I really wrote *When God Was a Woman* so women could learn to understand their inner selves. …

[Interviewer asks, 'What has the Goddess come to mean to you?' Merlin answers:] "She has become my life. I basically let her lead me. She is my guide through life. There is no particular image or name that I connect with her, but it is an inner understanding."

—*Aquarian Voices* (November/December 1989)

"The original idea of the book was basically to say to women, 'We are not second-class citizens; we were first-class citizens,' and to explain how this happened, how historically it happened. I started trusting that if I followed along with leaving my life open enough to random chance that the Goddess would keep feeding me information. …

"I really see the emergence of the Goddess as, at this point, not only political and feminist, but a whole level of transformation of di-mensional—almost into a fourth-dimensional—time perception of what's going on in the world and knowing that everything is in con-stant flux all the time and that we don't have to grasp it and make it stay still, but flow with it and allow ourselves to know that in any given moment we're going to be changing.

"We don't have to get hysterical and wild. We just have to say we know with dignity that we're correct."

—"Reclaiming the Goddess: An Interview with Merlin Stone,"
by Barbara Booher, *Common Ground* (Winter 1989/90)

"All living things embody the Goddess ... I do see the male energy as being possibly very positive. I think what's sad in our society is that males have been conditioned to be other than who they naturally are. Many men assume they have to take this sort of warrior stance. . . .

"I think there is some force in the universe, that I would call the Goddess, some flow that is saying, 'Women, wake up and start telling these people what they are doing. Point out the insanity of it.' We must think for ourselves, not follow the rules and regulations like sheep simply because the rules are there. I think we can keep making our world better and better, if everybody is willing. I don't see it as a con-frontation or a battle. I see it basically as consciousness-raising.

"We must get in touch with that divine spark within ourselves and realize we're better than the wars and fighting."

—*Inner Resources, Los Angeles* (Summer 1987)

"Hearing Her, seeing Her, praying to Her, worshipping Her, talking to Her, should be considered normal."

—*Merlin Stone, unpublished lecture notes* (1978)

"Spiritual imagery is, in a sense, visual prayer. Here, in this gallery, you are now surrounded by prayers of shapes and forms and colors, expressed by many fine artists. Try, for a very quiet moment or two, to 'hear' these prayers. You will find that what is sacred within you enables you to listen and respond to what is sacred within others. It is this sacred spark in each of us that joins together what we call Goddess."

—*The Goddess Show,* Merlin Stone, juror (Washington Women's Arts Center, 1984)

Excerpts from *At the Leading Edge*

by Michael Toms

MT: Merlin, how did you choose the title of your book *When God Was a Woman*?

MS: My original title was *The Paradise Papers*, which was meant to explain that it was an exposé of the story of Adam and Eve in the Garden of Eden. The book was first published in England under the title *The Paradise Papers: The Story of the Suppression of Women's Rites*. When it was later being prepared for publication in the United States, the editor decided *When God Was a Woman*—which is a line in the book—was the most wonderful line.

MT: What prompted you to do the many years of research required to put that book together? What was the motivation?

MS: I'm not exactly sure what really drove me on. It was like a compulsion or an addiction. So much information was just being sort of dumped in my lap; things just kept coming up on their own that were begging to be put into the book. Looking back, I have the feeling that there was a female energy in the universe that wanted this information out, and that, as long as I was willing to cooperate as an instrument of that goal, I would be used in that way.

MT: Did you have any idea, when the book was published, that it would have such a life of its own?

MS: When I was writing it, I thought that maybe ten people in the world would bother to wade through all these unfamiliar names and places. This material was something that almost no one knew about.... I'm very happy that the information about ancient Goddess reverence has become more familiar.

MT: How did it affect your life—both the act of writing it and its longevity? Did it transform your life?

MS: It certainly did. I think that it was the writing of the book, and the researching, that really transformed my life. I genuinely felt that there was an energy that was moving me along, an energy that I learned to trust after a while. I've just been sort of following an understanding—an understanding that I'm being used, moved along, and that I will be as long as I'm willing to be. I don't feel that it's anything against my will. I have to be willing to be used in this way, and I always am. The flow of energy of the Goddess is very much within, very much within our bodies. It can be experienced. It can be felt. That is the Goddess speaking to me, telling me what She wants me to do. I always know what I'm supposed to do. I always know what I'm supposed to do next because I get excited and energized by it. There really is a tremendous change happening in our society....

It's very simple: Men and women are people. All we have to do is simply act like people: deal with each other lovingly, relate to each other in cooperative rather than competitive ways, sympathize and empathize with the needs of one another—whether it be our lover, our husband, our wife, our children, or whomever....

One of the major concerns now within women's spirituality is the preservation of the planet. We're trying to develop a sense not only of planetary consciousness but also of planetary conscience. This will make us aware of what's happening to all other races of people, to all other species of animals, to the trees, to the rivers, and to all else that has suffered from our ignorance. Each of us acts or doesn't act, and that creates the future.

Earth is our home. Whether or not they want to build space colonies, we can't think of Earth as something to use up and toss away like so many other things in our toss-away society. We really have to wake up and think about this planet as our home, and as the home for our children and our children's children, because that is the Goddess energy. It is that life-energy. If we destroy life on the planet, we destroy our home; we destroy our Mother.

—*At the Leading Edge* (Larson Publications, 1991)

"I'm not any kind of separatist. I love men, women, everything and everyone. I am an ardent feminist. It's a matter of changing stereotypes. I'm for evolution. I think the divine is sacred in all of us. My personal spiritual beliefs give me a tremendous amount of strength."

—*In Print*, "Great Goddess" (Vanguard Press, 1986)

unraveling the myth of adam and eve

Unraveling the Myth of Adam and Eve

CHAPTER 10 FROM *WHEN GOD WAS A WOMAN*

*W*HEN FIRST I STARTED upon my investigation of the worship of the female deity, it was to a great extent motivated by the image of woman presented by Judaism and Christianity—the woman known as Eve. The further I explored the rites and symbolism of those who revered the Divine Ancestress, the more convinced I became that the Adam and Eve myth, most certainly a tale with a point of view, and with a most biased proclamation for its ending, had actually been designed to be used in the continuous Levite battle to suppress the female religion. It was, perhaps, a more updated version of the dragon or serpent myth whose vestiges are found in the biblical Psalms and the book of Job.

The female faith was a most complex theological structure, affecting many aspects of the lives of those who paid Her homage. It had developed over thousands of years and its symbolism was rich and intricate. Symbols such as serpents, sacred fruit trees and sexually tempting women who took advice from serpents may once have been understood by people of biblical times to symbolize the then familiar presence of the female deity. In the Paradise myth, these images may have explained allegorically that listening to women who revered the Goddess had once caused the expulsion of all humankind from the original home of bliss in Eden.

Sacred Snakes and Prophetic Vision

Let's begin with the serpent. It seems that in some lands all existence began with a serpent. Despite the insistent, perhaps hopeful, assumption that the serpent must have been regarded as a phallic symbol, it appears to have been primarily revered as a female in the Near and Middle East and generally linked to wisdom and prophetic counsel rather than fertility and growth as is so often suggested.

The Goddess Nidaba, the scribe of the Sumerian heaven, the Learned One of the Holy Chambers, who was worshipped as the first patron deity of writing, was at times depicted as a serpent. At the Sumerian town of Dir the Goddess was referred to as the Divine Serpent Lady. The Goddess as Ninlil, who at times is said to have brought the gift of agriculture and thus civilization to Her people, was said to have the tail of a serpent. In several Sumerian tablets the Goddess was simply called Great Mother Serpent of Heaven.

Stephen Langdon, the archaeologist who led some of the earliest excavations of Sumer and later taught at Oxford, asserted that Inanna, then known as Ininni, was closely connected with serpent worship. He also described Her as the Divine Mother who Reveals the Laws. He wrote that the Goddess known as Nina, another form of the name Inanna, perhaps an earlier one, was a serpent goddess in the most ancient Sumerian periods. He explained that, as Nina, She was esteemed as an oracular deity and an interpreter of dreams, recording this prayer from a Sumerian tablet: "O Nina of priestly rites, Lady of precious decrees, Prophetess of Deities art Thou," and commenting that, "The evidence points to an original serpent goddess as the interpreter of dreams of the unrevealed future." Several sculptures unearthed in Sumer, which date from about 4000 BC, portray a female figure with the head of a snake.

Writing of Elam, just east of Sumer, where in earliest times the Goddess reigned supreme, Dr. Walther Hinz tells us: "... part of this individuality [in Elam] consists of an uncommon reverence and respect for eternal womanhood and in a worship of snakes that has its roots in magic ... Even the pottery of the third and fourth millennia swarms with snakes ..."

Ishtar of Babylon, successor to Inanna, was identified with the planet known as Venus. In some Babylonian texts this planet was called Masat, literally defined as prophetess. Ishtar was depicted sitting upon the royal throne of heaven, holding a staff around which coiled two snakes. One seal from Babylon, which shows Ishtar holding the serpent-entwined scepter, was inscribed, "Lady of Vision of Kisurru." Ishtar was elsewhere recorded as "She who Directs the Oracles" and "Prophetess of Kua." Babylonian tablets offer numerous accounts of priestesses who offered prophetic advice at the shrines of Ishtar, some of these very significant in the records of political events.

Even in the Babylonian-Kassite myth, Tiamat was recorded as the first divine being. According to this legend, Tiamat originally possessed the Tablets of Destiny, which, after Her murder, were claimed as the property of Marduke. Tiamat was described in this myth as a dragon or serpent. The actual association of the serpent with the female deity, all through the texts and inscriptions of Sumer and Babylon, was probably the very reason this symbolism was used in the Indo-European myths.

On the island of Crete the snake appears in the worship of the female deity more repeatedly than anywhere else in the Mediterranean area. All over the island, artifacts have been unearthed that portray the Goddess or Her priestesses holding snakes in their hands or with them coiled about their bodies, revealing that they were an integral part of the religious rituals. Along with the statues of serpent-entwined priestesses, cylindrical clay objects, also wrapped about with serpents, have been discovered on Crete. Arthur Evans, the archaeologist who excavated the Cretan palace at Knossos, described them as "snake tubes" and suggested that they were used to feed the sacred serpents that were kept at the sanctuaries of the Cretan Goddess. The abundant evidence of the sacred nature of the serpent, along with the Goddess, has in fact appeared to such an extent on Crete that many archaeologists refer to the female deity there as the Serpent Goddess.

Evans, offering supportive evidence, asserted that the Lady of the Serpents on Crete was originally derived from the worship of the Cobra Goddess of the predynastic people of Egypt. He suggested that the worship of the Serpent Lady may have been brought to Crete in about 3000 B.C. This is much the same time that the First Dynasty of Egypt was forming, and he further suggested that Egyptian people may have fled to Crete as a result of the invasions at that time.

The use of the cobra in the religion of the Goddess in Egypt was so ancient that the sign that preceded the name of any Goddess was the cobra (i.e., a picture of a cobra was the hieroglyphic sign for the word Goddess). In predynastic Egypt the female deity of Lower Egypt (north) was the Cobra Goddess known as Ua Zit. Not a great deal is known about this most ancient Cobra Goddess, but we later see Her as the *uraeus* cobra worn upon the foreheads of other deities and Egyptian royalty. The cobra was known as the Eye, *uzait*, a symbol of mystic insight and wisdom. Later derivations of the Cobra Goddess, such as Hathor and Maat, were both known as the Eye. This term, in any context it is used, is always written in feminine form. The position of the Eye and its eventual association with male deities was explained in Chapter Four. The Goddess as Hathor was also associated with the male deity Horus; Her name actually means House of Hor. But one text preserved the story that Hathor had been the serpent who had existed before anything else had been created. She then made the heavens, the earth and all life that existed on it. In this account She was angry, though the text is not clear about the reason; She threatened to destroy all of creation and once more resume Her original form as a serpent.

A prophetic sanctuary stood in the Egyptian city of Buto, once the foremost religious center of the Cobra Goddess. The town was actually known as Per Uto in Egyptian, but the Greeks called it Buto, also applying this name to the Cobra Goddess Herself. This shrine was credited in classical Greek times to the Goddess known as Lato, but it is likely that the same site had once been the shrine of Oracular advice of the Goddess Ua Zit Herself. Herodotus reported that he saw enormous numbers of snake skeletons lying in a pass in that city.

In Greece, we are afforded the closest look at the derivatives of the Egyptian and Cretan Serpent Goddess. Though the nature of the religion had undergone some major transformations after the invasions of the Achaeans and Dorians, who brought with them the worship of Zeus, many vestiges of the earlier images and symbolism still survived. This was especially manifested in the heroic figure of Athena. Her serpent continually appeared in legends, drawings and sculptures. In some statues it peered out from beneath Her great bronze shield or stood by

Her side. A special building known as the Erechtheum stood on the Acropolis alongside Her temple, the Parthenon. This Erechtheum was considered to be the home of Athena's snake. But the snake of the Greek Goddess of Wisdom, who was revered on the majestic heights of the Athenian Acropolis, was not a creation of the classical Greek period. Despite the Indo-European Greek legend that suggests that Athena was born from the head of Zeus, the worship of the Goddess had arrived on the Acropolis long before—with the Cretan Goddess of the Mycenaean settlements. The classical temples of the Acropolis, consecrated to the Greek Athena, were actually built on Mycenaean foundations.

The connections begin to take form. As we read before, the Mycenaeans were the people who had lived on Crete at the palace of Knossos at about 1400 BC. They had integrated the earlier Minoan-Cretan culture into their own to such an extent that the worship is often described as the Minoan-Mycenaean religion. Clothing styles, signet rings, murals, seals and artifacts of all kinds reveal the great similarity of the Mycenaean religious beliefs to those of the Cretans. Once understanding these connections, we realize the significance of the fact that, beneath the ruins of the classical Greek temples of Athens and Delphi, as well as many other Greek shrines where the Goddess was most reverently associated with Her serpent, lay these older Mycenaean remains.

The shrine that perhaps offers the deepest insight into the connections of the female deity of Greece to the Serpent Goddess of Crete is Delphi. Under the classical temple and buildings of Delphi, Mycenaean artifacts and ruins of earlier shrines have been unearthed. In the earliest times, the Goddess at Delphi was held sacred as the one who supplied the divine revelations spoken by the priestesses who served Her. The woman who brought forth the oracles of divine wisdom was called the Pythia. Coiled about the tripod stool upon which she sat was a snake known as Python. Though in later Greek writings Python was male, in the earliest accounts Python was described as female. The serpent Python was of such importance that this city had once been known as Pytho. According to Pausanius the earliest temple at this site had been built by women, while Aeschylus recorded that at this holiest of shrines the Goddess was extolled as the Primeval Prophetess. In later times the priests of the male Apollo took over this shrine, and Greek legend tells us of the murder of Python by Apollo. The many sculptures and reliefs of women, generally described as "the Amazons," fighting against men at this shrine may actually depict the initial seizure.

Reports of Python, as well as the legend of Cassandra of Troy, reveal that snakes were familiar inhabitants of the oracular shrine at Delphi. Sacred snakes were also kept at a temple of the Goddess known as Hera, who was closely associated with Gaia of Delphi, the Primeval Prophetess. The sites of divination at Delphi, Olympia and Dodona were initially identified with the Goddess but were later confiscated by the priests of Zeus and Apollo (both of whom are described as having killed the serpent of the Goddess Gaia). Yet, even under the name of the male deities, it was still priestesses who most often supplied the respected counsel.

So far we have seen that the female deity, as She was known in Babylon, Egypt, Crete and Greece, was identified as or with serpents and closely associated with wisdom and prophecy. But it was not only in these lands that the Serpent Goddess was known. Again, when we look over to Canaan, which bordered on the Mediterranean Sea (as do Egypt, Crete and Greece), we discover evidence of the esteem paid to the Goddess as the Serpent Lady.

The manner in which the connections occur are intriguing. They are really deserving of an entire book rather than the few paragraphs we have room for here. From Neolithic times onward, people were quite mobile, trading and warring in areas many miles from their original homes. Distant colonies were founded and settled where timber, gold, spices and other valuable materials were found. Phoenician ships traversed not only the entire Mediterranean Sea and the inland rivers but made their way well around the coast of Spain as far as Cadiz, and possibly even up to the British Isles, many centuries before the birth of Christ and the Roman invasions. Even before the Phoenicians, who were actually the Canaanites of Tyre and Sidon, there were groups of people who sailed the Mediterranean waters freely and who were known simply as the Sea Peoples. They appear to have traveled widely, often leaving behind them the evident remains of their visit or settlement.

One such people were known as the Philistines. This name has been made familiar to us through the Bible, where they are continuously described as a treacherously evil people, obviously the archenemies of the Hebrews. But as Professor R.K. Harrison wrote, "Archaeological excavations in Philistine territory have shown that it is clearly a mistake to regard the Philistines as synonymous with barbarity or cultural deficiency, as is so frequently done in common speech."

The Philistine people present one of the most significant links between the worship of the Serpent Goddess of Crete and the female deity as She was revered in Canaan. The Philistines are recorded in the Old Testament to have come from the isle of Caphtor—which is generally believed to be Crete; the Egyptians called it Keftiu. The Bible described them as coming from Caphtor and Egypt. Though their major migrations to Canaan appear to have taken place about 1200 BC, Philistines are mentioned in Canaan in the time of Abraham. Several writers have suggested that the Philistines were actually a branch of the Mycenaeans, who were culturally active upon Crete and Greece at the same time. Some writers associate their name with the Pelasgians, the people who lived in Greece before the Indo-European invasions. During the periods of the greatest Philistine migrations into Canaan, they settled primarily in the southwest. This area came to be known as Philistia, the origin of the name Palestine. Evidence suggests that along with the Philistine people came the religion of the Serpent Goddess.

Some of the most revealing evidence of the connections of the worship of the Serpent Goddess of Crete to the female deity of Canaan, as well as the nearby island of Cyprus, has been the discovery in both places of "snake tubes"—nearly identical to those found on Crete. Of even greater significance is the fact that a snake tube was unearthed in a Philistine temple devoted to the worship of Ashtoreth.

Archaeologist R.W. Hutchinson pointed out some of the connections:

The snake tubes of Gournia [a town on Crete] have interesting parallels outside Crete and Evans collated a convincing series of examples of clay tubes connected with the household snake cult, some with modeled snakes crawling up them… Some of the more interesting examples of snake tubes, however, come not from Crete at all but from Late Bronze Age sites in Cyprus and Philistia. One tube found at Kition on Cyprus shows the snake tube converted into a dove cot… Another tube found in the House of Ashtoreth on the Philistine site of Beth Shan [Canaan] dated to the reign of Ramses II of Egypt (c. 1292–1225 BC) shows two snakes crawling round and into the tube…

Another piece found at Beth Shan portrayed the Goddess leaning from the window of a shrine, while a serpent emerged from a lower level. At this same site quite a few "Astarte plaques" were found, along with the statue of a woman, probably intended to represent a priestess—with a serpent coiled about her neck. Another interesting discovery made in this temple was a terra cotta serpent with female breasts. According to the Bible it was this House of Ashtoreth in Beth Shan where the armor of the defeated Hebrew King Saul was victoriously displayed by the Philistines (I Sam. 31:10).

On the nearby island of Cyprus, at another temple of Ashtoreth located in the town of Kition, near present-day Larnaca, not only a snake tube most similar to those found on Crete was discovered but also a small clay figure holding a snake. Recent excavations at Kition have unearthed another figure of Ashtoreth. We may not be too surprised to learn that the Ashtoreth temple at Kition was built on what are thought to be Mycenaean or Cretan foundations.

Though the presence of the Philistines alone might be sufficient to attest and explain the appearance of the Serpent Goddess in Canaan, Her worship gained entrance into the "promised land" through other channels as well. The Goddess Isis-Hathor, whose worship assimilated that of Ua Zit, the Cobra Goddess of Egypt, was well known in certain sections of Sinai and Canaan. Even as early as the Second Dynasty, some of these places are believed to have been seaports or even colonies of Egypt.

Some of the connections of the Goddess in Canaan with the female deity as She was known in Egypt are revealed through their names. In Egypt the Canaanite Ashtoreth was known as Asit, again much like Ua Zit and Au Set. The name Umm Attar, Mother Attar, was known in parts of Arabia, probably related to the name Hathor but also to another Canaanite name for Ashtoreth—Attoret.

Several ancient temples offer evidence of the connection between Isis-Hathor and the Goddess in Canaan. In both She appears as the Serpent Goddess. At the first, Serabit el Khadim, a shrine on the Sinai Peninsula close to the great Egyptian turquoise mines, bilingual Egyptian and Semitic inscriptions have been discovered. The inscriptions named the deity once worshipped at the shrine as the Goddess Hathor. In these bilingual inscriptions Hathor was also referred to as Baalat, meaning Lady or Goddess, as the word was then known in Canaan. J.R. Harris wrote of the temple on Sinai and discussed the relationship between the two names of the Goddess as She was known there. He explained, "Here she [Baalat] was evidently identified with the Egyptian Goddess Hathor at whose temple all the inscriptions were found." But perhaps most significant is the fact that, on the walls of this shrine, two prayers had been carved into the stone. In both of these the Goddess was invoked—as the Serpent Lady.

Sir Flinders Petri wrote of probable oracles at the enclosures of the Serabit complex. This shrine on the Sinai Peninsula, which lies between Egypt and Canaan, is particularly worth noting since many scholars have suggested that it may have been on the route the Hebrew tribes took upon their exodus from Egypt. The Bible records that it was during this period in the desert that Moses came to possess the "brazen serpent," which appeared seven hundred years later in the shrine in Jerusalem. It was eventually destroyed by the Hebrew reformer Hezekiah as a "pagan abomination" but it is not inconceivable that it may have come into the possession of the Hebrews at Serabit and even have been accepted temporarily by Moses as a means of placating the Hebrew people.

Yet this bronze serpent seems to have been identified with the Goddess religion, for the Bible reveals that it was kept in the same temple in Jerusalem where in 700 BC we find vessels for Ashtoreth and Baal, the *asherah*, the house of the sacred women and the women who wept for Tammuz.

The title of Baalat as another name for Hathor leads to yet another shrine of the Goddess, the one at the Canaanite port of Byblos, a site first settled as long ago as 6000 BC. As late as the fourth century BC, writings from Berytus (Beirut) stated that the Baalat was still the principal deity of Byblos. Overlooking the Mediterranean waters, on this coastal site of what is now Lebanon in what had once been Canaan, temple foundations date back to at least 2800 BC. Many records of Byblos tell us that it was, during most periods, closely aligned with Egypt.

At this temple in Byblos the Goddess was revered both as Baalat and as Isis-Hathor. Many symbols of the Goddess and Her cobra were found amid the ruins. One headband, adorned with the rising cobra, was constructed so that the snake would emerge from the forehead of the person who wore it, as the Eye of Wisdom. At this same site two golden cobras and an offering bowl decorated with snakes was also unearthed. According to Egyptian legend, it was to this city of Byblos in Canaan that Isis had once traveled to retrieve the body of Her dead brother/husband Osiris.

Elsewhere in Canaan evidence of snakes appears alongside the worship of the Goddess. It seems likely that the majority of the sculptures and artifacts associated with the female deity and Her serpent in Canaan may have met destruction at the time of the occupation of the Levite-led Hebrews; yet scattered remains offer silent testimony to Her one-time existence even in the cities of southern Canaan.

At Taanach a number of serpent heads were discovered, as well as a small figure holding a serpent. Here too was found a bronze figure of Ashtoreth along with an inscription that the Goddess gave the oracles by the pointing of Her finger.

At Beth Shemesh, jugs with serpents and a figure of the Goddess with a snake falling over Her shoulder and into Her lap were unearthed in excavations. At Tell Beit Mersim, another Philistine stronghold, there were many "Astarte plaques," as well as a plaque that Albright refers to as the Goddess, a serpent coiled about the lower half of the body. The piece is very badly mutilated and I would hesitate to say who the figure actually represents, though the snake is certainly clear enough.

Hutchinson draws a connection between this particular figure and the Serpent Goddess of Minoan Crete, writing, "A similar snake goddess seems to have been worshipped during the Bronze Age in Palestine where a stele was found at Tell Beit Mersim in a deposit dated about 1600 BC, carved with a representation of a goddess with her snake curling round her body. This stele was practically contemporary with the faience figure of the Snake Goddess found in the temple repositories at Knossos."

Another bronze serpent was found at Shushan, while at Shechem archaeologists unearthed a figure with a snake coiled about its body. At the town of Gezer, eighteen miles northwest of Jerusalem, a bronze serpent was found near a cave which had been used as a religious sanctuary. There was also a plaque of the Goddess with a cobra. Serpents also appear to have been depicted in the margins of the plaque. It has been suggested that in Her outstretched arms She once held serpents, as in so many of the other plaques of this type which combine the aspects of both Ashtoreth and Hathor, clay reliefs simply marked Qadesh—Holy. A bronze figure of Ashtoreth was also discovered at this same site.

Archaeologist R.A.S. Macalister described the excavation at Gezer in this way: "In an enclosure close to the standing stones was found a bronze model of a cobra which may have been a votive offering. It recalls the story of the brazen serpent of Moses to whose worship Hezekiah put an end in II Kings. Possibly this object was similar in appearance. Another remarkable find made within the precincts of the high place was the unique figure of the two horned Astarte."

Gezer had two large underground caverns; the cobra was found at a nearby circular structure. Again, several writers have suggested that oracular divination may have been practiced in the underground chambers where libation bowls decorated with snakes were discovered.

And in Jerusalem itself was the serpent of bronze, said to date back to the time of Moses and treasured as a sacred idol in the temple there until about 700 BC.

The symbol of the serpent entwined about accounts of oracular revelation appears throughout the Near and Middle East. To summarize, connections are drawn between the Cobra Goddess of Egypt and the Serpent Goddess of Crete. The Mycenaeans appear to have brought the oracular serpent with them from Crete to the shrines of pre-Greece, observed most clearly at the sites of Athens and Delphi. Other people, known as the Philistines, probably from Crete, brought the Serpent Goddess to Cyprus and Canaan, while the Egyptians carried the worship of the Serpent Lady across the Mediterranean Sea to Byblos and across the sands of Sinai to Serabit. Both in Babylon and Sumer we find the Goddess associated with snakes and with oracular prophecy. There is hardly an area in the Near and Middle East where we do not find accounts of the serpent and/or the shrines of divine wisdom as separate elements; yet both of these occur together often enough to suggest that the relationship between these two separate elements be recognized.

In questioning the nature and purpose of the oracular shrines and the priestesses who gave advice, historical records, especially in Babylon and Greece, explain that they were primarily utilized for vital political, governmental and military matters. It was not only the belief that the priestesses could see into the future that made oracular divination so popular but the idea that these women were understood to be in direct communication with the deity who possessed the wisdom of the universe. It is evident from the accounts of the people who believed in prophetic revelation that they did not view the future as totally predestined and determined by uncontrollable fates but rather as something that could be acted upon, as long as one knew the most advantageous action to take. The oracular priestesses were not consulted for a firm prediction of the future but for counsel as to the best strategy, considering the situation. This advice was available at shrines all the way from Greece to Mesopotamia.

Evidence of the Goddess in Sumer, under the names such as Nina, Ininni or Inanna, suggests that divine revelation was an aspect of the religion from the most ancient times. In later Babylon, records of Queens Sibtu and Nakia revealed the importance and influence of the oracular priestesses in the political affairs of Babylon and the city of Mari. Babylonian prophetesses were known as *appiltu* or *muhhtu*. It is rather interesting that the Hebrew word *zonah* is at times defined as "prostitute" and at times as "prophetess."

J. Hastings wrote that in Egypt, "In the Old and Middle Kingdoms, women of important families often bear the title 'prophetess.' It was nearly always the goddesses Hathor and Neith that they served in this capacity."

D.S. Russell wrote of the prophetesses who came to be known as the Sibyls. The Sibyls were often identified with a prophetess of Anatolia, named as Sybella, whom we may suspect has some connection with the Goddess known there as Cybele. It was, in fact, the Sibyls of Rome who were responsible for having the worship of the Anatolian Cybele brought into Rome. According to Russell,

> These sibylline oracles were written during the latter half of the second century BC in Alexandria. They are imitative of the Greek Sibyls who exercised a considerable influence upon pagan thought both before and after this time. The pagan Sibyl was a prophetess who, under the inspiration of the god, was able to impart wisdom to men and to reveal to them the divine will. There were many varieties of such oracles in different countries and in Egypt in particular they came to have an increasing interest and significance.

At the temple in Jerusalem in about 620 BC, Ezekiel spoke of the women who dared to prophesy "out of their own heads." Even the much later canons of St. Patrick, who is said to have brought Christianity to "pagan" Ireland, warned against "pythonesses." Pythoness is still defined in most contemporary English dictionaries as a prophetess or witch.

"My Mind Had Extraordinary Powers"

This continual appearance of the serpent with the Goddess, in association with prophecy and divine revelation, raises the question of the purpose and meaning of its repeated presence. The manner in which the serpent was used in oracular divination has never been made clear, but there are some clues hinting at the possible explanation.

One of these is from the story of Cassandra, a tale that may have survived from the period of the Achaeans and the Trojan War. The legend related that Cassandra was left overnight at the shrine of Delphi as a very young child. When her mother, the Trojan Queen Hecuba, arrived there in the morning, she is said to have found the child surrounded by the sacred snakes that were kept in the shrine. They were licking Cassandra's ears. This experience was offered as the explanation of how Cassandra gained the gift of prophecy.

A Greek prophet named Melampus was also recorded to have had his ears licked clean by serpents, thus allowing him to understand the language of birds. In the writings of Philostratus, he claimed that it was quite common for Arabians to understand divine revelations, especially the sounds of birds, explaining that they had acquired this ability by feeding themselves the heart or liver of serpents. The sounds of birds were very often associated with the oracular shrines of Greece, while on Crete and in Ascalon, Canaan, statues often included one or more doves perching on the head of the Goddess or priestess.

In both Hebrew and Arabic the terms for magic are derived from the words meaning serpent. In Brittany supernatural powers were said to be acquired by drinking broth prepared from serpents. Among the Sioux Indians in North America the word *wakan* means both wizard and serpent. Indians in the southwest United States had an initiation ritual in which a brave who had been chosen as eligible for the honor performed a dance in which he allowed himself to be bitten several times by a snake. As a result of this experience, provided he did not die, he was said to gain great wisdom and insight into the workings of the universe and the meaning of all things.

In addition to these connections between serpents and oracular revelation, contemporary science has perhaps provided the deepest insight into the possible relationship between the two elements. Normally, when a person receives a venomous snake bite, and subsequently the venom is introduced into the system, there are various reactions, depending upon the species of snake, including swelling, internal bleeding, difficulty in breathing and paralysis. These effects often prove fatal. But there are recent records of people who have been immunized, thus preventing the venom of a snake bite from causing death. When bitten after the immunization, especially by krait, cobra or other elapids, the subject experiences an emotional and mental state that has been compared to the effects of hallucinogenic drugs.

In an account kept by his wife, William Haast of the Florida Serpentarium (where venom is extracted for various medicinal uses) described his reaction to a krait bite, received after he had been repeatedly immunized for his work. The account was later recalled in H. Kursh's *Cobras in the Garden.* Kursh writes:

Suddenly he began to feel pleasantly light and weirdly buoyant, almost gay, as though he were slightly intoxicated ... he had developed an acute sense of hearing, almost painfully acute. The air about him was a charivari, a veritable jungle of discordant noises. It was as if he was under the influence of a strange narcotic ... He had one inexplicable sensation. It was a peculiar emotional reaction which he could not control. As he lay with his eyes involuntarily closed, he could "see" things. There were visions in front of him.

In another report on this same incident, Marshall Smith of *Life* magazine quoted Haast as saying, "I found myself making up the most wonderful verses. My mind had extraordinary powers." It may or may not be related, but the oracles of the shrines in Greece were said to be given in verse.

Much like mescaline (a product of the peyote cactus) or psilocybin (found in certain types of mushrooms), both used as sacraments in some North American Indian religions, the chemical makeup of certain types of snake venom, may have caused a person, especially someone in the expectant frame of mind, to feel in touch with the very forces of existence and a sensation of perceiving the events and meaning of the past, present and future with great clarity and comprehension. This type of sensation is certainly often reported by people using mescaline, psilocybin and lysergic acid diethylamide (LSD). The sacred serpents, apparently kept and fed at the oracular shrines of the Goddess, were perhaps not merely the symbols but actually the instruments through which the experiences of divine revelation were reached. This may explain the title of the Egyptian Cobra Goddess, who was at times known as the Lady of Spells.

According to an old Talmudic tradition, the venom of the serpent, which had corrupted Eve and all humanity, lost its strength through the revelation of Mount Sinai but regained it when Israel began to worship the golden calf.

The Flesh and Fluid of the Goddess

But the serpent is not the only link between the story of Adam and Eve and the worship of the Goddess. Another most important symbol in the story is that of the tree, the tree of knowledge of good and evil, from which hung the forbidden fruit. There are legends known from classical Greece about the golden apple tree of the Goddess Hera, about which the serpent Ladon coiled. The tree, incidentally, was said to be given to Hera by the Goddess Gaia, the Primeval Prophetess of the shrine at Delphi. Though legends of apple trees were known in classical Greece, I suggest that the tree of knowledge of good and evil in earliest times was not an apple but a fig.

A particular species of tree was continually mentioned as sacred in various ancient records, but deceptively under three different names, so that its singular identity has been overlooked. At times it was called the sycamore, at times the fig and sometimes the mulberry. This tree is actually the Near Eastern *ficus sicomorus*, the sycamore fig, sometimes denoted as the black mulberry. It differs from the common fig tree in that its reddish colored fruit grows in large clumps, sometimes like a cluster of grapes.

References to this sacred tree are found in the writings of Egypt, while representations of it appear on Egyptian murals. The Goddess Hathor of Egypt, revered both as the Eye of Wisdom and the Serpent Lady, was also known by another title—the Lady of the Sycamore. This tree was known as the Living Body of Hathor on Earth. To eat of its fruit was to eat of the flesh and fluid of the Goddess. Some Egyptian murals depicted the Goddess within this tree, passing out its sacred fruit to the dead as the food of eternity, immortality and continued life, even after death.

The type of tree represented on the signet rings of Crete was perhaps the same one, though depicted in a more symbolic form, simply showing the clusters of fruit. Evans suggested that the fig was sacred to the Cretans and described a section of a mural at Knossos where the tree alongside the altar was a fig. He also mentioned a group of sacred trees portrayed within the walls of a Cretan sanctuary, whose foliage showed them to be fig trees. Cretan seals and rings repeatedly depicted the Goddess or Her attendants alongside small fruit trees, caring for them, almost caressing them, as if in sacred devotion. In India, where the fig is known as the "pipal tree," it is still considered sacred.

Some of the most explanatory evidence of the symbolic meaning of this tree is the knowledge we have of the memorial rituals celebrated at the "annual death" of Osiris, brother/husband of Isis, a death closely related to the sacrifice of the annual king. According to Egyptian records, Osiris was first buried in a mulberry coffin. This coffin was later placed inside a living sycamore tree, symbolic of Isis-Hathor as his mother/wife. In this way She was to provide him with the food of eternity. This custom was closely linked with the legend that Isis went to Canaan to retrieve the tree in which Osiris had been buried, cut the coffin of Osiris from that tree and left the remainder of it as a sacred relic in Her temple at Byblos; this was the Canaanite shrine at which Isis-Hathor and Baalat were synonymous.

The sacred symbolism of this coffin tree of Hathor makes it likely that this was the tree repeatedly referred to in the Bible as the *asherah*. Ezekiel spoke harshly of the "idolators" in the temple at Jerusalem passing around the sacred branch of a tree, as if it were a great sin. Passages in Ezekiel threaten, "Never again will they defile my name with their prostitutions and with their funeral pillars of their kings," and "The House of Israel shall no more defile my holy name, neither they nor their kings, by their harlotry or by their dead bodies of their kings." Isaiah referred to the planting of small trees for Adonis, warning that "the sprigs of foreign gods" would bring a harvest of grief and desperate sorrow.

Evans mentioned gold fig leaves found at Mycenaean tombs in connection with a "funeral cult" there. The fig tree was regarded as a gift given by the Goddess, as She was worshipped at the Greek shrine of Eleusis, a temple also built on Mycenaean foundations. It was against a tree that Adonis and Attis both met their legendary deaths and on a tree that the annual effigy of Attis was displayed in Rome. Dionysus, a figure quite similar to Attis and Adonis, associated with the worship of the Goddess both at Delphi and Eleusis, was symbolically associated with the fig tree.

As I mentioned previously, the *asherah* or *asherim* of the Bible were planted or stood alongside the altar at the shrines of the Goddess. They were the despised pillars and poles which the Hebrews were continually ordered to destroy. Though we have no certain proof that these were sycamore fig trees, the evidence suggests that this was so. The fruit of this tree, described in Egyptian texts as "the flesh and fluid of Hathor," may even have been eaten as a type of "communion" with the Goddess, perhaps giving rise to the custom of the communion of the "flesh and the blood" of Jesus, taken in the form of wafers and wine even today. Most intriguing is the line in the Bible that relates that, when Adam and Eve realized their nakedness as a result of having eaten the forbidden fruit of the tree, they then made aprons to cover their sexual parts—with fig leaves.

Serpents, Sycamores, and Sexuality

It is here that our understanding of the sacred sexual customs and matrilineal descent patterns enters the matter, further clarifying the symbolism of the forbidden fruit. In each area in which the Goddess was known and revered, She was extolled not only as the prophetess of great wisdom, closely identified with the serpent, but as the original Creatress, and the patroness of sexual pleasures and reproduction as well. The Divine Ancestress was identified as She who brought life as well as She who decreed the destinies and directions of those lives, a not unnatural combination. Hathor was credited with having taught people how to procreate. Ishtar, Ashtoreth and Inanna were each esteemed as the tutelary deity of sexuality and new life. The sacred women celebrated this aspect of Her being by making love in the temples.

Considering the hatred the Hebrews felt toward the *asherim*, a major symbol of the female religion, it would not be too surprising if the symbolism of the tree of forbidden fruit, said to offer the knowledge of good and evil, yet clearly represented in the myth as the provider of sexual consciousness, was included in the creation story to warn that eating the fruit of this tree had caused the downfall of all humanity. Eating of the tree of the Goddess, which stood by each altar, was as dangerously "pagan" as were Her sexual customs and Her oracular serpents.

So into the myth of how the world began, the story that the Levites offered as the explanation of the creation of all existence, they place the advisory serpent and woman who accepted its counsel, eating of the tree that gave her the understanding of what "only the gods knew"—the secret of sex—*how* to create life.

As the advocates of Yahweh destroyed the shrines of the female deity wherever they could, murdering when they could not convert, the Levite priesthood wrote the tale of creation. They announced that male supremacy was not a new idea, but in fact had been divinely decreed by the male deity at the very dawn of existence. The domination of the male over the female, as Hebrew women found themselves without the rights of their neighbors, rights that they too may have once held, was not simply added as another Hebrew law but written into the Bible as one of the first major acts and proclamations of the male creator. With blatant disregard for actual history, the Levite leaders announced that woman must be ruled by man, declaring that it was in agreement with the original decree of Yahweh, who, according to these new legends, had first created the world and people. The myth of Adam and Eve, in which male domination was explained and justified, informed women and men alike that male ownership and control of submissively obedient women was to be regarded as the divine and natural state of the human species.

But in order to achieve their position, the priests of the male deity had been forced to convince themselves and to try to convince their congregations that sex, the very means of procreating new life, was immoral, the "original sin." Thus, in the attempt to institute a male kinship system, Judaism, and following it Christianity, developed as religions that regarded the process of conception as somewhat shameful or sinful. They evolved a code of philosophical and theological ideas that inherently espoused discomfort or guilt about being human beings—who do, at least at the present time, conceive new life by the act of sexual intercourse—whether it is considered immoral or not.

This then was the unfortunate, unnatural and uncomfortable trap of its own making into which the patriarchal religion fell. Even today we may read in the Common Prayer Book of Westminster Abbey under the Solemnization of Matrimony, "Secondly it was ordained for a remedy against sin, and to avoid fornication; that such persons that have not the *gift of continency* might marry, and keep themselves undefiled members of Christ's body" (my Italics).

The picture takes form before us, each tiny piece falling into place. Without virginity for the unmarried female and strict sexual restraints upon married women, male ownership of name and property and male control of the divine right to the throne could not exist. Wandering further into the Garden of Eden, where the oracular cobra curled about the sycamore fig, we soon discover that the various events of the Paradise myth, one by one, betray the political intentions of those who first invented the myth.

A Levite Account of Creation— Theology or Politics?

Let us take a closer look at the tale of creation and the subsequent loss of Paradise as related by the Hebrew leaders and later adopted and cherished by the advocates of Christianity. As we compare the Levite creation story with accounts of the Goddess religion, we notice how at each turn, in each sentence of the biblical myth, the original tenets of the Goddess religion were attacked.

Stephen Langdon wrote, "Thus beyond all doubt the Nippurian school of Sumerian theology originally regarded man as having been created from clay by the great mother goddess." Professor Kramer tells us, "In a tablet which gives a list of Sumerian gods the goddess Nammu, written with the ideogram for 'sea' is described as 'the mother who gave birth to heaven and earth.'" One Sumerian prayer goes as follows: "Hear O ye regions, the praise of Queen Nana, Magnify the Creatress, exalt the dignified, Exalt the glorious One, draw nigh unto the Mighty Lady." The Egyptians wrote, "In the beginning there was Isis, Oldest of the Old. She was the Goddess from whom all becoming arose." Even in Babylonian periods there were prayers to Mami or Aruru as the creator of human life. Yet the worshippers of Yahweh, perhaps one thousand years later, asserted that it was a male who initially created the world. It was the first claim to male kinship— maleness was primal.

According to legends of Sumer and Babylon, women and men had been created simultaneously, in pairs—by the Goddess. But in the male religion it was of ultimate importance that the male was made first, and in the image of his creator—the second and third claims to male kinship rights. We are next told that from a small rather insignificant part of man, his rib, woman was formed. Despite all that we know about the biological facts of birth, facts the Levites certainly knew as well, we are assured that the male does not come from the female, but the female from the male. We may be reminded of the Indo-European Greek story of Athena being born from the head of Zeus.

Any unpleasant remnant or reminder of being born of woman had to be denied and changed. Just as in the myth of the creation through an act of masturbation by the Egyptian Ptah, the Divine Ancestress was written out of reality. We are then informed that the woman made in this manner was presented as a gift to the man, declaring and assuring her status—among those who accepted the myth—as the property of the male. It tells us that she was given to him to keep him from being lonely, as "a helper fit for him." Thus we are expected to understand that the sole and divine purpose of women's existence is to help or serve men in some way.

The couple so designed was placed in the Garden of Eden—paradise—where the male deity warned them not to eat any of the fruit of the tree of knowledge of good and evil. To the ancient Hebrews this tree was probably understood to represent the sacred sycamore fig of the Goddess, the familiar *asherah* which stood beside the altars of the temples of the Goddess and Her Baal. The sacred branch being passed around in the temple, as described by Ezekiel, may have been the manner in which the fruit was taken as "communion." According to Egyptian texts, to eat of this fruit was to eat of the flesh and the fluid of the Goddess, the patroness of sexual pleasure and reproduction. According to the Bible story, the forbidden fruit caused the couple's conscious comprehension of sexuality. Upon eating the fruit, Adam and Eve became aware of the sexual nature of their own bodies, "And they knew that they were naked." So it was that when the male deity found them, they had modestly covered their genitals with aprons of fig leaves.

But it was vitally important to the construction of the Levite myth that they did not both decide to eat the forbidden fruit together, which would have been a more logical turn for the tale to take since the fruit symbolized sexual consciousness. No, the priestly scribes make it exceedingly clear that the woman Eve ate of the fruit first—upon the advice and counsel of the serpent.

It can hardly have been chance or coincidence that it was a serpent who offered Eve the advice. For people of that time knew that the serpent was the symbol, perhaps even the instrument, of divine counsel in the religion of the Goddess. It was surely intended in the Paradise myth, as in the Indo-European serpent and dragon myths, that the serpent, as the familiar counselor of women, be seen as a source of evil and be placed in such a menacing and villainous role that to listen to the prophetesses of the female deity would be to violate the religion of the male deity in a most dangerous manner.

The relationship between the woman and the serpent is shown to be an important factor, for the Old Testament related that the male deity spoke directly to the serpent, saying, "I will put enmity between you and the woman and between your seed and her seed." In this way the oracular priestesses, the prophetesses whose advice and counsel had been identified with the symbolism and use of the serpent for several millennia, were now to be regarded as the downfall of the whole human species. Woman, as sagacious advisor or wise counselor, human interpreter of the divine will of the Goddess, was no longer to be respected, but to be hated, feared or at best doubted or ignored. This demand for silence on the part of women, especially in the churches, is later reflected in the passages of Paul in the New Testament. According to the Judaic and Christian theology, women's judgment had led to disaster for the whole human species.

We are told that, by eating the fruit first, woman possessed sexual consciousness before man and in turn tempted man to partake of the forbidden fruit, that is, to join her sinfully in sexual pleasures. This image of Eve as the sexually tempting but God-defying seductress was surely intended as a warning to all Hebrew men to stay away from the sacred women of the temples, for if they succumbed to the temptations of these women, they simultaneously accepted the female deity—Her fruit, Her sexuality and, perhaps most important, the resulting matrilineal identity for any children who might be conceived in this manner. It must also, perhaps even more pointedly, have been directed at Hebrew women, cautioning them not to take part in the ancient religion and its sexual customs, as they appear to have continued to do, despite the warnings and punishments meted out by the Levite priests.

The Hebrew creation myth, which blamed the female of the species for initial sexual consciousness in order to suppress the worship of the Queen of Heaven, Her sacred women and matrilineal customs, from that time on assigned to women the role of sexual temptress. It cast her as the cunning and contriving arouser of the physical desires of men, she who offers the appealing but dangerous fruit. In the male religions, sexual drive was not to be regarded as the natural biological desires of women and men that encouraged the species to reproduce itself but was to be viewed as women's fault.

Not only was the blame for having eaten the fruit of sexuality, and for tempting Adam to do the same, laid heavily upon women, but the proof or admission of her guilt was supposedly made evident in the pain of childbirth, which women were assured as their eternal chastisement for teaching men such bad habits. Eve was to be severely punished as the male deity decreed: "I will greatly multiply your pain in childbearing; in pain you shall bring forth children, yet your desire shall be for your husband and he shall rule over you."

Making use of the natural occurrence of the pains of the pressure of a human child passing from the womb, through a narrow channel, into the outside world, the Levite writer pretended to prove the omnipotent power of his deity. Not only was woman to bear the guilt for sexual consciousness, but according to the male deity her pain in bearing a child was to be regarded as punishment, so that all women giving birth would thus be forced to identify with Eve.

But perhaps most significant was the fact that the story also stated that it was the will of the male deity that Eve would henceforth desire *only* her husband, redundantly reminding us that this whole fable was designed and propagated to provide "divine" sanction for male supremacy and a male kinship system, possible only with a certain knowledge of paternity.

We are perhaps all too familiar with the last line of the decree, which announced that from that time on, as a result of her sin and in eternal payment for the defiant crime which she had committed against the male deity, her husband was awarded the divine right to dominate her, to "rule over" her to totally assert his authority. And in guilt for what she had supposedly done in the very beginning of time, as if in confession of her poor judgment, she was expected to submit obediently. We may consider here the more practical reality that, once the economic security of women had been undermined by the institution of male kinship, women were forced into the position of accepting this one stable male provider as the one who "ruled the roost."

Once these edicts had been issued, the couple was expelled from the Garden of Eden, the original paradise where life had been so easy. From that time on they were to labor for their livelihood, a most severe warning to any woman who might still have been tempted to defy the Levite Yahweh. For hadn't it been just such a woman, listening to the advice of the serpent, eating the forbidden fruit, suggesting that men try it too and join her in sexual consciousness, who had once caused the downfall and misery of all humankind?

ancient mirrors
of womanhood

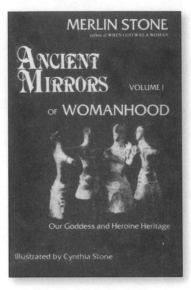

Ancient Mirrors, Vol. 1

Ancient Mirrors, Vol. 2

Original covers designed by Merlin Stone for the two-volume set *Ancient Mirrors of Womanhood: Our Goddess and Heroine Heritage,* published by her own New Sibylline Books in 1979.

Ancient Mirrors of Womanhood:

A Reflection on the
Poetic Genius of Merlin Stone

by David B. Axelrod

A wealth of inspiration for your own creative work in fiction,
dance, poetry, song, drama, painting, graphics.
(Merlin's description of her book
on a promotional bookmark)

*M*ERLIN STONE IS REMEMBERED for her thorough scholarship, which finally gave credence to the importance of the Goddess through the ages, but her second book, *Ancient Mirrors of Womanhood*, may well be a work of even greater genius. Much more information about the Goddess was needed to counter the tremendous weight of the patriarchy, which suppressed Goddess religions. In her second book, Merlin presented her facts in an even more accessible and enjoyable format.

The study of the Goddess, for a long time prior to Merlin and a few other feminist writers, was heavily biased. When Otto Rank wrote his study on *The Myth of the Birth of the Hero* (1909), he barely mentioned women as having a place in what was clearly a patriarchal mythos. Nor did Joseph Campbell give much attention to women who completed what he identified as an archetypal "hero cycle" in his own *The Hero with a Thousand Faces* (1949). The list of major studies in mythology and comparative religion that did not acknowledge the true function of the Goddess is so long that it clearly demonstrates the importance of Merlin Stone's work. In a patriarchal world dating back well before Thomas Bulfinch's *Stories of Gods and Heroes* (1855), the "hero" reigns supreme. Where are the "heroines," the stories of women of bravery, power, wisdom, and influence? It was absolutely necessary for Merlin to provide us with even more explication of our Goddess heritage.

In *When God Was a Woman*, Merlin presents her extensive research about the Goddess religion from a distinctly feminist point of view, culminating in her unraveling the myth of Adam and Eve. Anticipating the furor that might result from these pronouncements, Merlin was careful to provide extensive research and documentation of pre-patriarchal Goddess religions. Without Merlin's attention to detail, we might not fully understand or even believe her conclusions about the conscious suppression of women in the Judeo-Christian myth of our creation. Merlin begins *Ancient Mirrors* with a quote from an early feminist author, Clara Colby: "Nothing would be more interesting in connection with the *Woman's Bible*, than a comparative study of the accounts of creation held by people of different races and faiths" (from *The Woman's Bible*, "Comments on Genesis," 1895). *Ancient Mirrors* answers that prophetic call for more clarity.

However, the intention of *Ancient Mirrors* actually goes beyond the self-assigned mission of Merlin's first book. Knowing that some readers might find the style of *When God Was a Woman* to be a challenge—a "scholarly" read—Merlin recast her wealth of knowledge into a much more accessible form when she wrote *Ancient Mirrors*. One could think of *Ancient Mirrors* as a sequel to Merlin's first, groundbreaking book. Even Merlin said that she had so much information still left to impart after her first book, she felt she had to create another volume. But it would be a mistake to think that *Ancient Mirrors* is only a sequel. We often hear people praise the eloquence and poetry in the Songs of Solomon. We can also praise the "Songs of Stone."

It would be useful to consider the arc of Merlin Stone's life as a way to better understand the depth of her creative genius in creating *An-*

cient Mirrors. If we all—rich and poor, educated and uneducated—seek some vision of the truth, one could make the case that all four central elements of Merlin's life and training came together in her writing the book: work, study, inspiration, and even a touch of "madness." The "ordinary" working person may toil on in relative obscurity, but that person also wants to believe life is meaningful. Of course, those who live a life of letters, pursuing degrees or devoted to the arts, seek the truth. Whether it is superstition or there is some science that explains it, it is often believed that mental illness allows an uncommon glimpse into a deeper realm. Certainly, a different brain thinks outside the box. Then there are those who devote themselves to religion or are truly inspired. In an unpublished novel, excerpts from which are included in *Merlin Stone Remembered*, Merlin identified the need that many people have to set out on a quest. And what greater quest is there than to find some eternal "Truth"? At intervals in her life, Merlin never shirked or diminished the importance of basic, hard work—even as a waitress or, when Lenny met her, as a switchboard operator in a Miami Beach hotel. Working people, as much as any of us, quest for meaning in their lives. As central to Merlin's existence was her art and her studies—a life of the mind. She achieved not just her bachelor's degree and a master of fine arts degree, but through her vigorous independent study, she was rightfully awarded an honorary doctorate. Her scholarship was certainly a quest to bring us all a central Truth.

However, for all Merlin's scholarship, to this day, some people still attempt to dismiss her findings as "madness." For her scholarship and writings, in another age, Merlin would have been burned at the stake, or certainly locked away as a lunatic. Of course, one person's madwoman is another's prophet, and it is here we should acknowledge the sheer inspiration exhibited by Merlin Stone in creating forty-seven poems for many of the nearly one hundred twenty goddesses she presents in *Ancient Mirrors*. Her work is the nexus of all Merlin's experience as an artisan, a scholar, a "mad" risk-taker, and an inspired teacher of the Truth about the Goddess. In her Introduction, Merlin admits that she "reject[ed] the idea of a strictly academic presentation of the information that I had found." She read the numerous scholarly studies where the "entire footnote biased emphasis" was on male-oriented figures. "Thus, I openly admit to my own bias in choosing to study only female images.... It was also clear to me that, if I was going to present material at all, I was going to do so with respect—the respect of seriously considering the religious ideas of others as more than intellectual curiosities.... People had prayed to, honored, held as sacred [these goddesses]" (Stone, "Introduction," vol. I, p. 12).

Ancient Mirrors presents the story, function, and rituals for goddesses covering a substantial period of time and in an extensive range of countries and cultures. Not only has Merlin found the facts that document the existence of each goddess, she has actually created a "liturgy" for many of them—poems and prayers that can be recited to honor the goddess and invoke her powers. For example, she reverentially invokes Neit, the Egyptian goddess:

> Most ancient Mother,
> Great Radiant One,
> Lady of the Stars,
> Mistress of the Celestial Ocean....
> The Earth nestles between Her thighs,
> as daily She gives birth to the Sun.
> (*Ancient Mirrors*, vol. II, pp. 75–76)

The poem/prayer itself is seventy-one lines long, and in place of a simple, scholarly enumeration of Neit's attributes, Merlin brings us into the metaphoric world of the goddess whose powers created and, daily, re-create our existence for us:

> Her eye creating the Nile,
> the stars glowing with emerald light
> set into her very body,
> the single word 'beauty' marked as a glyph
> between Her sacred horns.
> (*Ancient Mirrors*, vol. II, p. 76)

The "eye" becomes the Nile. The "stars glowing" are the body of the Goddess herself. All "beauty" exists within her. The sense that the very body of the Goddess provides us with our world is a central concept that poetry, with its devices of synecdoche (allowing the part to represent the whole) and personification, fosters. But more so, Merlin had an artist's sense of texture and color so that her poems take on a sculptural and tactile feeling.

For the Hebrew goddess Shekhina, known in the Bible as "the Bride of Sabbath," Merlin laments:

> too long has She been in exile,
> too long have Her people
> sorrowed at Her absence...
> Still the candles are lit,
> still the sacred braided loaf is baked,
> in hopes that Her ancient Sabbath spirit
> will enter each home—
> filling it with the Mother love
> that is the very presence of the Shekhina.
> (*Ancient Mirrors*, vol. I, p. 128)

Merlin's poetry teaches, coaches, and sings the long-lost, the banished, the often-forbidden goddesses back into our lives.

For the Indian goddess Kali, Merlin cautions us not to succumb to racist associations with dark color being a lesser human form—or a lower caste in India itself. When Merlin invokes Kali, it is with a love for the darkness and the very sound of her name:

> Black as the petal of a blue lotus at night,
> black as the night touched by the light of the moon,
> Kali is the essence of Night,
> She who is called Sleep.
> She who is named Dream,
> She who is the joyous dancer of the cremation ground...
> She is Maha Kali, Great Mother Time,
> She is Nitya Kali, Everlasting Time,

She is Raksa Kali, Goblin yet Protector
during quake, famine or flood,
She is Smyama Kali, the Dark One who dispels fear,
She is Smasana Kali, Ever-Joyous Dancer.
(*Ancient Mirrors*, vol. II, pp. 23–24)

And so the poem goes on, creating a rhythm that could enthrall those reciting together and summon the spirit of the Goddess herself.

The usual form of Merlin's poems first invokes the goddess, identifying her attributes and role in her people's creation and culture. Then, Merlin may need to correct misinformation or defend a goddess who is falsely accused of wrongs. Two of Merlin's poems are hundreds of lines long—essentially goddess epics that tell each goddess's major story in verse. It is not to diminish the importance of scholarship that we can praise what Merlin has done—transcending mere fact to bring the Goddess back to life. A first encounter with any of her poems in her book might leave a reader to think that Merlin simply copied texts and incantations from ancient sources. Her genius, in fact, was in composing just the words that adherents might have recited in praise of each goddess. Merlin's grasp of each goddess and of the nature of Goddess religion was so completely empathetic that she could credibly summon and honor each goddess.

Beacon Press, recognizing the genius of Merlin's creations, bought the rights to her privately published two volumes and reissued them in a single paperback edition in 1984. Reviews quoted on the book's promotional literature immediately identified its significance. Erica Jong, called it "an essential book for anyone interested in the female aspect of the deity" and applauded Merlin's "passion." The Akiko Dance Company of Hawaii noted the book was an "inspiration for an entire repertory of dances." Poet and novelist Ruth Pettis said the book "can provide an endless source of ideas and inspiration for women image-makers—for poets and ... for those in the visual arts." Reviewer Karen Lindsey, writing for *Sojourner Magazine*, said, "These are stories to grow up with, to have around to reread ... to nurture ourselves and our daughters." It should be mentioned that *Ancient Mirrors* contains artwork created by Cynthia, Merlin's daughter—a suite of twelve pen-and-ink drawings depicting goddesses and scenes within their related stories—as well as "Ruler of the House of Life," a tapestry of Isis done by Merlin's daughter Jenny. Together they are yet another testimonial to the love and talent of both the mother and the daughters.

three thousand years of racism

Editor's Note

While Merlin Stone may be best known for research into the thousands of years of lost goddess religions, she was also very keenly aware of the scourge of racism. In a 1979 article she wrote for *Plexus: A Bay Area Women's Newspaper*, Merlin attests to the fact that "the issue of racism within the women's movement is one that touches me deeply.... After years of concern, compassion and guilt about racism (long before my consciousness of sexism), it recently dawned on me that perhaps I was in a position to do something about it." ("Racism," Vol. 5, No. 10, p. 5) She was writing to encourage women's groups to include more women from Third-World countries and to be sure they paid minority speakers an equal stipend. Acknowledging her own position of importance in the women's movement, she raised her voice for racial equality.

The parallels between gender discrimination and racial discrimination were obvious to Merlin as she wrote her books. In *Ancient Mirrors of Womanhood*, Merlin was thorough in establishing the importance of goddesses of numerous ethnicities. In her commentary on goddesses in India, for example, she notes how Kali was relegated to a lower, "darker" place as a further way for people of a lighter complexion to assert their supremacy (Stone, *Ancient Mirrors*, p. 222). *When God Was a Woman* was equally notable for the documentation of the worship of the Goddess among people of diverse cultures and races.

In 1981, Merlin published *Three Thousand Years of Racism: Recurring Patterns in Racism*—an essay of approximately ten thousand words—as a twenty-eight-page pamphlet including two pages of annotated bibliography. She used her own imprint, New Sibylline Books, "in conjunction with *Women Against Racism*."

The actual facts about that organization and the historical events that precipitated the release of the essay seem to be lost. However, books and essays were appearing at that time that asserted a new identity among African-American women, including, in that same year, Gloria Watkins's *Ain't I a Woman?: Black Women and Feminism* (under the nom de plume Bell Hooks, South End Press, 1981) and Angela

Davis's *Women, Race and Class* (Random House, 1981). In her own promotional statement for *Three Thousand Years*, Merlin states: "Our western educational system leaves many people with the idea that white people have a proud cultural heritage. ... Educators must ... [stress] the proud cultural heritages that all races possess." (New Sibylline flier, 1982)

She achieved some success with educators. State University of Colorado adopted her pamphlet as a part of its freshman orientation. The University of Santa Clara, California, proposed that Merlin visit to hold "contact meetings" to better educate students on campus. Even years after the pamphlet's publication, the County of Santa Clara got Merlin's permission to give its social workers a copy as "an excellent tool to help workers ... build bridges with one another." (Letter requesting permission, June 1991) In addition to her concerns about racism within the women's movement itself and the implicit racism of America's educational system, Merlin was highly concerned about the broader struggle toward racial equality in the U.S. and abroad. Women worldwide were uniting to take a stand against apartheid and for racial as well as gender equality.

It should also be noted that while Merlin Stone, born Marilyn Jacobson in 1931, was not a practitioner of a specific religion, she was born Jewish. Her childhood and most formative years would bear witness to the rise and fall of the Third Reich. She was fourteen when the concentration camps were liberated and the full consequence of the Holocaust emerged for the world. Her analysis of Hitler's Aryan empire, as part of *Three Thousand Years of Racism,* together with her identifying the clear patterns of racism, were absolutely a natural consequence of Merlin Stone's personal and scholarly life.

—*David B. Axelrod*

Three Thousand Years of Racism:
RECURRING PATTERNS IN RACISM
by Merlin Stone

*A*FTER THE LAST FEW decades of efforts to erase or lessen the many overt and covert forms of racism in the U.S., many of us are now watching in horror as the reports of various forms of racist attitudes and violence seem to be increasing rather than fading away. We may blame it on the rise in unemployment, inflation, or extreme neo-conservative trends. But beneath our consideration of each of these factors lies the nagging question of the efficacy of the strategies and tactics that we have been using to battle against racism. Is there something that we should do that we have not done? Is there something that we have done that we should not have done? And perhaps most important have we ever arrived at a full and clear enough analysis of racism that provides a firm foundation for the formulation of effective anti-racist efforts?

We have long believed that our comprehension of racist acts and attitudes had been too limited. It had been based primarily upon observations of racism in the U.S. over the past few centuries and, for the most part, focused upon the effects of racism upon the victims rather than on the methods and behavior of the perpetrators. It was for this reason that we began to examine some of the records of racist acts and racist statements that had been written in many areas of the world and throughout recorded history. Some of these records dated back to over 3,000 years ago. As a result of this examination we believe that the chronologically and geographically broader perspective provided by these records may be of use in our comprehension of racism and thus in our formulation of viable strategies and tactics to combat racism in all its manifestations.

The written accounts of racism throughout world history are numerous and will require many years of work to fully present and discuss. But due to the urgency of the issue we feel that some of the basic insights gleaned from this examination should be presented now. In our effort to do this we will first describe and explain what appear to be rather consistent patterns in the many accounts of racism, following this with some specific historical examples of racism that we feel may be of particular significance in our understanding of racist behavior. The final focus of this paper will be on the records of racism among the ancient Aryan groups of about 1200–600 B.C., the accounts that we feel may offer especially useful insights into the methods and strategies of racist oppressors today.

The Process

One of the first realizations that the examination of a broad spectrum of historical records provides is that racism is not, and never has been, a static attitude, a monolithic form of behavior, or a body of random events. The records make it clear that racism occurs as a long-term *process* comprised of specific stages. Not truly perceiving racism as a process may be at the core of our problems in confronting it successfully for just when we think we are lessening racism, as it exists in one of its stages, it may surprise us by moving into another stage. But the examination of the historical records also reveals that the many stages of the entire racist process follow a surprisingly consistent repertoire, i.e., specific stages of racism occurring at specific points in the process. By first perceiving racism as a long-term process, then becoming familiar with the full repertoire of the numerous stages within the process, and finally better understanding when each stage will be used, we can begin to see the predictability in racist behavior. We believe that it is this predictability that will be of value in our formulation of anti-racist activities.

To understand racism as a process, we should first delineate the two major aspects within it. Although these two aspects are closely interwoven in nearly all racist oppression, perceiving the specific nature of each aspect is necessary for a clear comprehension of the process. The first aspect, and nearly always the underlying purpose of racism, is *economic racism*, the theft of the land, property, resources and/or labor from people of a racial or ethnic group other than one's own. The second aspect is *cultural racism*, the act of propagandizing and/or believing that a racial or ethnic group other than one's own is innately inferior in human development. This second aspect may range from assertions of an innate lack of mental or creative capacities to an innate lack of various "moral" capacities. It is the assertion that the lack of these qualities is innate, i.e., genetic, as much a biologically determined factor as skin coloring, that is the core of cultural racism.

Once distinguishing between these two aspects of racism so that we may define each, we may then observe the progressive stages within each aspect—and how each specific stage of cultural racism is strategically dovetailed to support each specific stage of economic racism. Within the context of this paper we have simplified the progression of the process into two major stages but, as we shall explain, many substages exist within each stage and the transitions within and between the stages occur on a gradual continuum, at times even overlapping.

The first stage of economic racism is the initial theft of the land, property, resources and/or labor belonging to another racial or ethnic group by violence as extreme as that required to accomplish the theft, e.g., unprovoked aggression, invasion, full scale war, massacre and/or kidnapping. This theft is supported by the first stage of cultural racism. This is the assertion that the victims of the theft are innately immoral, even innately evil, e.g., demons, cannibals, head hunters, savages, bloodthirsty, merciless, sadistic, vicious, child killers, rapists, heathen, in league with the devil, criminal, devious, sly, sexually perverse, dishonest, cunning, etc.

In this first stage of cultural racism there is little or no emphasis on a supposedly innate mental superiority of the aggressors; innate moral superiority is the issue. The aggressors declare that they are innately moral. The victims are supposedly lacking in fully developed human capacities for morals and ethics, leading to the aggressors' declaration that they must be controlled or annihilated. The aggressors claim to be combatting this evil and immorality for the sake of all humankind or in the name of some supposedly higher divine force.

The purpose of first stage cultural racism is to incite fervor among the aggressors that will fuel and justify the unprovoked aggression and extreme violence of first stage economic racism. The various sub-stages within this stage encompass the aggressors' first assertions of evil or immorality, along with their initial physical attack, and continue until the final defeat and subjugation of the victims. As increasing areas of the victims' territories are conquered and/or greater numbers of the victims are subjugated, the assertions of evil and immorality lessen by degree, creating sub-stages that may range from the aggressors' initial assertions of "demons" or "savages" to somewhat milder assertions such as innate dishonesty or cunning. The length of time of the entire first stage encompasses the initial attack until the final conquest, a time period that may range from several weeks to several centuries, i.e., as long as there is serious resistance by the victims.

The second stage of economic racism is the long-term control by the aggressors/conquerors of what they have taken by force and then claim is rightfully theirs. The land, property and resources of the victims are legally in the conquerors' name no matter that they wrote the new laws themselves. The labor of the victims, now living in the conquerors' land, is reimbursed with just enough to keep the victims alive, able to work, and to produce more laborers whether for cheap or slave labor. (This includes the conquerors' control and regulations of the number of laborers, leading to enforced pregnancies when more laborers are wanted by the conquerors, or enforced sterilization and/or less concern for the food supply and health care of the victims when less laborers are wanted.) The level of overt violence in this second stage is lower than in the first stage but is always present as an example or threat against rebellion by the victims.

The second stage of cultural racism supports the second stage of economic racism. This is the assertion that the members of the subjugated population are innately mentally inferior, e.g., less able to learn, less inventive, less creative toward cultural accomplishments, at a lower level of human development, etc. The menial jobs allotted to the conquered victims supposedly affirm this innate mental inferiority. These assertions of the victims' supposed inferiority are structured into the social institutions of the conquerors, as well as the laws, customs, educational and economic systems and, at times, the religious systems.

Deprived of their ancestral lands, property and resources, of their own cultures and customs, even of control of their own lives, the victims and their descendants gradually internalize the conquerors' assertions of their superiority. The level of this internalization creates various sub-stages, forming a direct ratio to the level of repressive violence, i.e., the greater the internalization, the less overt the violence—and vice versa. (This does not apply to the less obvious violence of enforced pregnancies, sterilization, or lack of concern for food and health care used to control the labor supply.) The length of time of this second stage is determined by the ability of the aggressors/conquerors to maintain the subjugation of the victims and to fend off rebellion.

But the most important factor in understanding the entire process of racism is perceiving the conquerors' strategy of revising both aspects of first stage racism upon any serious intransigence or rebellion by the victims at any time during the second stage, i.e., an acceleration of repressive violence accompanied by a reversion to the various forms of assertions of an innate evil or immorality in the rebellious victims.

We have long been aware of the increase in repressive violence as the conquerors' response to confrontations of their racist behavior. What we have not seen as clearly is the conquerors' strategy of vacillation between the two sets of quite different stereotypes of cultural racism: the correlations of assertions of an innate mental inferiority upon the passivity or cooperation of the victims; the assertions of an innate evil or immorality when the victims refuse to be victimized.

Observing the tactic of this vacillation to maintain economic racism and to repress all efforts to battle against it is vital to our understanding of the entire racist process for the historical records suggest that economic racism has seldom, if ever, existed without the support of some form of cultural racism.

Acts of economic racism have been recorded throughout written history. Written records supporting cultural racism are less plentiful but do surface in statements made shortly before, or at the time of, various conquests, and in the records of the legal, martial, religious, social and educational systems of the aggressors/conquerors. Observing some of the specific accounts of cultural racism, as it has been used and re-used to support economic racism for over 3,000 years, gives us some idea of the repertoire of various cultural racist assertions and when each will be used.

First Stage

The use of first stage cultural racism appears in the accounts of the Germanic Saxons' battles with Asian Turkic Magyars in the Tenth Century. To fuel their battles against the Magyars, the Saxons asserted the Magyars were "cannibals and vampires," "the devilish offspring of Gothic witches who had mated with fiends in the wastes of Asia."[1]

This assertion of an innate evil in the Asian groups that were to the north and east of the Teutonic/Germanic tribes was to be revived time and again. It was used to fuel the Crusades that began at the end of the Eleventh Century. At the call of Pope Urban II in 1095, white European men began to gather in troops and make their way across the thousands of miles of Europe and Asia to conquer the "evil Asian infidel," i.e., the Asian Seljuk Turkic peoples who were accused of threatening Christianity in Byzantine Turkey. It was not long before Semitic Jews in Europe, as well as Semitic Jews and Arabs of the Near East, were also regarded as "evil Asian infidels" by European Crusaders who attacked and murdered many Jews and Arabs along with Asian Turks.

After several centuries of 'Holy Wars,' the crusading Teutonic Knights of Germany ruled over large areas on the eastern bank of the Baltic Sea, extending their conquests well into western Russia, while the Levantine area that is now Israel, Lebanon and west Syria was conquered by the leaders of the Crusades who eventually crowned themselves as kings or princes of many eastern Mediterranean towns and provinces. Godfrey of Lorraine became King of Jerusalem. Tancred of Normandy was crowned Prince of Galilee. Guy de Lusignan ruled Cyprus, Raymond of Toulouse claimed Tripoli. De la Roche became Duke of Athens, as Baldwin of Flanders took the throne of the Emperor of Constantinople, declaring himself as ruler of the entire Byzantine Christian Empire.[2]

But the white European assertion that Asian peoples were evil did not originate with Christianity. It had existed among the Norse and Swedes in the pre-Christian Viking period. Norse accounts of the Ninth Century describe the Inuit (Eskimos) and the Asian Finns, who lived to the north and east of the Norse and Swedes, as skraelings, literally "wretched savages." Declaring that the Asians' darker coloring made them "evil in appearance," Norse Vikings gradually occupied the Asian Finnish areas of Scandinavia. This attitude apparently justified the unprovoked Viking murders of "skraelings" in Vinland (now thought to have been Newfoundland), which the Vikings had also attempted to colonize.[3]

Much this same form of cultural racism was used to fuel and justify the four centuries of violent conquest of the entire western hemisphere. The concept of "Manifest Destiny" as the justification for white Europeans to invade and take the lands and resources of Native Americans by ruse and violence was rife with images of the indigenous populations of the western hemisphere as "bloodthirsty heathen savages." Despite the reports of Columbus who spoke of the Arawak tribe of the Caribbean as peaceful and generous, despite the writings of the Sixteenth Century Montaigne who described the Native Americans as the most honest and forthright of people, the general attitude of the white European adventurists, and of the European royalty and business interests that funded them, was that the Native Americans were "heathen savages" worshipping "accursed idols" and practicing immoral social and religious customs, i.e., non-Christian. This attitude of first stage cultural racism appears to have been most prevalent among the Puritan "colonists" from Britain, but also appears continually in Spanish accounts of the conquest of Mexico and the Yucatan.[4]

The refusal of most Native Americans to be forced from their own lands, and their refusal to be used as slave labor for the Europeans, led to a prolonged first stage of economic and cultural racism that began shortly after 1492 and continued until the last half of the Nineteenth

Century. The remnants of this attitude lasted well into the Twentieth Century, surfacing time and again in "Cowboy and Indian" films. Since so much more than Native American labor was to be gained by the European invaders of the entire western hemisphere, the first stages of economic and cultural racism continued to the point of an almost total extermination of the indigenous population of North America and much of Central and South America. Although many Native Americans, especially in Mexico, were taken as slaves by the Spanish troops, and "good looking Indian women" were taken as war booty, most Native Americans resisted enslavement so furiously that they were not generally regarded as potential slave laborers by the Europeans.[5]

But while Native Americans remained in the extreme violence of first stage racism for so many centuries, European "colonists" then kidnapped people from Africa to serve as the slave labor on the lands they had taken from the Native Americans. European ships sailed the Atlantic, repeatedly carrying the silver and gold taken from the Native Americans to Europe, returning with cargoes of healthy young people kidnapped from Africa.[6] Forcibly removed from their homelands, hence in an even more powerless position than the Native Americans, the kidnapped Africans and their descendants in North, Central and South America more quickly became the victims of second stage racism. Thus, as the Native Americans were still being described as "bloodthirsty heathens," and gradually being exterminated by the continuation of first stage violence against them, it was primarily African people who were used as slaves. The European "colonists" were quick to assert that the kidnapped black people were at a lower level of mental development.

The pattern of the stages of the racist process remained consistent, for when the Native American populations became so small that they were no longer able to physically resist the theft and aggression, the survivors were then stereotyped as mentally and motivationally inferior, while Afro-Americans, especially since the recent demands for civil rights, have been increasingly stereotyped as vicious or dishonest.

Equating the people of darker races, or darkness per se, with the devil, or some supernatural force of evil or immorality, has been used repeatedly in first stage cultural racism, not only in the Christian period but by pre-Christian white groups as well. As we will explain more fully, this form of first stage cultural racism appears throughout the religious accounts of the ancient Aryans. The ancient Aryan records provide a great deal of insight into the astonishing ideas invented by racist minds to support their abuse, conquests, and oppression of other peoples. But before discussing the early Aryan records, a look at some later records of second stage cultural racism may be helpful in better understanding the significance of the Aryan accounts and the role they played in contemporary racist attitudes.

Second Stage

Between the sixteenth and nineteenth centuries white Europeans invaded and conquered many areas of the world, in most cases those belonging to people of darker races who constitute the majority of the Earth's population.

There was hardly a mile of the 5000 mile long continent of Africa that had not been appropriated by one European nation or another,[7] as the conquerors eventually declared the innate mental inferiority of the indigenous African populations despite the reality that they had physically and culturally flourished on their own lands for thousands of years. From the Indian Ocean to the Pacific, from major portions of the mainland such as India and Burma, to the vast land areas of Australia and New Zealand, to large islands such as Borneo, New Guinea and The Philippines, to even the smallest of islands of the Polynesians in the mid-Pacific, the governments and troops of European countries such as England, France, Holland, Spain, Portugal, Germany, Belgium and Italy battled over which one of them owned the land, property, resources and labor of the people who had lived there for so many millennia.[8] Initially spoken of as savages, cannibals, head hunters, or simply heathens, the people of the many conquered populations eventually became the cheap or slave labor force for the European conquerors.

By the beginning of the Nineteenth Century, when many "colonies" were in the firm grasp of the descendants of white Europeans, the claims of second stage cultural racism were widely propagated and believed among most white Europeans, those still in Europe, and those who ruled the indigenous populations of the "colonies," some of which had become separate white-ruled nations. These second stage cultural racist claims were often deeply internalized by the descendants of those who had been conquered and subjugated in their own homelands, and by the descendants of those who had been kidnapped for slave labor in other lands.

It was in the early Nineteenth Century that second stage cultural racism, which had previously been institutionalized primarily by the laws and social structures of the aggressors/conquerors, emerged in yet another social institution of white people—the universities of Europe. Formulated as an "academic subject," and described as "racial theory," second stage cultural racism was reinforced by members of the European academic community as several highly respected university professors claimed that the mental and creative superiority of white people could be "proven" by "documented evidence." It is somewhat ironic that the use of this so called academic evidence and the educational system to further institutionalize second stage cultural racism eventually led to a complete academic refutation of this "evidence," as we shall explain.

The creation of "racial theory" as an academic subject appears to have begun with a Chairman of the Department of Philosophy at the University of Berlin (the direct predecessor of Hegel)—Johann Gottlieb Fichte. It may be significant that in this particular form of second stage cultural racism, along with the then familiar white European assertions that the people of all darker races were supposedly mentally inferior to white Europeans, that there were further assertions that the lighter people of the white race were supposedly mentally superior to the darker people of the white race. According to Fichte, the descendants of the Teutonic/Germanic tribes, i.e, the lightest people of the white race, were supposedly superior to all others peoples on Earth. Fichte asserted that the French, Latin and Jewish "races" were inferior, their generally darker coloring revealing their genetic heritage from the supposedly inferior darker races. Putting forth these ideas in a series of university lectures in 1807 (later published and widely read),

Fichte stated that it was only the Germanic people "in whom the seed of human perfection exists."[9]

Second stage cultural racism, in the guise of "racial theory" remained in the more generalized domain of philosophy for some forty years. But in 1847 a professor of ancient civilizations and philosophy (historical linguistics) at the University of Bonn, Christian Lassen, finally supplied what "racial theorists" had desperately wanted—historical "evidence" of an extremely ancient white civilization to legitimate their claims. It had been somewhat difficult, although apparently not impossible, to assert that the white race was the most mentally advanced form of human, when all available evidence showed that the earliest cultural inventions and developments—from law codes to the invention of the wheel—of the most ancient civilizations had been initiated by the darker peoples of the Near and Middle East. For the "racial theorists" of northern Europe this problem was all the more disturbing alongside the historical records about the Teutonic/Germanic tribes that described them as illiterate primitive people as late as the Roman period. By their own standards of the cultural and technological accomplishments that supposedly reveal basic human intelligence, the northern European "racial theorists" could produce no historical support for their claims. To establish an extreme antiquity, hopefully even a primacy, for white cultural development was a much longed for discovery among the "racial theorists" of the early Nineteenth Century.

The writings of Professor Christian Lassen provided this "discovery." Lassen's work was based upon information that was becoming increasingly available in Europe in the late eighteenth and early nineteenth centuries, the Sanskrit writings of the ancient Aryans of India. The information that most pleased the "racial theorists" was that the Sanskrit language of the Aryans was linguistically related to European languages.

The fact that Sanskrit was an Indo-European language had first been noted by William Jones and Charles Wilkins in late Eighteenth Century England. It was confirmed by the work of Franz Bopp of Bavaria in 1816.[10] Publishing his work in four volumes entitled *Indische Altertum-*

skunde (Indian Antiquities), Lassen stressed the great antiquity, even the probable primacy, of Aryan culture. According to Lassen, the Aryans were responsible for having initiated and developed many of the earliest cultural and technological accomplishments of humankind. Drawing upon the work of Jones, Wilkins and Bopp, Lassen wrote that the linguistic connections between Aryan Sanskrit and European languages showed that the Aryans were the ancestors of the white race.[11] Thus were the assertions of the second stage cultural racism based upon what was believed to be "documented evidence" of the primacy of the white race in cultural and technological development.

As we mentioned, basing claims of an innate superiority on archaeological and philological evidence of ancient cultures was to lead to further discoveries that completely refuted the "evidence" of white Aryan cultural and technological primacy. The "racial theorists" who used the then available knowledge of the ancient Aryans as proof of the innate superiority of what soon became known as the Teutonic/Germanic/Aryan people would have been deeply shocked, certainly disappointed, had they lived long enough to read the three volumes on the Harappan civilization of India written by archaeologist Jon Marshall and published in 1931.[12]

In these volumes, Marshall described the results of his years of excavations of the Harappan civilization of India, excavations that proved that the Aryans had invaded India as aggressive, illiterate nomads at about 1700 B.C. The Aryans had violently conquered the inhabitants of the Harappan civilization during several centuries of attack—eventually appropriating the cultural and technological accomplishments of the Harappans. Marshall's work was later affirmed by the work of Mortimer Wheeler in 1946–1953.[13]

Not only had the Harappans used a written language, wheeled vehicles, metallurgical processes, a brick architecture that included large civic and religious buildings and two and three story private homes, paved streets, and a system of drain sewers that led to inside bathrooms in most homes, but the Harappan civilization had existed for close to a thousand years before the Aryans had even arrived in India. Even more shocking to "racial theorists" would have been Marshall's and Wheeler's evidence that the Harappan civilization had been developed by a mixture of Mediterranean and Proto-Australoid peoples who were the ancestors of the dark Dravidian people still present in south India today.

But Marshall's discoveries, and the publication of them, were not to be made until some eighty years after northern European ideas about the ancient Aryans were used as a foundation for a form of second stage cultural racism that was propogated by some of the most highly respected professors of Europe.

The impact that the incorrect evidence about the Aryans had upon "racial theory" was widespread. Count Arthur de Gobineau published the first book of another four-volume treatise in France in 1855, this one boldly entitled *Essai sur l'Inegalite des Races Humaines* (Essay on the Inequality of the Human Races). Basing his theories on the supposed primacy of Aryan cultural development, Gobineau wrote, "History shows that all civilization flows from the white race, that no civilization can exist without the cooperation of this race." Gobineau also asserted that the lighter people of the Germanic and Celtic groups were the last "pure" remnant of the supposedly culture founding Aryans, i.e., the way all Aryans must have looked before some mixed with other races, extending Fichte's "seed of human perfection" to all lighter colored people of northern France, northern Germany, Scandinavia, Holland, northern Switzerland, England, Ireland and Scotland.[14]

The erroneous evidence of Aryan antiquity in cultural and technological development provided by writers such as Lassen and Gobineau influenced many other European scholars of the Nineteenth Century. Among these was a Professor of History at the University of Berlin between 1874 and 1896. In his extremely well attended lectures, and in his articles in the *Preussische Jahrbucher*, Dr. Heinrich von Treitschke deeply influenced northern European thought, basing his conclusions of a Teutonic superiority upon the idea that the Aryans had been the original "bearers of culture."

Treitschke's colleague at the University of Berlin, Professor of Economics Eugen Karl Duhring, added "racial theory" to his analysis of economics, asserting that the Oriental or Asiatic nature of Jewish people was morally inferior, thus undermining the European economy.[15] One can almost hear the echoes of Vikings, Saxons, and Crusaders, asserting that there is an innate evil or immorality among Asian peoples. It was perhaps not too surprising that some of the later Nazi propaganda used against the Jewish people of Europe stated that their original homeland had been in the heart of central Asia rather than in the actual Semitic homeland of the eastern Mediterranean.

Claims of a contemporary Teutonic/Aryan superiority wandered even further from factual evidence as "racial theory" was further developed and popularized by an Englishman living in Germany, Houston Stewart Chamberlain.[16] In the 1200 pages of his two-volume *Grundlagen des Neunzehnten Jahrhunderts* (Foundations of the Nineteenth Century), published in 1897, Chamberlain even challenged the New Testament. Despite the specific Hebrew genealogy listed in The Gospel According to Matthew, Chamberlain declared that the morals of Jesus "proved" that he was not a Semitic Hebrew. What was he then? Judging by his morals, Chamberlain asserted, he must have been an Aryan. Errors exist throughout Chamberlain's writings. Speaking of the Amorites who produced the Law Code of Hammurabi, well known as a Semitic people, Chamberlain described them as "tall, blond, magnificent Aryans." Of the Hittites of Anatolia, Chamberlain wrote that they were obviously Semitic, supposedly proved by their long noses. (The Hittites were later shown to be an Aryan group by the work of philologist B. Hrozny in 1915.) Yet despite the many errors and wild speculations in Chamberlain's books, an English translation of the two volumes was made available in England and the U.S. by 1910, while the original German edition was in its 24th printing in 1938.

It was not a difficult leap for Adolf Hitler when writing *Mein Kampf* in 1924 to assert that the Slavic, French, Hungarian and Baltic "races" were inferior to the Germans. Hitler asserted that African people were "half-apes," insisting that it was "a sin against all reason … a sin against the will of the Eternal Creator" to educate black people.[17] But Hitler's racism was not his own invention or the original product of a warped mind. He leaned heavily upon the "academic" cultural racism that had been accepted by much of northern Europe.

Thus Hitler could write, "All human culture, all the result of art, science and technology that we see before us today are almost exclusively the product of the Aryan ... He is the Prometheus of mankind from whose bright forehead the divine spark of genius has sprung at all times ... If we were to divide mankind into three groups, the founders of culture, the bearers of culture and the destroyers of culture, only the Aryan could be considered as representative of the first group."[18]

How ironic that such words were being written in 1924, the very year that Marshall began his excavations of the Harappan civilization, the excavations that revealed that the Aryans in India had been illiterate, barbaric nomads who had learned nearly all that they were credited with inventing from the dark Harappans. It is worth noting that in Mein Kampf, while referring to all other peoples as mentally inferior, Hitler singled out the Jewish people as being "in league with the Devil." Could this sole assertion of first stage cultural racism have been noted and confronted before the horrors of the holocaust had we been more aware of the stages of cultural racism?

The Aryans

At this point we must examine the records of the ancient Aryans. Who were these people who were so joyfully adopted by many white Europeans to confirm the assertions of second stage cultural racism? As we shall see, the Aryans did not initiate or found cultural or technological development for humankind, but they may well have been the inventors of the process of racism that has been used repeatedly for over three thousand years.

We should begin by clarifying that the ancient Aryans were actually specific groups of the second millennium B.C. (2000–1000). Their identifications as Aryans are based primarily upon the evidence of the languages that they used. Aryan languages have been discovered to be the only known languages from ancient periods that are related to the Indo-European languages of today.

The Indo-European languages are widespread and numerous. Most of them fall into three major categories:

The first category is composed of the ancient Aryan/Indo-European groups that initially entered recorded history in the second millennium B.C., some invading India, some invading Anatolia (Turkey), some invading Greece, and some invading or migrating into Iran. Their languages are known respectively as Sanskrit, Hittite, Mycenaean Greek and Indo-Iranian.

The second category of Indo-European languages are the Slavic and Baltic (Lettic) languages still used by people who now live primarily in the areas of Russia, Poland, Latvia, Lithuania, Czechoslovakia and Yugoslavia.

The third category includes most contemporary western European languages, English, German, Danish, Swedish, Norse, Dutch, French, Italian, Spanish, Portuguese, Rumanian, and the older languages of Latin and Gaelic. Greek, Persian, Armenian, Hindi, Bengali, Kurdish, Urdu and Romany are also Indo-European languages. Most archaeologists and philologists agree that the earliest Indo-European speaking people were originally a nomadic group whose earliest known homeland was probably on the steppes of southern Russia near the Aral Sea.

It was upon the extremely tenuous argument of a specific connection between the Aryans who had used Indo-European Sanskrit, and the Nineteenth and Twentieth Century people who used Indo-European Germanic languages, that "racial theorists" declared that the lightest skinned, lightest haired, lightest eyed members of the Teutonic/German peoples were the most direct descendants of ancient Aryan peoples. This claim of a direct Aryan ancestry for the lightest people of the white race may or may not be true. But even allowing, for the sake of discussion, that any specific group of people today are the last "pure" remnant of the ancient Aryans, what is this Aryan heritage?

One group of Aryans is known to have entered the area of Iran (hence the name Iran, from Aryan) before the second millennium B.C. They do not appear to have developed any major cultures there for several thousand years. This was despite the fact that the nearby cultures of the Sumerians in southern Iraq, the Semitic Akkadians in central Iraq, the Elamites in southwestern Iran, and the Harappans in India, had been using written language and building highly developed civilizations from about 3000 B.C. The archaeological evidence of Iran suggests that the Aryan migration or invasion into the area may even have brought earlier Neolithic developments there to somewhat of a dead end, e.g., Jarmo, Susa, Sialk, and Tepe Hissar.[19] As we shall explain more fully, the earliest evidence of Iranian/Aryan literacy dates to about the Seventh Century B.C.

A second group of Aryans are known to have invaded Anatolia (Turkey) at about 1800–1500 B.C. Anatolia had experienced gradual Neolithic cultural and technological development by non-Aryan groups from about 5000 B.C., e.g., Hacilar and Catal Huyuk. According to the archaeological evidence and written records of about 1400 B.C. the Aryans had arrived in Anatolia as aggressive, illiterate nomads, killing and terrorizing as they moved southward. After a period of several centuries they eventually subjugated the people of the earlier culture of Hatti in central Anatolia. After this conquest the Aryans adopted the cuneiform writing of the Semitic Akkadians to their south. It was from these cuneiform tablets written by the Aryans in Anatolia, who referred to themselves as the "Rulers of the Land of Hatti," that archaeologists dubbed the Aryans of Anatolia as Hittites. Their records reveal that once the Aryans had conquered the people of Hatti, the Aryans assumed the roles of aristocracy and ruling class, enslaving many of the indigenous inhabitants who were of Mediterranean origin.

Were the Hittite Aryans a superior people? If the violent conquest of citizens of developed urban and agricultural communities by invading nomads using horses for speed and power and javelins for murder and terror is indicative of a superior people then the Hittite Aryans were superior. It is true that once they had conquered the indigenous Hattians, the Aryans ruled for several centuries, but such a people can hardly be described as the founders or inventors of culture, or as the essence of innate morality.[20]

The most substantial body of evidence of the early Aryans comes from India, the group of Aryans that became the subject of Lassen's study and, in turn, so deeply affected the development of "racial theory." In India, both archaeological and written evidence confirm the invasion and conquest of the ancient Harappan civilization by the no-madic Aryans. Although Harappan writing has been discovered it has not yet been deciphered, thus the oldest available written records of ancient India are the Aryan writings that date from about 1200 B.C. onward. These were written in a script believed to have been adopted from Mesopotamia. From archaeological excavations, and from the written records of the Aryans, we know that the Aryan invasion of India occurred in much the same gradual pattern as the Aryan inva-sion of Anatolia, and at approximately the same period. Since the Aryan/Indo-European entries into Greece are also dated to about this same time, it is clear that the Aryans had broken up into several groups at about this time or slightly earlier.

One extremely interesting aspect of the Aryan records from India is the description of a sacred Aryan ritual known as the Asvamedha. This ritual consisted of a specially consecrated horse being allowed to roam free for one year, followed by a band of Aryan warriors on horseback. As the horse wandered onto the territories of other peoples the ritual re-quired that the band of Aryan warriors insist upon a payment of tribute from the inhabitants of the territory. If tribute was refused, the Aryans then broke into open warfare. If the Aryans achieved a martial victory the territory was then claimed as an addition to Aryan lands. (If the horse and warriors were still alive at the end of the year, the warriors brought the horse back to their tribal chieftain who then sacrificed it in ritual ceremony.)[21] Perhaps related to this custom, the Aryans gradually swept through the entire Harappan culture that had been built along some 950 miles of the banks of the Indus River. The archeological evi-dence suggests that the killing and looting of both urban and agricul-tural communities continued for several centuries.

It is interesting to note that the Aryans, even in the much later pe-riod when they had adopted writing, described any rebellious inhabit-ants as *rakshas*, demons who drank blood and killed infants, or *yaksas* who were said to eat children, or *vetalas*—vampires. Later Aryan leg-ends tell of a "Demon King" named Ravana who was associated with the large island of Ceylon that lies just off the southernmost tip of India. Although the "Demon King" is portrayed as a mythical figure in

Aryan legend, his connection with the southern area of India that experienced the least Aryan intrusion is interesting, especially as the later Dravidian writer Kamban portrayed Ravana as a somewhat heroic figure defending his people.[22]

Upon the eventual subjugation of the indigenous peoples of India, the Aryans instituted the *Varna* class structure (sometimes referred to as the caste system). The Varna structure (Varna literally means color) divided the population of India into four major classes. The highest class was that of the *Brahmins*, Aryans who were regarded as the priestly class. The second class was the *Ksatriyas*, Aryans regarded as warriors. The third class was the *Vaisyas*, the shepherds and merchants. The Vaisyas were generally of mixed Aryan/Harappan heritage, the offspring of an interbreeding that had occurred during the centuries of battle and conquest. The fourth class was the *Sudra*, or slaves. This class was primarily composed of the dark indigenous inhabitants of India—the Dravidians. The Varna structure was affirmed by Aryan religion in the form of a simple creation legend that supposedly explained the origins of the four classes from a primeval cosmic father, Purusha. An Aryan hymn in the Rg Veda explained, "The Brahmin was his mouth, of his arms came the Ksatriyas, his thighs became the Vaisyas, and of his feet the Sudras were born."[23]

Laws based on the Varna structure appear in an early Aryan text known as the Laws of Manu. According to these laws the Sudras had been created solely to serve the other classes. If they did not please or satisfy the wishes and demands of the higher classes, they were "to be expelled or slain at will." The Laws of Manu declared, "A Sudra who tries to make money or to better his lot in life is distressing to the Brahmin priests ... It is better to do one's own class duty badly than to do another's well." (This same Aryan belief in blindly fulfilling the duty of one's own class also justified all aggression and battles for the Aryan Ksatriya warriors, as so clearly explained in the Bhagavad Gita.) Along with the various laws against "confusion of class," i.e., social or sexual mixing between the classes, the Laws of Manu even provided information on the exact amount of interest that each class was to pay if they borrowed any material goods or money: Brahmins 24%,

Ksatriyas 36%, Vaisyas 48%, Sudras 60%. So much for later claims in Europe that usurious interest rates on money lending was a Semitic idea that was unnatural to the Aryan mind.[24]

The laws of Manu also declared: "Of [all] creatures the animate are said to be the best, of animate being those who live on their wits, of those who live on their wits men, and among men Brahmans are best ... The very birth of a Brahman is an eternal form of *dharma*; born for the sake of *dharma* he is conformed to becoming Brahman. When a Brahman is born he is born superior to the whole Earth, he is the lord of all creatures, and he has to guard the treasury of *dharma*. Everything that exists throughout the world is the private property of the Brahman. By the high excellence of his birth he is entitled to everything. What he enjoys, what he wears, and what he gives away are his own private property, and it is through the mercy of the Brahman that others enjoy [anything at all] (*Manu*, I. 96–101)."

The second stage cultural racism of the Varna structure was further embedded in the Aryan Vedic religion in the form of beliefs about reincarnation. There is some evidence suggesting that the concept of reincarnation had existed among the people of the earlier Harappan civilization. The concept is not mentioned in the earliest Aryan writings. When it does appear as an integral aspect of the Aryan Brahman and later Hindu religious tenets, the idea of a "pie in the sky" class mobility is inherent within it. According to Brahmanic and Hindu texts, if the Sudras lived their lives fulfilling their proper class duty, i.e serving the other classes obediently, they might find their reward in a future incarnation—being born lighter and thus in a higher class.[25]

The vast body of records from ancient India that refer to those who would not accept the Aryan invasion and domination as bloodthirsty demons and vampires, and then using both religion and laws to support an ongoing second stage of economic racism by the Aryans, are probably the earliest written accounts of a conscious and tangible use of the various stages of cultural racism to support economic racism.

In the later written accounts from the Aryans that entered Iran we may be observing an even more basic concept underlying all Aryan racism. Although the earliest written materials from the Aryans of

Iran are as late as the Seventh Century B.C., they are thought to reflect very ancient Aryan beliefs that may have been preserved through oral recitations. Although nothing as tangibly racist as the Laws of Manu are known from this earliest literate period of Iran, the religious concepts of Zoroastrianism based on the Aryan/Iranian writings in the Zend Avesta, and the later writings in the Bundahisn and Denkart, appear to reveal a form of cultural racism that was not only justified but encouraged by Aryan/Iranian beliefs about the very structure and purpose of the universe.[26]

The Zend Avesta is attributed to a prophet known as Zarathustra (Zoroaster) and is generally dated to about 600 B.C. According to the Avesta, in the beginning of all time there were two gods, the God of Light, Spenta Mainyu (Ahura Mazda), who represented all that is "light, good and beautiful," and the God of Darkness, Angra Mainyu (Ahriman), who represented all that is "dark, evil and repulsive." The Avesta states that when Ahura Mazda realized that the dark and evil Ahriman existed, he created the entire universe, Earth and stars, as a battleground on which to suppress and defeat Ahriman. It was supposedly at that time that the souls of all people came to Earth to aid Ahura Mazda battle against Ahriman. But the Aryan account goes on to tell that Ahriman then invaded the "light and perfect creation" of Ahura Mazda, "mixing and mingling his darkness" with what had been pure light, thus supposedly contaminating the Earth and the universe with darkness. According to Zoroastrianism, the presence of Ahriman's contamination could be seen in all things dark, while the presence of Ahura Mazda existed in all things light.[27]

In the Bundahisn and the Denkart it is stated that those who worshipped Ahura Mazda were representatives of light and goodness, while those who did not were a "dark race," "the people of Ahriman," "the demons and fiends of evil." According to Zoroastrianism, the cosmic struggle between light and darkness was taking place continually, and the souls that had not been "contaminated" by the darkness of Ahriman would eventually conquer the "dark demons."

Another legend in the Avesta might give us a glimpse into the idea of Aryan expansionism as a "Manifest Destiny" concept of some 2500 years ago. This is the legend of the Aryan Yima, known as the "son of the sun." Yima was said to be the first ruler of the Aryan people, personally appointed by Ahura Mazda to "rule the world." To help him achieve this wordly rule, Ahura Mazda is said to have supplied Yima with two sacred instruments—a whip and a goad. According to the legend, when Yima felt that his people were too crowded, he "extended" the Earth by one third more than it was before. He did this three times by using the whip and the goad.[28]

It is also interesting to note that the First Woman in the Aryan/Iranian cosmology is Jeh, "The Demon Whore Queen," the consort of Ahriman. Not only was Jeh blamed with contaminating the First Man with her "whoredom" but as the First Woman she was said to contaminate all women who, in turn, would defile all men. Along with this Aryan attitude towards women's sexuality, it was also said that Jeh's first menstruation was caused by the kiss of Ahriman when he was pleased that she had defiled the First Man. Thus women's menstrual periods were viewed by the Aryans as having been caused by the kiss of the Aryan devil, Ahriman.[29]

Records of the class structure of the Iranian/Persian empire as it existed in the Sassanian Period of about 250 A.D. may reveal the remnants of a class structure similar to that of the Varna structure in India. The four Iranian classes (Pistras) consisted of the highest class, the warriors who were the second class, the farmers and cattle breeders as the third class, and the artisans and laborers were the fourth. This structure did not include a slave class such as the Sudra but the Iranian Pistras class structure is strikingly similar to that of the Varna structure of India. The fact that the Pistras structure was also accompanied by a legend of a cosmic man from whom the four classes had emerged, much as they supposedly had from Purusha, has caused some scholars to state that both the class structure and the legend had been adopted from India at a later period. Although the Iranian Aryans and the Aryans of India had once been members of a single cohesive group, the idea that the Pistras class structure was adopted is quite plausible. It may well have supplanted earlier class ideas that appear in the Bundahisn. This is an even more extreme class hierarchy consisting of ten species of human. The highest species was said to be represented by the First Man, Gayo Mareta, "the pale eyed seed of the Aryan lands." The lowest species of "man" as listed in this Aryan race/class hierarchy, was the monkey.[30] Aside from any argument or discussion about which Aryan class structure was the older, it is clear that a class structure based upon physical identities was a long familiar Aryan concept.

The later Iranian religion of Manicheism, based upon Zoroastrian beliefs, also pitted Ahura Mazda, as Ohrmazd, against Ahriman. Ohrmazd was said to be "pure light," living in heaven, while Ahriman was referred to as "The Prince of Darkness," living in the darkest depths of the earth surrounded by his dark demons.[31] The eventual spread of Iranian Manicheism to Rome, and even later to other areas of Europe, had far reaching effects upon Christian concepts of a powerful God in Heaven and an almost equally powerful Devil in Hell, a devil often referred to in Christian writings as The Prince of Darkness. In consideration of this influence of Iranian/Aryan religion upon the development of Christianity we may want to examine the accounts of Magi appearing at the birth of Jesus more closely.

Perhaps influenced by Iranian Manicheism, perhaps influenced by even earlier Aryan connections, we should note that the Twelfth Century writer Helmold described pre-Christian Slavic religion holding the same duality, worshipping Byelbog as the God of Light and Good, Chernobog as the God of Dark and Evil.[32] Several mythologists and psychologists have described this duality as a natural archetype, or instinctual universal, basing their conclusions almost entirely upon Indo-European cultures.

It was perhaps the tragedy of timing (although no excuse for racist attitudes or acts can or should ever serve to apologize for basic greed and inhumanity) that knowledge of the great ancient civilization of the Harappans of India, and the even earlier civilization of the Sumerians of southern Iraq, were not discovered until the early Twentieth Century. It was not until 1924 that Marshall began his excavations that revealed the astonishing information about the ancient civilization along the Indus River. Marshall's work, and the later work of Wheeler, turned archaeologists' beliefs about the nature of the ancient

Aryans upside down. Yet even after these discoveries, some European archaeologists and historians glorified the warlike abilities of the Aryans, some even praising how fair they were to their slaves once they had conquered their lands.

The discoveries of the Sumerian culture became known at much the same time as those of the Harappans. It is now generally believed that the earliest development of written language, and the cultural and technological accomplishments of Egypt, Harappa and Akkad, were influenced by the even earlier Sumerian civilization which began to flower about 3200 B.C. Shown not to have used either an Indo-European or a Semitic language (the two major language groups of the Near East), the Sumerian people have never been racially identified. Their language has been most closely compared to the Ural-Altaic languages of central and north Asian peoples, but even this link is extremely tenuous.[33]

In stark contrast to these ancient civilizations to whom we owe such a great debt of gratitude for the legacy of inventions and cultural developments to which we became heir, *The Germania* of Tacitus records that the Teutonic/Germanic peoples of northern Europe still lived in primitive, illiterate, tribal groups some three thousand years later. According to Tacitus, the men of the Germanic tribes thought it "tame and spiritless to accumulate slowly by the sweat of his brow what can be got quickly by the loss of a little blood … When not engaged in warfare they spend a certain amount of time hunting but much more in idleness, thinking of nothing else but sleeping and eating. For the boldest and most warlike men have no regular employment, the care of home and fields being left to the women, old men and weaklings of the family. In thus dawdling away their time they show a strange inconsistency—at one and the same time loving indolence and hating peace."[34]

It was not until the Fifth Century A.D., that the Angles and some of the Saxons, both Teutonic/Germanic tribes, left their territories in Denmark and northern Germany to become the Anglo-Saxons of Britain. While the Angles and Saxons were invading the then- Celtic island of Britain, Teutonic/Germanic tribes such as the Visigoths, Ostrogoths, Suevi, Franks, Asding Vandals and Siling Vandals were invading and conquering the areas now known as France, Italy and Spain.[35] A few centuries later, the groups of Dane and Swedes known as Varangians colonized along the great rivers of Russia, eventually forming an aristocracy under King Oleg in 880 A.D.

These Teutonic/Germanic invasions and conquests in central and southern Europe and western Russia resulted in an accentuated spectrum of skin and hair color in these areas even today. Although groups such as the Visigoths or Ostrogoths no longer exist as such, it is interesting to note the social and/or economic positions of the people on the lighter end of the spectrum in the various countries of Europe and in Russia. Could it have been from these invasions that we find a type of pecking order of racism that occurs as a domino effect from the lightest to the darkest people in so many areas? Are we still infested with ancient ideas of light as good and dark as bad and archaic concepts of some cosmic class structure based upon coloring?

Summary

The need to feel proud of one's ancestry seems to be a basic drive in all human beings. The desire to establish a claim of proud antiquity appears to run deep within the human creature. From children squabbling about their parent's jobs or status to efforts to trace a family tree to some royal line—the desire is observable.

Early Christian writers used the assertion of primacy when challenging the religious beliefs of the pagan Romans. Drawing upon the antiquity of the Hebrew Scripture (Old Testament), at the time thought to be even older than it actually is, Tertullian claimed that Christianity was the more worthwhile religion for it was as old as "the nativity of the world itself." St. Augustine also challenged the religious beliefs of the Greeks and the Romans by claiming that the antiquity of the Old Testament was far greater than that of Greece. One might even be tempted to consider if the very existence of Jewish people, once the Christian Church had been formed, remained as the one obstacle to an unchallenged Christian claim to the Old Testament. Is the Old Testament one piece of property that even first stage cultural racism has not made possible to fully appropriate? Can this be the underlying core of anti-Semitism? There is certainly a puzzling irony in a Christian embrace of the Ten Commandments on one hand, alongside anti-Semitic assertions of innate immoralities of Jewish people on the other.

Even in the past decade, in ideas as seemingly innocent and certainly wildly speculative as theories of space travelers implanting culture on Earth, there lingers a continuing refusal by some white people to believe that people of darker races could have been responsible for the cultural and technological developments of ancient civilizations. The originator of such theories, Von Daniken, comments upon the astronomical knowledge of the Mayan peoples of the Yucatan, saying, "it is difficult to believe that it originated from a jungle people." And in describing some ancient artifacts from Indonesia, Von Daniken writes, "One cannot imagine savages making them." For those who cannot imagine "jungle people" or "savages" as culturally inventive or intelligently observant, Von Daniken subtly provided an alternative answer. Not only were the culture founders of Earth supposedly from outer space but they were a rather specific type of outer space being. In a passage concerning the Incas, Von Daniken provided his sole suggestion of a physical identity for these culture-founding space travelers. "Never before had they heard of gigantic *white men* who came from somewhere in the sky." Dare we ask, had the remains of a great ancient civilization been discovered in some field outside Berlin or Amsterdam, would Von Daniken have been so willing to attribute it to ancient space travelers?

As Twentieth Century study of ancient history and early civilizations came more and more to focus on the periods of archaic and classical Greece as the foundations of western culture, over two thousand years of the cultural invention and developments of Sumerian, Egyptians, Harappans and Akkadians have been almost completely ignored in education. If discussed at all, the ancient beginnings of culture and technology are presented in somewhat of a chronological vacuum, seldom explained as the two to three thousand year old cultural and technological foundations of Greece and Rome that they had been. Our western education systems leave many people with the idea that only white people have a proud cultural heritage. One of the first steps that we must take in combatting racism is to ensure that students of all grade levels—from elementary to university—are more knowledgeable about the cultural histories that all races possess. Explaining that the earliest known cultural accomplishments of humankind were those initiated and developed by darker skinned peoples is vital in combatting racist ideas. Early education about the most ancient cultures mentioned above, as well as those of the Orient and the western hemisphere, that developed quite apart from white European influence, could make second stage cultural racism difficult if not impossible for children first formulating their views of the world. But this cannot be done until those who educate children are truly familiar with the non-European civilizations of the past.

Combatting first stage cultural racism may be more difficult. No race or ethnic group has been totally morally and ethically perfect. But more honest accounts of the aggressions of the Indo-European ruled Persian, Greek and Roman Empires, as well as of the Vikings, the Crusades, and the centuries of European "colonization" of much of the world, are vital in avoiding pretensions of a white European ethical or moral supremacy. This might also be accompanied by a more careful study of the records of the ethics and morals of pre- and non-Christian religions. The repeated emphasis on the importance of charity, compassion and honesty in the religious texts of Egypt and Sumer, as well as in the written and oral accounts of the early religious beliefs of many other cultures, may help to erase the erroneous assumption that white Europeans invented these ideals.

We might also become more conscious of any and all self-righteous claims of a superior morality, or accusations of a basic immorality in others. The subtle propagation of such ideas has long heralded the beginnings of more overt and violent racist acts. Many of our anti-racist efforts of the past few decades have been aimed at showing the equality of mental abilities in all races. It is perhaps time to stress the truth about the moral qualities inherent in all peoples. For as the simultaneous growth of automated production and greater population lead to a need for less labor, we may want to be wary of a return to first stage racism as a control of the labor supply.

It is perhaps divine providence of a sort that leaves us in doubt about the racial or ethnic identity of the Sumerians, the people who, at least to date, appear to have played such a major and primal role in cultural and technological development. As long as the identity of the Sumerians remains unknown, no race can state a claim of superiority based upon an ultimate primacy of either mental ingenuity or moral ethics. But whatever evidence is found in the future, it is surely time that we understood the equal capacities of all races and ethnic groups. Or will it take an actual encounter with beings from outer space to force us to see each other and ourselves as no more and no less than the fascinating life form that we are—as Earthlings.

Annotations and Bibliogray

1. Keen, Maurice. *The History of Medieval Europe* London: Routledge & Kegal Paul, 1968, pg. 41.

2. Ibid. See Runciman, S. *A History of the Crusades.* Cambridge: Cambridge University Press, 1987, pgs. 117–133.

3. Magnusson, M. & Palsson, H. *The Vinland Sagas.* London: Penquin/U.K., 1965. See Kendrick, T.D. *A History of the Vikings.* London, 1930.

4. Farb, Peter. *Man's Rise to Civilization.* New York: E. P. Dutton & Co., 1968, pgs. 257–278. See Hanke, L. *Aristotle and the American Indian.* Bloomington: Indiana University Press, 1959. Morison, S.E. *The European Discovery of America: The Northern Voyages.* Oxford University Press, 1971. Morison, S.E. *The European Discovery of America: The Southern Voyages,*1974.

5. Diaz del Castillo, Bernal. *The Conquest of New Spain.* Trans., J. M. Cohen. London: Penquin/U.K., 1963.

6. Mannix, Daniel. *Black Cargoes.* New York: Viking Press, 1962. See Davidson, Basil. *Black Mother.* Boston: Atlantic-Little Brown, 1961. Murdock, George. *Africa: Its Peoples and Their Cultures.* New York: McGraw Hill, 1959. McEvedy, Colin. *The Penquin Atlas of African History.* New York: Penquin, 1980.

7. Goode, J. Paul, ed. *Rand McNally Atlas.* Chicago: Rand McNally, 1932.

8. McEvedy, Colin. *The Penguin Atlas of Modern History.* New York: Penquin, 1972, pg. 48.

9. Dawidowicz, L. *The War Against the Jews.* New York: Holt Rinehart & Winston, 1975, pg. 26. Shirer, Wm. *The Rise and Fall of the Third Reich.* New York: Simon & Schuster, 1959, pg. 143. See Fichte, J.G. *Reden an die Deutsche Nation.* Berlin: 1808. Mosse, G. L. *The Crisis of German Ideology.* New York, 1964.

10. Basham, A.L. *The Wonder That Was India.* New York: Grove, 1954, pgs. 4–7.

11. Lassen, Christian. *Indische Altertumskunde.* Koenig. 1847–62, 42 Vols.

12. Marshall, John. *Mohenjo Daro and The Indus Civilization.* Probsthain, 1931, 3 Vols.

13. Wheeler, Mortimer. *Harappa Journal of Ancient India III.* 1947. *The Indus Civilization.* Cambridge, 1953.

14. de Gobineau, Arthur. *Essay on the Inequality of the Human Races.* Paris, 1853–55. See Bidess, Michael D. *The Father of Racist Ideology: The Social and Political Thought of Count Gobineau.* New York, 1970.

15. Dawidowicz, L. op. cit. p. 38f. See Duhring, E.K. *The Jewish Question.* Berlin, 1881.

16. Shirer, Wm. Op. cit. p. 152ff. See Chamberlain, H. S. *Foundations of the Nineteenth Century.* New York, 1910, 4 Vols.

17. Hitler, Adolf. *Mein Kampf.* Houghton Mifflin, 1971, pg. 430.

18. Ibid., p. 290.

19. Childe, V. Gordon. *New Light on the Most Ancient East.* W.W. Norton, 1969, pgs. 189–206. Mellaart, James. *Earliest Civilizations of the Near East.* Thames and Hudson, 1965, pgs. 69–76.

20. Gurney, O. R. *The Hittites.* New York: Penquin, 1952. Garstang, J. *The Land of the Hittites* Constable, 1910. Mellaart, J. *Anatolian Chronology in the Bronze Age.* Anatolian Studies, Oxford: VII, 1957.

21. Basham, A. L. op. cit. pg. 42.

22. Ibid., p. 318, pg. 475. O'Flaherty, W. *Hindu Myths.* New York: Penguin, 1975, pgs. 198–204.

23. Basham, A. L. op. cit. p. 137ff. Clayton, A. C. *The Rg Veda and Vedic Religion.* Madras, 1913.

24. Buhler, G. "The Laws of Manu." *Sacred Books of the East.* Oxford: VII, 1880.

25. Speiser, F. *Living Religions of the World.* Thames and Hudson, 1957, pg. 85ff. O'Flaherty, W. op. cit., pg. 251ff.

26. Zaehner, R. C. *The Teachings of the Magi.* George Allen & Unwin, 1956. Ibid. *The Dawn and Twilight of Zoroastrianism.* London, 1961. See Mills, L. H. "The Zend Avesta." *Sacred Books of the East,* XXXI. Oxford, 1887. Dhalla, M. N. *Zoroastrian Theology,* New York, 1914. Moulton, J. M. *Early Zoroastrianism.* Williams and Norgate, 1913.

27. Zaehner, R. C. op. cit. Brandon, S. G. F. *Creation Legends of the Near East.* Hodder & Stoughton, 1963. Dresden, M. J. in *Mythologies of the Ancient World.* ed. Kramer, S. N. Doubleday, 1961, pgs. 333–364.

28. Dresden, M. J. op. cit. pg. 344f.

29. Zaehner, R. C. *The Teachings of the Magi.* op. cit. pgs. 42–46. Dresden, M.J. op. cit. pg. 343f.

30. Zaehner, R. C. op. cit. pg. 75. Dresden, M.J. op. cit. pg. 342f.

31. Speiser, F. op. cit. pgs. 451–467. Dresden, M. J. op. cit. pg. 341f. Burkitt, F. C. *The Religion of the Manichees.* Cambridge University Press, 1925.

32. Warner, Rex. ed. *Encyclopedia of World Anthology.* Phoebus, 1971, pg. 183.

33. Kramer, S. N. *The Sumerians, Their History, Culture and Character.* University of Chicago Press, 1963.

34. Tacitus, P. Cornelius. *The Agricola and the Germania.* Trans. by Mattingly, H., revised, Handford, S. A. Penguin, 1970, pg. 114. See Suetonius. *The Twelve Caesars.* Trans. by Graves, R. Penguin, 1957. *Caesar the Conquest of Gaul.* Trans. by Handford, S. A. Penguin, 1951. Tacitus, P. C. *The Annals of Imperial Rome.* Trans. by Grant, M. Penguin, 1956.

35. Keen, M. op. cit. p. 19.

unpublished writings

Merlin with her books.

Unpublished Writings

BY MERLIN STONE

Inner Voice: Intuition

Editor's note: The following is a lecture delivered by Merlin Stone at a 1978 conference on "Feminist Visions of the Future" in Chico, California. We've left these lecture notes exactly as they were written by Merlin. In the original copy of this essay, Merlin used phonetic spellings to facilitate her presentation of the essay as a lecture. We acknowledge here that there are many variant spellings of the names of figures and even variations on how they functioned in each original telling. Thus, you will read Merlin's interpretations exactly as she rendered them, but using spellings we feel are acceptable to identify the various goddesses, prophetesses, and seers themselves. —David B. Axelrod

INTRODUCTION *Inner Voice - Intuition*

Before I begin my talk this morning, I feel that I must explain
that this is not the paper I had ˄originally intended to present. Although it
contains information gleaned through academic research and study,
as you will soon see, it is not what one might refer to as a purely
academic paper. Three months ago, as I began to organize the notes
I had been preparing for this morning, ˄in fact just as I had finished typing
˄most of the introduction to the intended paper, I had an experience that I
felt, and feel, that I must share with you. I hope that the researched
information that the paper does contain will be of interest to you,
but ,though hesitant about revealing myself so publicly, I cannot
help but feel that it is the experience itself that is ˄truly the underlying
thesis of what I will be reading to you.
    Throughout the experience, I felt compelled to record what was
happening, as it happened, and now feel that ˄sharing the way in which it
happened, may be more meaningful than any more typically academic
presentation would have been. I left the first page of the introductory
statements as they were, and from there on in, tried to record all
that was happening as accurately as I could. When I am finished
reading this, you may decide that a strait jacket is in order, but
I hope, that by being as open and vulnerable as I will be in reading
what I wrote, the account of the experience will be as meaningful
to all of you as it was, and is, to me, as we embark upon our voyage
into the future.

England   Talk at Chico/CA March 1978

Notes for a lecture on "Inner Voice: Intuition" by Merlin Stone.

Inner Voice: Intuition

by Merlin Stone

$\mathcal{B}$EFORE I BEGIN MY talk this morning, I feel I must explain that this is not the paper I had originally intended to present. Although it contains information gleaned through academic research and study, as you will soon see, it is not what one might refer to as a purely academic paper. Three months ago, as I began to organize the notes I had been preparing for this morning, in fact, just as I had finished typing most of the introduction to the intended paper, I had an experience that I felt, and feel, I must share with you. I hope that the researched information the paper does contain will be of interest to you but, though I'm hesitant about revealing myself so publicly, I cannot help but feel that it is the experience itself that is truly the underlying thesis of what I will be reading to you.

Throughout the experience I felt compelled to record what was happening, as it happened, and now feel that sharing the way in which it happened may be more meaningful than any more typically academic presentation would have been. I left the first page of the introductory statements as they were, and from there on, tried to record all that was happening as accurately as I could. When I am finished reading this you may decide that a straitjacket is in order, but I hope that by being as open and vulnerable as I will be in reading what I wrote, that the account of the experience will be as meaningful to all of you as it was, and is, to me as we embark upon our voyage into the future.

We have gathered here this weekend not just to present but to share and discuss our feminist visions of the future. As we consider our images of the future we will probably each be drawing upon all that we know about life on Earth—in the present and in the past—in order to form our visions of some yet unformed, unknown tomorrow. From the wide range of our personal experiences, and what others have told us by word of mouth, television, newspapers, books, film, radio, or wherever else we gather our information about the nature of human and planetary realities, we form our images—our visions—of the possibilities for the future. Most of us would probably describe our "visions" as actually being our thoughts and hopes about a future that could be better in so many ways than what we have so far known. Some of us, or is it only me, may find some of the more utopian visions set in a somewhat Disney-like scene of plush green hills, dotted with clusters of wildflowers blowing in the clearest of air, where it never seems to rain but there is always a glowing rainbow arching in the background. There may be a few of us who envision the plight of humanity and Earth as even worse in the future than it is today and even those of us—all too aware of the state of technology and the paranoia of so-called rational minds—who feel there may be no future at all.

Although I too have many personal thoughts and hopes about the possibilities of the future, I would like to use this time to talk about the actual process—the act of women thinking and speaking out about visions of the future—and the role that our self-esteem and trust in our own judgment plays in this process. Here we are, a group of women who up until the last decade or so were probably encouraged to believe that it was natural for us, as women, or as girls looking forward to becoming women, to limit our visions of the future and our own lives. We were encouraged to include images of a husband, a home of our own, and a few children playing in the garden or sitting at the table in the kitchen enjoying a dinner that we would cook and serve. If our visions dared to be a bit grander they might have included images of our husbands, or sons, becoming professors, doctors or even winning Nobel prizes, or whatever it was that they wanted, or we had wanted, to be or do. If we dared to allow our visions to go much beyond these limits we often met with disapproval, or perhaps worse—lack of interest and disbelief—and most of us learned to keep any more unusual ideas about the future to ourselves.

Who are we to now not only consider, but speak aloud of, visions of the future for an entire society—perhaps an entire planet? Can we, as women, so long used to limiting ourselves to quite narrow, individual visions of the future, trust ourselves enough to not only contemplate visions that challenge the very structure of society as we know it but dare to voice these ideas aloud to so many others? As I sit at my typewriter typing this last sentence, imagining myself addressing many other women almost three months from now, I ask this question not only of my imagined audience but I suppose, primarily, of myself. And as I do, I suddenly hear a voice that seems to be inside me, definitely a woman's voice, telling me not only that "of course we can" but that "we must." The voice is one I have often tried to ignore, but over the last few years one that I have come to know quite well. When first I asked who it was that was speaking to me this woman's voice told me that her name did not matter, but that if a name would make me more comfortable, most people called her Intuition.

~

Now that I have put my doubts into words to introduce my talk on the need for all and each of us to truly and deeply trust our own perceptions and judgments as we talk about the future, I hear this woman's voice again. In a somewhat jesting tone she says, "If women are at all hesitant about our ability to make serious suggestions and plans for the future, we might do well to observe where the visions and speeches of the men who believe they do this naturally, and well, have led us to today." Though the voice comes from nowhere but inside myself, I reply, "Who really listens to women's views on anything, much less something as vast and abstract as the future of humanity and the planet?" Masking my own doubts and hesitations with the cautious use of a literary reference, I argue, "Remember what happened to Cassandra when she tried to speak out on the future?" Almost hoping the voice will go away so that I can get on with the paper, I hear it even more clearly saying, "The story of Cassandra was intended as a warning, as a threat to women in a then still developing patriarchal structure, but what of the multitude of accounts of women, who were actually sought out, and relied upon to foretell of events to come?"

Full of advice as ever, she then says to my surprise and dismay, "Put aside your other notes on the importance of confronting and changing false stereotypes of women with greater knowledge of the powerful and courageous images of the Goddess, and the effect this will have on women's self-esteem in the future—and talk instead about the roles of mortal women as prophets of the future and how it was once understood that the messages given by these women were those given to them by the Goddess. This is the part of our vast woman heritage that will provide courage to women who might hesitate, as you so often do, to trust their own judgment and foresight. Offer them this image to take with them—to take beyond the nurturing wall of a women's conference—to use to combat any doubts in the long years of work still ahead."

I consider this for a moment and, despite the pile of notes I have been preparing for months, I begin to think of the numerous references to women foretelling the future, not only in the classic, ancient cultures, but in cultures all over the world. But then, with my usual stubborn cynicism that I know she has heard all too often, I reply, "It is strengthening to know about times and places where women's prophecies of the future were highly respected, and even carefully heeded, but I do have a bit of trouble with the way they picked up their information. The cooing of doves and their movements in flight? Listening to the sounds of leaves blowing in the wind? Reading palm kernels and corn kernels? It really is a bit difficult for a woman of today to take these methods of foretelling the future very seriously."

Intuition counters with the challenge that the editorials we read and hear about in newspapers and on television might not be any more reliable, and adds, "Remember, in the days of ancient prophecy, it was the woman as priestess, or prophetess, who interpreted what she saw or heard and explained it to others. At least she had direct access to the sources of her information." I frown a bit, not sure if I believe Intuition's analogy really fits. But, unconcerned with my doubts about her logic, she continues: "It seems to me that these same people who might find it strange that a prophetess found meaning in the pattern of birds in flight might, at the same time, be willing to consider the patterns of the planets on the day they were born as meaningful—or not be able to resist taking a look at those impossible mass horoscope columns in the daily papers." I argue that despite its ever growing popularity and acceptance, many people still consider astrology to be utter nonsense. "Yes," she agrees. "I have heard people reject the possibility that the movements and placement of the astral bodies might affect their lives, but I must admit the ones who did seemed to be the sort with the type of mind that would reject anything they could not see or touch or that had not been told to them by someone in a certified position of authority. Then, I hear her laughing at her own private joke about what she refers to as a "techno-rational" mind as she says something about "how difficult a time such people must have with all those strange un-technological, irrational images and feelings they experience in their own dreams every night."

"Maybe they're the ones who can never remember their dreams," I say, trying to be helpful, but she is already well into reminding me that dreams, above all other signs or omens, were regarded as messages, foretelling the future.

Just as I decide that she is really quite old-fashioned and still living in the past and that I should get on with my work, she suddenly remembers what started this particular conversation and her voice, now revealing some impatience with me, asks, "Whether or not you believe in the validity of any of the ancient methods of prophecy, will you at least concede that the records from many cultures reveal that it was primarily women who were regarded as able to interpret signs and omens and to foretell the future?" I am forced by the truth of what she says to nod my head in silent agreement. "And will you," she continues, "also concede that the actual evidence about the women in these many cultures, who were respected for this ability to speak knowingly of the future, might just have some bearing on a conference entitled 'Feminist Visions of the Future'?" I am a bit less comfortable about this second question, realizing that it means completely revising my notes and outline, but I do begin to consider it seriously enough to wonder whether if some women who attend the conference do not think it is pertinent or helpful, they might at least find it interesting in terms of understanding the past, if not the future.

At this point, I begin to seriously consider putting aside my original notes to speak instead on the specific historical evidence of "woman as prophetess." I start to go through the pages of my still unedited, massive manuscript on the evidence of Goddess and heroine images from all over the world. So much of the information that I have included on women foretelling the future is connected to the various images of the Goddess, the priestess so often understood to be conveying the messages of the Goddess. What I locate, even in the rather hurried initial scanning, ranges all the way from material on the oracular priestesses, of the great temples of the ancient Near and Middle East, to an account of women reading the pattern of the cross-cut grain of a saptur tree in Panama. I start to take outline notes from my sections on the Goddess in Babylon, Scandinavia, Africa, Mexico, and, of course, from so-called rational, logical Greece and martial Rome.

I come across more material about the Germanic and Celtic women prophets, and yet more from ancient Sumer, Canaan, and Anatolia. But after quickly marking down the numbers of the pages where I located each passage, along with a reminder of what was where so I can return once again to reread each statement and passage more carefully to decide what to include in the talk, I suddenly stop short and reconsider the idea of changing the subject of the talk. "Ancient oracles foreboding doom and absolute destiny"—the words float through my mind as I strangely revert to ideas I had about the actual nature of ancient prophecy, long before I began studying the many documents and artifacts of ancient religious beliefs. The prophesied tragedy of Oedipus and Jocasta, and its strange fulfillment, enter my thoughts as one of the few references to ancient prophecy that I had known at the time. "This is not the point of the conference," I begin to argue again. We are not going to be discussing the prediction of events in the future. If we believed in a fixed fate, a totally predestined future, why would we bother to have the conference at all? Our reasons for wanting to get together to talk about the future are to share some ideas about the way we would like it to be and how best to make those things happen." I hear Intuition laugh, making some half-audible remark about my predicting what people will be wanting to do in California in March as I sit at my typewriter in New York in January. Through the embarrassment of having her catch me doing just that, I hear her say, "Have you forgotten all those texts and documents on the oracles in Greece and Babylon and Sumer? Wasn't it you who wrote, 'It is evident from the accounts of the people who believed in prophetic revelation that they did not view the future as totally predestined, but rather as something that could be acted upon as long as one knew the most advantageous action to take. The oracular priestesses were not consulted for a firm prediction of the future, but for counsel as to the best strategy considering the situation.'"

Vaguely remembering writing these lines some four or five years ago, then locating and rereading them in my own book, I struggle to recall what I had based those statements on. I begin to go through my old files. Memory slowly returns. Most of the prophecies that were recorded in ancient periods were concerned with wars, colonizing, royalty, and a few with the building of the new temples, but it is clear in nearly every actual record of an oracle that within the revelation of the future was the very specific advisory counsel of the priestess.

I reread the statements of Plutarch in which he told of the Germanic holy women reading the eddies and currents of the streams about 2,000 years ago, studying both the sounds and the movement and, from what they found, warned against engaging in a battle until the time of the new moon. The more cynical of us might say that the women believed that by the time of the new moon it would be warmer, or colder, or even just darker, but, according to Plutarch, the advice was given—and taken. I reread the passages on the prophecy of the Sibyl who claimed that the twelve-year-long Punic War would not come to an end until the sacred stone of the goddess Kybele was brought to Rome from the city of Pessinus in Turkey, and added that a great temple must be built to house the stone, and to honor the Anatolian goddess Kybele, in the heart of Rome. Incidentally, although the advice of the Germanic holy women was given as the reason that the Germanic tribes lost a battle to Caesar's advancing army, the Sibylline oracle was honored. Not only did the twelve-year-long war end shortly after the black meteorite arrived in Rome, a year of exceptional prosperity following, but a great temple to the Anatolian goddess Kybele was completed thirteen years later in the area now known as Vatican City. Tablets found in 1603 AD suggested it was not far from, and possibly directly beneath, where St. Peter's stands today.

As I continue to go through the pages of the manuscript, I locate passages on the many women who were consulted not by royalty or leaders of armies, but by poorer folk who wanted to hear about the future of a child still in the womb, or of the best time to plant seeds, so that the family harvest would be plentiful enough to last through the dry season. In our own language, we might use the word "prophetess" to describe an individual woman who foretells the future. The Babylonians referred to such women as "Sha'iltu" or "Apiltu." The Celts of Ireland called them "Banfathi" and the Scandinavians knew them as "Voolvah." It is obvious that not everyone had access to such famed and wealthy oracular temples as the Grecian Delphi, Roman Cumae, or Babylonian Arbela, but there are records of women counted upon for their foresight into the future, and their wise counsel on it, from cultures all over the world.

The voice, which had been silent as I had been reading and typing all this time, suddenly says, "Don't you see? It is the evidence of these mortal women having been regarded as authorities and counselors on the future that must be shared with the women at the conference. It is this information that will assure women that it was for so long considered to be the natural role of women to look into the future, not just predict it but to provide advice and counsel on how to proceed. It seems to me that denying this natural role of woman is what led the world into the confusion it is in today. This image of mortal women, though often viewed as speaking the messages of the Goddess, will offer strength and certainty to women, not only to consider and speak out about what is going to happen but to expect and, if necessary, demand that women's voices be heard again in all planning of the future of the world."

Suddenly, a "vision" begins to reel across the visual screen of my mind. It is of a woman addressing a large audience of women and men. As she speaks, her age, her face, and her size keep changing. She is tall, short, heavy, thin, young, old, black, white, brown, gold, but all the while her voice continues, her words filled with both logic and compassion— while everyone present listens in respectful concentration to what she is saying. I especially check to see if the men are making any snide remarks, but they appear to be just as anxious not to miss a word of what she is saying as the women are. The "vision" makes me smile, though I am sitting alone, and I feel as if a reserve supply of energy just entered my body. With this heightened energy I continue to read through my material on women and prophecy and realize that I will speak on women and prophets of the past. Intuition has won the argument and I hear her sigh with relief as I type this. Then she suggests that I include this play-by-play description of how and why I decided to change the topic of my talk—as part of it. "Did I not initially say I was planning to discuss 'process'?" she reminds me. I reserve the right to put off my decision on this until I read over what I have written.

I start to reread the records of the oracles from the Ishtar temple at Arbela. I notice how many start with the priestess announcing, "I am the Goddess Ishtar of Arbela," so that there is no doubt that the voices of the priestesses of Arbela were understood to be conveying messages from the Goddess Herself. As I am reading, the voice of Intuition nudges me again gently. I wince a bit at the prospect of even more advice, but what she asks of me this time is more easily done.

"Tell them the names of the priestesses who spoke the oracles at Arbela," she says, "the ones whose names are recorded at the end of each ancient temple tablet. How many women today know the names that were buried on those clay tablets all these years—or even that the names are there to be known?" As I look over the names on the translations from the tablets discovered in excavations of the Ishtar temple in Arbela, I hear Intuition's voice reading along with me, lingering nostalgically over each name as if over the names of old friends one has not heard mentioned for a long time. It is as if there is a deep, cavernous echo in my head as I hear her read the names aloud: "Belitabisha, Sinkisha-Amur, Ishtar-bel-daini, Ishtar Latashyat, Urkittu Sharrat, Baja, and Rimute-allate." Perhaps to ease the intensity of still hearing the names echoing in my mind—as if in a long time tunnel—I find myself trying to regain my balance by a somewhat facetious query about whether or not any of these women saw far enough into the future to know that their names would be recited at a women's conference in California almost three thousand years after these records were inscribed.

Intuition ignores my question and instead suggests that I add the fact that the titles that were carved along with the images of Ishtar reflected her role as the actual source of the words and advice conveyed by the priestesses: Goddess of Oracles, Lady of Vision of Kissuru, Prophetess of Kua. "Also," she points out, "include the lines of the prayer to the Goddess who used the voices of women to speak,

'With Ishtar there is counsel and wisdom, the fate of everything she holds in Her hands.'" Writing down these lines of this ancient Babylonian prayer helps to remind me that the planet we call Venus was sacred to Ishtar and that, in Babylon, Venus was known as Masat, Prophetess. In turn, I recall that the earliest charts of the movements of astral bodies made in Babylon—which most scholars believe to be the place of origin of the concept of the zodiac—were charts of the appearance and positions of the planet Venus, Masat.

I look through the pages on Sumer, only to hear Intuition once again pointing the way. "Dreams," she says. "Dreams, just as I told you." Of course, she is right again. All the information I have so far found on prophecy in Sumer is connected to the interpretations of dreams. I located the inscriptions to the Sumerian goddess Nina, as Prophetess of Deities, Mother Interpreter of Dreams. But these same documents reveal that the goddess Nina was also revered as the one who actually arranged destiny. The Sumerian goddess known as Nanshe is also mentioned in various texts as the Interpreter of Dreams. Nanshe may actually be a later image of Nina, for although the temple in the city of Lagash was dedicated to the goddess Nanshe, the sacred section of the city where the temple stood was known as Nina. Both Nina and Nanshe are recorded as Goddess names rather than names of mortal priestesses, but in the Sumerian accounts they did interpret the dreams of mortal people. This use of the name of the goddess as the interpreter may be the result of the Sumerian belief that the high priestess was actually the incarnation of the Goddess on Earth. In the hymn of the high priestess Enheduanna, from about 2400 BC, Enheduanna told of her sorrow at a time when she had been forced to flee from the temple "like a swallow from its nest." In the hymn, she wrote, "No longer am I able to interpret the commands of Ningal to the people." The goddess name of Ningal was specifically associated with the Sumerian city of Ur, as Nanshe was specifically associated with Lagash. The name of Nina seems to have first been known from the town of Eridu, the earliest settlement of the Sumerians. The name of Ninsun occurs in a few Sumerian texts as a goddess name, but in the *Epic of Gilgamesh*, Gilgamesh went to a mortal, Ninsun, at the temple in the city of Erech, addressed her as "mother," and asked her to interpret his dreams—which she did. It was perhaps from this more ancient culture of Sumer, in which the priestess was so closely identified with the Goddess, that the later Babylonian custom of each oracular priestess announcing herself as speaking as the Goddess, had been derived.

I go through the pages on ancient Canaan, the land along the Mediterranean that now contains both Israel and Lebanon. I locate the lines in which the Goddess, known there as Asherah, is described as having given the oracle with the "pointing of Her finger." The line was found on a badly cracked fragment of a tablet and there is nothing to clarify whether the finger belonged to a priestess or a priest. Intuition comments that she has heard so much lately about how important it is for the clergy to be of the same gender as the deity, and that surely something as specific as a female finger, as compared to a male's, would have been an important consideration. I have the feeling that she is being a bit sarcastic, but I do remember that the goddess Asherah was described in the more plentiful and detailed tablets of the Canaanite city of Ugarit as the Mother of All Deities and, as the contemporary translation puts it, Patroness of Diviners. I feel on firmer ground when I reach the passages on the temple in the southern Canaanite city of Ascalon where priestesses gave prophecies based upon the flight patterns and sounds of specially tended doves. It was this same method of foretelling the future that was also used at the Greek shrine of Dodona where the Peliades, the Dove Priestesses, spoke the oracles. This use of doves in oracular divination was probably the source of the numerous dove images that accompanied goddess figures and reliefs found in the goddess temples of Cyprus, Crete, and Greece. Doves were an especially important symbol in the artifacts of the worship of the Goddess as Aphrodite, and it is not surprising that, on the islands of Cyprus and Cythera, the Greek shrines of Aphrodite were closely linked with the Canaanite goddess Asherah or Ashtoreth. Though the Greek shrine at Dodona eventually came under the control of priests of Zeus, it was said to have once been the shrine of the goddess Dione, often described as the Mother of Aphrodite. To confuse the matter even further, the priestesses who prophesied at Dodona about

2,500 years ago, Promenia, Timarete, and Nicandra, spoke of the first dove flying to Dodona from Thebes in Egypt.

In the pages on the Goddess in Anatolia (Turkey), I locate a few lines based on some quite early fragments, possibly of pre-Hittite origin. They describe two heavenly sisters, Istustaya and Papaya, as holding "filled mirrors," possibly bowls of liquid that cast reflections, bringing to mind images of a crystal ball. While keeping their eyes upon these filled mirrors, Istustaya held the spindle, while Papaya wove the years of life. The Anatolian women, known simply as the Elderly Women, were not only regarded as healers, and worth having present at times of birth and death, but for those who would not think to venture into the wealthy official oracular temples, the Anatolian Elderly Women were there to consult for advice upon the future. It was not just the advice of their years of experience that was asked of them, though surely that was valuable and inherent in what was said, but, according to ancient Anatolian tablets, the Elderly Women looked into the future by using a method described as "drawing lots."

The prophecy of the Sibyl, as I mentioned earlier in connection with the end of the Punic War, suggests a link between the Sibyl of the Romans and the worship of the Anatolian goddess Kybele in the city of Pessinus. I have not yet found evidence of oracular priestesses in Pessinus, but the Sibyl's familiarity with, and respect for, the sacred stone suggests that prophecy may have been an aspect of the worship of Kybele in Pessinus as well. The stone itself may be significant in light of the documents from Byblos, in Canaan. These state that the sacred stone of the goddess Baalat, in the temple of Byblos, had "fallen from heaven," suggesting that the stone was a meteorite, as was the sacred stone from Pessinus. The stone of Byblos was said to contain the essence of the Goddess and was able to heal upon contact. It was also described as "breathing with the knowledge of the future." There is the possibility that the Anatolian name Kybele, at times spelled with a "C" rather than a "K," and pronounced Cybele outside of Turkey just as Kyprus becomes Cyprus, may even be the origin of the name of the prophetesses known as Sibyls. Heraclitus wrote that the word "Sibyl" had been derived from a famed prophetess known as Sybella who lived on the western coast of Anatolia.

When I turn from the pages on the Ancient Near and Middle East to the Goddess reverences in Central America, I find the passage explaining that, among members of the Cuna tribe of Panama, rituals enacted for a young woman as she first began her menses, included the cutting down of a single saptur tree from a special grove sacred to the Cuna goddess Mu Olo Kurtilisop, or Giant Blue Butterfly Lady. The pattern of the grain of the cross section where the tree was cut was then read by the elderly women of the tribe to foretell the future life of the young woman. I next locate the lines about the goddess Teteu Innan, known among the Aztecs of Mexico but thought to be a survivor of the earlier Tula people. Teteu Innan, known as a goddess of birth and healing, was associated with a method of prophecy accomplished by reading the patterns of the kernels of corn. This method of prophesying the future may have been similar to one mentioned in accounts of Dahomey in Africa. In the Dahomey account, the woman Minona was said to have taught the reading of palm kernels to the people of Dahomey. Minona was described as a daughter of the woman Gbadu, who, in turn, was described as a messenger and helper of the Dahomey creator goddess Mawu.

Among the Teutonic peoples of Scandinavia, the three women known as the Norns—Urth, Skuld, and Verthandi—were portrayed not only as the ones who watered the roots of the Tree of Life but as the weavers of all destiny. In other Teutonic accounts it was the Goddess as Frigga who sat high upon a stool in her Palace Fensalir and spun the golden thread of fate. Though this might sound as if the Teutonic people considered fate to be absolute, it was also said that Frigga relied upon the divine woman Gna to ride about on her horse, Hofvarpnir, to gather information about what was happening on Earth and to bring this to Frigga as she wove. Evidence of Teutonic women being associated with prophecy is found in descriptions of the rite of the mystic Seydur. The women who participated in this directly as prophets of the future were known as Voolvah. The Voolvah would chant for hours in a deep trance and, in this state, would tell the villagers who gathered about them what was to come.

The use of signs from springs and streams that I mentioned earlier, though attributed by Plutarch to the holy Germanic (Teutonic) women, may have been the result of influence by the Celtic tribes who, at that time, were still living in areas throughout France and Germany, as well as in northern Italy. The worship of the Goddess among the Celts was especially linked to sacred springs and rivers. The area in which Plutarch described the incident as having occurred was not far from the territory of the Celtic Sequani, who revered the goddess Sequana as their Divine Ancestress. When the Sequani moved further west to an area near Dijon, France, a shrine was built to the goddess Sequana at the source of a great river that was then named in her honor. Though there is definite evidence that the shrine was a noted place of healing, we might guess that it was also a shrine of prophecy based on the currents and sounds of the waters, so filled with Sequana's spirit that they bore her name, the River Sequana, eventually known as the River Seine.

Celtic accounts include images of women as combined prophetesses and poetesses. For example, the woman Fedelm, in the stories of Queen Maeve, is described as having three irises in each eye. Fedelm, it is explained to Queen Maeve as they chanced to meet upon the road, just returned from studying "vision and verse in Alba." This idea of linking vision and verse—prophesy and poetry—is one that occurs throughout Celtic texts, where such women are referred to as Banfathi. But the material I find most fascinating is that pertaining to the male Taliesin, who claims not only knowledge of both past and future but the position of being the greatest poet of the Celts while, at the same time, admitting that he stole his powers of genius and insight from the cauldron of the goddess/sorceress Cerridwen.

Another figure in Celtic legend also reveals woman's image as the voice of the future. This is the rarely discussed Morgan le Fée. The Celtic evidence on Morgan le Fée is so complicated, and composed of so many fragments, that it took several pages to cover in the book. Perhaps the simplest way to explain the core of the image of Morgan Le Fée is to trace her connection to Morgana La Fee of France, who, in turn, was associated with Fata Morgana of Italy. The road goes further yet, as Fata Morgana was, in turn, linked with the Roman goddess Fortuna. The names alone—Fay and Fata—cognate with both Faerie and Fate. And Fortuna and Fortune, meaning chance or destiny, reveal this image of woman to once again be that of Arranger of Events and Life, whether as Nina, Mawu, Frigga, Teteu Innan, Ishtar, or even the pale survival of Lady Luck to some fervent gambler of today. The Roman goddess Fortuna was revered in her temple at the city of Praeneste, modern Palestrina, and in Cerveteri (both in Italy), not far from the more noted shrine of the Sibyl of Cumae. In Cerveteri the priestesses provided information about the future from "lots that rose from the hot springs there."

The image of Fortuna was, in turn, closely associated with the Roman image of the Three Fates, who, like the Three Norns, wove the threads of future events—Clotho holding the distaff, Lachesis spinning, while Atropos stood by to clip the thread. The Fates, known in Greece as the Moirae (or in Rome as the Parcae), were said to be the daughters of the goddess Themis, she who owned the scale of justice, acting as both judge and counselor. Some accounts describe Themis as sitting on Olympus directly next to Zeus, her nephew, and providing him with advice and counsel. One gathers from the Greek myths that Zeus did not pay much attention to her, but at least Themis fared better than another, probably earlier image of the Goddess of "Wisdom and Counsel," Metis. Metis was described as having been swallowed by Zeus and forced to give him advice from inside his bloated belly.

The material on the goddess Themis leads to the most renowned oracular shrine of all—Delphi—which literally means "womb." Tucked away in the foothills of the craggy Phedriades Mountains of Greece, Delphi, though most often described as a temple of the male Apollo, dates back to the Mycenaean period of Greece (about 1400 BC), when it was a holy place of the Mother of Themis, the creator goddess known as Gaia. Since it took ten pages in the book to cover the evidence on Gaia and the accounts of the loss of the shrine of Delphi to the priests of Apollo, I will simply say here that it was Gaia who was described by Aeschylus as the Primeval Prophetess and that the first priestesses, the Pythias, who gave the prophetic oracles at Delphi, conveyed the messages of Gaia—not Apollo. The conquest of the shrine by Dorian invaders and its eventual control by the priests of Apollo may be reflected in mythic accounts such as that of Daphne fleeing from Apollo's attempt to rape her. Or there is the priestess Delphyna, who stood in Apollo's way and was shot down by his fiery arrow, and the story of Cassandra, who was tortured with the curse of being able to foresee the future but never to be believed. Greek myth tells us this curse was placed upon Cassandra for resisting the sexual advances of, who else but, Apollo.

So full circle, though very briefly covered under the pressure of orally describing thousands of years and many unfamiliar names and places in such a short period of allotted time, I return to thoughts of the haunting image of Cassandra. And suddenly the voice of Intuition, silent since the last crack about the clergy being in the image of the deity, now says, "Well, that should at least get the point across that it was, and is, the natural role of woman to look into the future and to offer the wisdom of women's counsel on it." With fingers tired from typing, papers and books now scattered all over the room, I say, "Intuition, I'm truly glad you suggested doing this, but now I am feeling very hesitant about leaving in the beginning of this paper and admitting to all the women at the Chico conference that I hear voices—your voice to be specific—and even more damning that I answer back and argue with you." She does not answer, and now I worry that she is offended by this challenge to her very existence. Trying to veer over to a less painful subject, I ask, "Why do so many people speak of intuition as 'women's intuition'? If all women hear your voice, and women are the majority of people on this Earth, then perhaps hearing voices should be considered normal." She is still silent, and my mind travels back to some of the places and times I have just been writing about, remembering how often priestesses were thought to be conveying messages of the Goddess.

Really feeling a bit crazy at this point and quite exhausted, I say defensively, "But it's true: they do say 'women's intuition,' almost always 'women's intuition.'" Still no answer. I decide to look up the word in a massive old Webster's Dictionary. Webster's says "intuition" is "inner tuition," and suggests I look up "tuition." I wonder, as I turn the pages to *T*, if following Webster's advice is really any sounder than following Intuition's. "Tuition—the watch or care of a tutor or guardian, watchful, protective." I digest the meaning of "intuition" as an inner tutor, an inner guardian or adviser. At this point, I am not sure if it is my voice or hers that whispers, "The Goddess within each woman." Of course, I think, Intuition is a woman's balance of perceiving existent external realities while, at the same time, being advised or tutored about what we see from within. Women listened to her voice before they (we) were frightened by stories of Cassandra or were told that if we heard a woman's voice it must be our imagination because Ezekiel, Jeremiah, Isaiah, and the rest said that true prophecy came from hearing a man's voice. But, all my life, this woman's voice has been telling me to listen to her. In exhaustion and total exasperation, I plead, "Intuition, truly you are driving me crazy. Are you my own voice? Are you the voice of the Goddess? Do you really exist?" Finally, an answer, as I hear the voice say, "That's a rather complex theological, philosophical, and psychological question, one that I think we had better save for another time. But before you finish this paper, do add that as women demand to have their voices heard in the future, I, too, would like to be heard and to have my ideas considered seriously. I don't mind arguing or having to defend my point of view, but I do resent being ignored. And, oh, one more thing before you get up from the typewriter: don't forget to mention that the future always was, is, and will be beginning right now."

I would like to finish by saying that by sharing this with you, I am not advocating an undigested acceptance of the voice of Intuition in each of us. But by exploring the areas that our intuitions suggest, taking the time and trouble to examine our intuitive ideas, balancing what we know from Intuition with our tuition of all that is happening around us, we may find that we, as women, possess the most perfectly balanced compass for navigation into the future.

The Global Garden

by Merlin Stone

(An unpublished article dated May 2, 1992)

BERTRAND RUSSELL ONCE ASKED, "Do you think of your skin as separating you from the rest of the world, or as connecting you to it?" At the time I heard this, perhaps forty years ago, I laughed and decided that I simply thought of my skin as something to keep me from leaking.

Since that time I have given a great deal of thought to this question of separation and connection, especially in relation to how this matter might emerge in times to come. So much spiritual contemplation arrives at the perception of everyone, everything, being connected, interwoven in a sacred web of life. Yet so many people perceive themselves as separate, not only from most or all other people, but from other species, from other forms of nature, even from our planet.

It seems to me that one of the most powerful emotions that acts as a lens for a perception of separateness is fear—a deep, unconscious fear of things getting out of control, a fear of a dangerous chaos. It is this fear of chaos that leads to emotional and material fortressing. It leads to building walls of protection around the heart and mind. It leads to an amassing of material goods and wealth as walls to protect one's comforts, body, and ego. The greater the fear of chaos, the greater the fortressing.

The fear of a dangerous chaos leads people to try to maintain a rigid control of themselves. It also leads to an effort to control everyone and everything else by judging, shaming, and humiliating them, as well as by constructing hierarchies based on gender, race, nationality, ethnicity, religion, economics, class, education, species, and other aspects of life. Feelings of trust or compassion become close to impossible if they in any way seem to threaten any one of the numerous fortresses constructed to achieve a sense of control.

One of the most noticeable manifestations of a fear of chaos is a resistance to flow, to process, to change. What could be more threatening to frightened efforts to maintain control? If there is one change that I would like to see in the future, it would be a lessening of the fear of chaos, even the ability to embrace it as a stage of incipient creation. This would allow for a deeper comprehension and trust of time and process, a greater courage to continually consider all possibilities and options. It would encourage a greater spontaneity and creativity in thinking about the way we live. We would not embrace change merely for the sake of change, but would be free to choose those changes that work best for all life on the planet, free to move in more compassionate, life-nurturing directions, and to embark upon these paths with courage, hope, and trust.

If we could stop being so protective of our separated selves, we could tear down the individual fortresses, step out into the lush global garden of infinite possibilities, and finally experience what it means to be fully alive.

Women in Armed Combat

by Merlin Stone

Written in 1991, the source notes for this essay have been lost, but based on the thorough scholarship of Merlin's other published works, we confidently publish this essay here. —David B. Axelrod

*W*OMEN IN COMBAT? It's a prospect that anti-feminists and some feminists have found equally unthinkable for opposing reasons: women's physical "inferiority" and need for protection on one hand, and women's moral "superiority" and opposition to violence on the other. Both viewpoints could benefit from historical records. Women have fought and killed in battle; that much is clear. Was it out of aggression or self-defense? Was there actually a need to conquer, or was it fueled by a will to survive? Only by looking at the reasons for violence can we fully understand why women may be both physically capable of fighting and killing in combat as well as culturally likely to resort to it for different reasons.

One of the better known accounts of an ancient woman soldier is that of Boudicca (Boadicea), Queen of the Celtic Iceni tribe that inhabited the area that is now Norfolk in Great Britain. The Roman writer Dio Cassius reported that Boudicca personally led a mass rebellion against the invading Roman army in 61 AD and burned the town of Llundein (London) to the ground. He described her as "huge of frame, terrifying of aspect, and possessing a harsh voice." He further explained that a mass of red hair fell to her knees, that she held a long spear to frighten all who came before her, and that she prayed to the Celtic battle goddess Andrasta before entering battle. Perhaps she was also influenced by the fact that Roman soldiers had raped her daughters.

Cartimandua, a Celtic woman who lived during the same period as Boudicca, was queen of the large Brigante tribe that lived in the area now called Yorkshire. Tacitus recorded that Cartimandua chose to sign a peace treaty with the invading Romans, divorcing her husband (who preferred to fight) in order to do so. The Celtic text known as the Tain Bo Cualnge includes many passages about Medb, queen of the Irish county of Connaught. Though initially put into written form in the seventh century AD, the Tain is a compilation of accounts that had long been retained through oral recitations. Judging from the place names and events described in it, Celtic scholars believe that some of the accounts may be as old as the Le Tene Period of about 500 BC. According to the Tain, Medb led the mounted Connaught troops in battle against the troops of Ulster. References to other well-known women soldiers such as Scathach, Aoife, and the Gwyddynod of Gloucester are also recorded in Roman and Celtic records. Ammianus Marcellinus, writing of the Roman invasions of Celtic territories, commented, "An entire troop of foreigners would not be able to withstand a single Gaul (Celt) if he called his wife to his assistance."

Tomyris, chief of the Massagetae tribes that lived near the Caspian Sea, led the battle that resulted in the retreat of invading Persian armies and the death of their leader, Cyrus of Persia, in 530 BC. According to the Greek historian Herodotus, writing in about 425 BC, Tomyris decided to engage the Persian troops in battle after a series of attempts at peaceful negotiations. Her decision to attack was made after discovering that her son, Spagapides, had been captured by Cyrus and had died in the enemy camp. The battle was a bloody one that began with mounted troops using bows and arrows and ended with spears and daggers in hand to hand combat. When the battle was over, Tomyris sought out the body of Cyrus on the battlefield. Her rage was so great that she then beheaded the slain king. The account of this incident, as recorded by Herodotus, includes the words that Tomyris spoke at that moment: "Though I have conquered you and I still live, truly you have defeated me by killing my son."

Artemisia, sovereign of Halicarnassus, appears in the accounts of Herodotus as a naval commander of five ships in a Persian-led retaliation against a Greek incursion of Aegean islands. She is described not only as an extremely competent naval officer but also as an outstanding strategist of naval battle. Her expertise became so renowned that the Greeks offered a reward of ten thousand drachmae to anyone who could capture her alive. The reward was never claimed. After the battle at Salamis, in 480 BC, Artemisia returned safely to her homeland in Anatolia (now Turkey).

Numerous lengthy passages that appear in many of the Greek and Roman classics refer to women as "amazons." These accounts, along with bas reliefs and paintings depicting women in battle, have been dismissed as fantasy by many writers of the nineteenth and twentieth centuries. Yet well-known classical writers—Callimachus, Diodorus Siculus, Herodotus, Homer, Pausanius, Pindar, Plutarch, Strabo, and others—described women warriors in various areas of the Near East and Caucasus regions, some not far from the Massagetae territories of the later Tomyris. The oldest of the Greek accounts is that of Homer. Since several different groups of women are described in these accounts, each would require a separate dating analysis. Homer's passages, linked to the Trojan War, are generally believed to refer to the Mycenaean Period of about the fourteenth century BC. The very specific geographical areas designated, and the extremely detailed accounts of some of the battles, do not allow a casual dismissal of women as soldiers.

Archaeological evidence supports descriptions of ancient female deities—most often associated with fertility, wisdom, and compassion—that include attributes so martial that contemporary scholars often refer to them as battle goddesses. Although ancient goddess figures might be regarded today as theological inventions, the question remains: Why were such powerful, martial deities in so many different cultures perceived as female? The classical Greek Athena is perhaps the battle goddess most familiar to us, but the image of female deity as warrior was far from unique in ancient periods. The image of the helmeted Athena has been traced back to earlier Minoan Crete, and to several artifacts that depict the Minoan goddess with helmet and spear. In turn, both the Minoan goddess and Athena are thought to have been derived from the warrior goddess Neith, who was known in early dynastic periods of Egypt and Libya.

Tablets of the fourteenth-century-BC city-state of Ugarit in northern Canaan, currently Ras Shamra in Syria, contain detailed accounts of battles of the Semitic goddess Anath. One major epic described how she defended her temple against invaders. Bas reliefs of Anath depict her with spear and battle helmet in portrayals similar to those of Athena. Japanese literature describes the sun goddess Amaterasu appearing in the heavens holding a bow in one hand, five hundred arrows in the other, and a quiver of one thousand arrows on her back. The Purana texts of India offer several different versions of the battles fought by the goddess Durga against various manifestations of the demon of evil. A seventh-century-AD carved stone relief adorns a temple at Mamalla-puram on the coast of India, some thirty miles from Madras. It depicts troops of the demon in retreat as Durga rides forth upon a lion. The weapons attributed to Durga were bow and arrows, spear and trident. Babylonian cuneiform tablets depicting the goddess Ishtar were inscribed: "When at the front of combat she is seen, she is a flood of light whose strength is mighty. Ishtar is the one who cannot be opposed. She is the whirlwind that roars against all wrong."

Along with these accounts are those of Strabo's passages regarding the women warriors of India; Briffault's accounts of women soldiers in Indonesia and Polynesia; the oral traditions about the woman Potai (war chief) Pohaha of the Cottonwood Clan of the Native American Pueblo; accounts of women soldiers such as Mary E. Wise, Elizabeth Compton, Sophie Thompson, Frances Hook, and Anna Ella Carroll, all of whom took part in the U.S. Civil War; and, of course, the more familiar accounts of Joan of Arc. French and English reports of nine-teenth-century Dahomey told of the royal bodyguard of one hundred women who fought alongside King Gueso in the battle at Abeokuta, a town in Nigeria close to the Dahomey border. The martial skills and courage of these women were said to be equaled only by their prowess in the elephant hunts. An account of the Dahomean women soldiers appeared in the Paris edition of the *New York Herald Tribune* on December 2, 1964. The story told of an elite corps of women soldiers who fought in the war for the independence of Malawi (Nyasaland).

Women of the Native American Iroquois tribes of the northeastern U.S. participated in martial strategy in a somewhat unusual way. Although it was the Iroquois males who actually participated in combat, the women had total control of the food supply. Refusing to supply food to the warriors constituted a veto against that particular conflict, thus canceling many a battle.

Historical evidence makes it clear that women are both physically and psychologically capable of engaging in war and armed combat. It helps us to understand that when a majority of women in the past and present have avoided war as the solution to world problems, this has not been by default, but by choice. In this era of technological warfare, women are perhaps even more capable of participating in war, while the reasons for speaking out against it have become increasingly obvious. Perhaps when we consciously acknowledge that women are inherently capable of engaging in combat, women's voices calling for peaceful solutions will be given more serious consideration.

Two Poems by Merlin Stone
I Trust the Voice

(1987)

We are the Goddess
creating the world ever new.
Our strength and our courage
grow when we do what we do.
I trust the voice inside of me.
I trust the voice inside of you.

As sisters we grow together
weaving our wisdom so old,
shaping a new world together
with patterns and colors so bold.
I trust the voice inside of me.
I trust the voice inside of you.

Together we're dancing the future,
with pragmatic magic we glide.
The song of the Goddess within us—
no longer can She be denied.
I trust the voice inside of me.
I trust the voice inside of you.

For When I pass on   1985   M. STONE

Don't grieve over me
I did what I wanted to do
followed my excitement,
my thoughts and desires
lived as I wanted to ~~live~~
re~~fused~~ jected traditions and rules
neither a meteor nor a dud
I let my loves flow
my furies explode
smashing icons and celebrity
appearing and withdrawing
as the mood suited me

Don't grieve over me
I have never felt regret
and even in times of despair
a candle of hope remained lit
I relished intensity + integrity
truth with gentle diplomacy
compassion, with demands
that potential be fulfilled
I thought rude questions,
smashed superficiality and pretense
laughed at established lies
decided, that most people/were afraid to live

Don't grieve over me
I was blessed with a full measure
of the ~~passion~~ juices of conscious life.

Original text of "For When I Pass On."

For When I Pass On

(1985)

Don't grieve over me.
I did what I wanted to do,
followed my excitement.
my thoughts and desires
lived as I wanted to
rejected traditions and rules
neither a meteor nor a dud.
I let my loves flow
my furies explode
smashing icons and celebrity
appearing and withdrawing
as the mood suited me.

Don't grieve over me.
I have never felt regret
and even in times of despair
a candle of hope remained lit.
I relished intensity and integrity
truth with gentle diplomacy
compassion, with demands
that potential be fulfilled.
I thought rude questions
smashed superficiality and pretense
laughed at established lies
decided that most people
were afraid to live.

Don't grieve over me.
I was blessed with a full measure
of the juices of conscious life.

Merlin in her room, circa 1995, when she finished her novel.

One Summer on the Way to Utopia, or *Dreams of Getting There*
EXCERPTS FROM AN UNPUBLISHED NOVEL
BY MERLIN STONE
with commentary by David B. Axelrod

*D*R. ADDIE SEDGEWICK WEAVER, clinical psychologist, expert and lecturer on cults and cult behavior, and social commentator, tells us:

> I've always been extremely curious about people who seem to be on the path of some compelling quest, always wanting to know what it is that pushes, or perhaps magically pulls, each quester to take just one more step again and again and again. Whether that quest is to arrive at the point of experiencing the spiritual enlightenment of nirvana, or to discover who really wrote the plays attributed to William Shakespeare, or to accumulate millions of dollars, or achieve enormous fame, or develop a cure for a particular disease…the expression of a sometimes obsessive and frequently intense dedication of a person toward a very specific goal has always intrigued me.

Addie is the protagonist in a novel written by Merlin Stone. By all accounts, Merlin worked on the book off and on for two years, completing a second draft by 1995.

Merlin created Addie, a clinical psychologist, professor, and expert on cults and cult behavior, to give a first-person account of social and women's issues. Addie recounts a number of sessions with her patients. In addition, she watches her husband's quest for an "Elixir of Immortality," and advises a friend who is drawn into an ongoing investigation of cult activities.

We are witness to clinical sessions Addie conducts. We join her in the course she teaches on cult behavior. We witness Addie's own personal relationships. Each situation provides a context for us to consider the ways people seek happiness. Addie's commentary continues:

> Although the actual journey of any quest—the experiences along the way, the encounters with various people, the lessons, the tests, the adventures, the epiphanies—is often said to be the true purpose of the quest, still I find myself more curious about the intensity of the drive, the fierce motivation that forces the quester along like a small piece of paper in the wind of a hurricane or a lover in search of the lost beloved.
>
> What initially aroused my interest in quest people were the intense rushes of excitement I could see they were experiencing, wildly surging tides of adrenalin, endorphins, long highs of an almost ecstatic anticipation that seemed to accompany every probability, even any possibility, along the way. I am still quite puzzled about the nature of that quest energy, that heightened sense of existence, which primarily reveals itself in the single-minded determination of each quester to explore along some very specific pathway, each wave of excitation manifesting itself in an insatiable thirsting for just one more bit of information, just one more obstacle to overcome, just one more acquisition, just one more mountain to climb, just one more idea to try, with the continually repeated expectation of reaching an ultimate sense of satisfaction, an ever-present yearning to achieve the envisioned promise of the finish line. (pp. 3–4)

The observations continue:

> How do people get started on these quests? What is it that seeps into their innermost drives, pulling them, sustaining them, on these sometimes dangerous and certainly long and arduous journeys?

At times I've surmised that the essential nature of the goal of each quest might be innate, genetic, that early clues could have been observed in the very young child. My most serious and thoughtful guess would be that it was probably the result of a random group of events and experiences, people being in certain places at certain times, especially in their earlier years, that sent them off on their individual quests. In my more imaginative moments, I've even wondered if each compelling quest is a single component of some overall cosmic plan, a predestined role that is being communicated to, and carried out by, each of the questing individuals without them even being aware of what is driving them along on their paths. (pp. 7–8)

It is, of course, a fallacy to assume that the words of any fictional character automatically speak for the author herself. But there seems to be little doubt that Merlin, who pursued her own vigorous quest and research on goddesses and goddess worship, is speaking at least somewhat through Addie when she observes:

Although I have never thought of myself as a quest person, perhaps every life may be regarded as a quest, a seeking to decipher what life is about, why we are here, what we are supposed to be doing while we are here. Perhaps my own compelling quest is to comprehend what it is that drives the most noticeably questing people ever onward, to gain more insight into the intrinsic nature of human quest itself and, in so doing, to better understand why some lives seem more exciting, more satisfying, than others. (p. 10)

Of Addie's patients, the one person most useful in terms of sketching out women's issues and views is the character Andrea. In session after session, Andrea questions her own identity, delves into the nature of man-woman and woman-woman relationships, and recounts her discovery of the women's movement and her growing female consciousness.

Addie begins a session by noting that:

> We do live in a society where women are much more likely to be treated as children, even as incompetents. Therefore, it is more often the woman who is likely not to trust her own perceptions and judgment. The question is whether or not this can be done to a woman who was reflected positively during her childhood, encouraged to trust her own perceptions and judgment.... Sometimes it's difficult to believe that ... a man who says he loves a woman would do that to her. I guess that's the first perception we begin to doubt, that it's happening at all. (p. 41)

Later, commenting more generally, Addie herself observes:

> Too many humans become callous and arrogant, belittling others, striving for status and power, caring for no one but themselves, in their quests to feed and comfort their own egos. Who, other than beings with superhuman powers, could rescue us as a species? Perhaps that is why Superman and Wonder Woman are so beloved by children, even by adults who read about them as children. Perhaps it is why so many people have recently become interested in the idea of angels.... It seems that so many people are desperately hoping, searching, for a savior, a messiah, a Melchizadek, a Superman, someone to save them, someone capable of making this a better world or leading them to one that was already perfect—a utopia, an Eden, a paradise. Women, especially before this last wave of women's liberation, often waited to be rescued and carried off by some knight in shining armor riding up on his white horse—a Prince Charming.

How anxious some people seem to be to find and accept a leader for their quest, to believe in the sweet promises of evangelists or those of smooth-tongued politicians, each seductively describing how they will create a better world if you will just follow them. The Pied Piper arrives in many forms, a shape-shifter if there ever was one. (pp. 74–75)

~

Again, in a clinical session with Andrea, Addie lets us glimpse some interesting thoughts on the women's movement. Here is an account in which Andrea describes her attendance at a women's gathering. Andrea says:

As it turned out, only nine women showed up in all, mostly women who lived in that area. Mindy said they usually had more. For a long time we sat outside, cold as it was. We sat around a ring of huge rock slabs, with this tremendous fire blazing in the middle, crackling and sparking into the night sky while two women were drumming, and all the women were singing these songs I'd never heard before. I hadn't worn warm enough clothing, and when Lucy saw that I was shivering, she brought a blanket out from the house and wrapped it around my shoulders without my even asking. Sitting there in front of this great fire, with that striped woolen blanket draped around my shoulders, I felt as if I were in a dream, almost as if we were the women of some primitive tribe, or people in another time. I'd never had an experience like that before. There was such a sense of closeness between the women, and that included me. All the "I must impress you" competition at the parties I have to attend here in the city seemed a world away.

There was one thing that did bother me a bit.... It was kind of silly. Some of the songs they were singing were about the moon as a goddess. They used Greek and Roman goddess names—Artemis and Diana. As I've told you, my family was never very religious, Episcopalian, but we hardly ever went to church. I don't know if my discomfort was from thinking it was too pagan, or too religious. I can't imagine that those women were raised worshiping Diana any more than I was, yet they all seemed quite comfortable with the songs, even Mindy. In any case, when it was over, Lucy invited us to stay at the house, so we didn't get back to the city until this morning. I didn't want to return. It was so idyllic. ...

I remembered how much I missed being near trees and the smell of the earth and the air. Did I mention that they did this strange thing for me? They asked if I wanted them to do a healing for my divorce. They all seemed to know about it from Mindy, who, to put it politely, doesn't believe in secrets. I suppose I was so totally absorbed in the whole experience by that time, I must have agreed. They formed a circle on the grass not far from the fire, holding hands the way children do in their games. Then they stood me in the center of the circle and kept dancing around me, singing, moving in closer and closer until I felt incredibly safe and cared for, as though I had eight loving mothers.

When we went into the house after the ritual and I was lying in bed looking up at the full moon through the window, I realized that I need more friends, friends like Mindy, friends like these women who made me feel so connected, not only to them but to myself. (pp. 6–7)

Here are Addie's comments after the session with her patient Andrea:

It sounded rather odd. I had read an article about something similar, women forming groups like that. It seemed to be connected to the women's rights movement, of which I heartily approve. Women's rights were something my mother had often spoken of as extremely important. She had participated in some of the marches to get the vote for women.

It's still hard for me to believe that women gained the right to vote only about twelve years before I was born. I was in my late thirties when the women's rights movement began to spread again, and I often wished that my mother had been alive to see it. I've attended some feminist conferences and panel discussions, read quite a few articles about it, but I wasn't sure what I thought about a group of contemporary women dancing around under the full moon. ...

I had a vague notion, almost a visual image, of Andrea standing at a crossroads, standing there trying to decide which path to take, possibly changing the course of her direction. Was this simply another road on her quest, or was she completely changing the destination—the goal—of that quest? (pp. 134–137)

~

If creating Addie serves in any way as an alter ego for Merlin herself, it is touching to listen in on Addie's private musings. Addie asks:

"Just who am I?" I found myself wondering, setting down my teacup and walking over to the mirror ... to look at myself. I examined the small lines that formed around my eyes and mouth, the gray in my hair, and then noticed that the black scarf I had worn in the kitchen was still hanging around my neck where I had pushed it down to eat my snack. A whimsical impulse made me pull it up over my nose again just to see how it looked.

Again, I saw myself as the Lone Ranger. Did I need to be like the Lone Ranger, constantly trying to help people in distress? Is that what made me feel worthwhile? A funny image of myself dashing about on a white horse drifted through my mind, along with the old cry of *Hi-Yo, Silver! Away!* Rescuers. Saviors. White horses. ... Did I need a white horse like Silver to ride on? Perhaps I did, as long as Greg [her husband] needed his alchemical gold.

I heard Greg moving around in the kitchen, probably turn-
ing off the heat under his bowl of green mush, his effort to
concoct an Elixir of Immortality that he thought might keep
him alive and young forever. . . .

No, I wasn't the Lone Ranger. I was more like the writer of
Chaucer's *Canterbury Tales*, listening to the story of each pilgrim
as they made their way on their quests, their pilgrimages. But
Chaucer's pilgrims were all traveling to the same place. What if
each one had been going in a different direction, as mine seemed
to be? (pp. 146–147)

Certainly, if Addie speaks for Merlin at all, the way she characterizes
her relationship with her husband, Greg, also would speak well for
Merlin's own relationship with her life partner of thirty-four years,
Len Schneir:

I should explain that much of my ability to keep up with all
these people and activities has been facilitated by the wonderful relationship I have with my husband. After almost thirty
years of marriage, and having heard about hundreds of marital
problems in couples counseling, I realize how lucky I've been. I
believe that each of us continually encouraging the other to
fully develop our innate potential, to feel free to explore whatever is of interest to us as individuals, has been of enormous
benefit to the solidity of our relationship. (p. 23)

Indeed, in Merlin's novel, Addie tells us that her patient Andrea "had
come into therapy to help her get in touch with whatever made her
choose a man like Roger [the husband she just divorced] so she could
be more careful in the future." (p. 161)

The exchange between patient and therapist is revealing. The exchange is worth reading in its entirety. In the dialogue with Addie,
Andrea says:

"I don't think I'm a lesbian. ... I just think that men are damaged goods. They simply don't understand what an egalitarian relationship is. They're always out to win, and we become the losers because we don't even realize a game is being played."

"You've always described your own father as very gentle and kind."

"That's a different generation. Besides, my mother always placated him with the patience of Griselda. She was right there behind him all the time doing just about anything he requested. I don't intend to do that for any man."

"I'm not suggesting that you sacrifice yourself, but there are relationships where men and women can give equally to each other."

Andrea pursed her lips, shaking her head from side to side. "I think it always works to the man's advantage. I've been reading this book about how men are always thinking they're in some sort of contest, while women are more concerned about relationships, trying to make them work better. The author presents it as if we're simply different, men and women, but how can you relate to someone who's always thinking about everything, even making love, as a competition? You can see they're always jockeying for position in sports, in business, in politics, in everything. Sexually, they're competing with any man you've ever been with and anyone you might meet."

She paused for breath, but not for long, taking up her tirade with renewed vigor. "And look at who commits most of the violence—boys and men, right? Mindy calls it testosterone poisoning. They say they feel protective toward women, but then there's all that terrible wife battering and rape, even sexually abusing young girls. It's all part of their contest, their need to control, to have power over everyone and everything around them. They're always competing about something, whether it's over material things or even ideas.

"It's why we have wars—their ultimate contest! And all that rubbish about women wanting to control men! You know what that's about, don't you? They want to control everything you do and exactly the way you do it. That's winning the contest. If you ask for one little thing, suddenly they feel pressured, nagged, controlled, just by your asking. So they accuse you of being a controlling woman, which is just another way of controlling you, of winning the contest."

I'd never seen Andrea so full of rage, even more furious than when she had initially been talking about Roger [her ex-husband]. This was a scathing indictment of all men. These were issues of morality in conflict with psychological notions about emotional health and mental stability. I'm beginning to see politics as yet another aspect of why people behave as they do. I don't mean politics in the sense of who's running in an election, but politics in its most basic presence in our lives—who's in charge, who makes the decisions, and who has the power.

My studies in psychology never dealt with questions of how groups of people actually do have less power in a given situation, or have to defend themselves against negative stereotypes, whether it's because of race, gender, economics, class, ethnicity, age, disabilities, or whatever affects the people of that group as individuals. I'm beginning to see now that the all too numerous structures of hierarchy, those that leave many people with very little or completely without status or power in various ways, do exist. To pretend they do not, or to pretend they have no impact on an individual's personal life, is as much a pattern of disassociation and denial as when these patterns occur in young children who have been abused.

Yet, as a therapist who has spent so much of my time doing couples counseling, and despite the recent peculiarities at home, I truly enjoyed my relationship with my husband for nearly thirty years. I wondered what I might say to Andrea that would be honest and helpful.

"Of course you'll make your own decisions about relating to men. You're certainly functioning well in managing your life, your new apartment, and new friendships. And I can see that since you left Roger, your sense of satisfaction with your life seems healthy and constructive. Your view of men may be just a state in your recovery from the divorce, or perhaps you'll continue to feel this way. Time will tell. But I've been meaning to ask you since you haven't mentioned your work for quite a while, how's it going?"

"It's all right. I'm getting a little bored with my job at the magazine. And, of course, with all the changes I've had to make since I left Roger, I haven't had much time to do any writing of my own. Actually, I haven't written much of anything. It's a little hard to concentrate. I'm sure I'll start again soon. I have some ideas for a play."

"That sounds interesting. As I said before, the decision of whether or not to stop therapy is also completely up to you. It's funny; I recently had lunch with a woman who helped me through much of my pain after my divorce when I was just about your age, and she wasn't a therapist at all. In fact, she was a very poor seventeen-year-old Native American woman—a waitress at a place where I was staying for a few months, although now she's become very active in the environmental movement in British Columbia."

"I didn't realize you had been divorced. You always seem as though you know yourself so well, that you would go through life making all the right decisions."

"Andrea, I'm almost sixty years old. If I haven't learned something about myself over all these years, I'd be a rather unobservant person. Everyone makes mistakes. The trick is to notice them as soon as possible. What's that old saying, "That's why they put erasers on pencils"?

"Now we have computers. We get into the habit of changing and changing and changing and never being completely satisfied," Andrea said. She thought for a moment and then added, "You know, I think I would like to continue our sessions for at least a little while longer if that's all right with you." (pp. 161–165)

~

One could make a case that many details of Merlin's own life are interwoven in her novel. Merlin's own brave quest to research and document Goddess worship could easily relate to her hero Addie's own meditation on what motivates people on a quest. Addie's perceptions of what makes a successful male-female relationship are very likely tempered by Merlin's own happy personal relationship with her lifemate, Lenny. Merlin had her ups and downs, her first divorce and a second brief marriage that was also connected to time she spent in British Columbia. Parallel after parallel may be drawn, and, indeed, there is an entire field in literature, biographical criticism, that builds interpretations of works of fiction around the facts of an author's life. As authors often live private lives and, after their passing, are obviously not available to validate one theory or interpretation or another, it may be a safer task to simply read and discuss the passages themselves to glean whatever wisdom they may contain. Critics can't claim fiction as fact any more than they can read an author's mind.

That said, Merlin may well have left us some fascinating glimpses into her own personal views in the perceptions she attributes to Addie, who observes:

Time span. Looking backward, deep into the past. Looking forward, far into the future. Was it like a perspective point in a drawing, allowing us to see as far into the future as we could see into the past? Are all quests actually different efforts to understand this vast expanse of time and to try to make some sense of how yesterday links with tomorrow? It's like a bridge being constructed from both banks with the hope that they'll meet in the middle of the river, each of us trying to weld the two parts together in our own way and in our own lives. (p. 199)

Looking back over her lectures in her class on cult behavior, Addie observes:

I was increasingly aware that many people did seem to be on a quest for power and control, not unlike cult leaders. I felt I needed to present a more overall view of the quest for power and control, how it relates to a quest for status, and the impetus for the creation of hierarchy.

It had recently been brought to my attention in so many different ways. There had been a breakthrough with women realizing that many males had set up a hierarchy that regarded females as inferior. There were people ... who realized that a hierarchy had been set up by many Caucasians based upon portraying other races as inferior. There were the hierarchical attitudes of many Anglo-Saxons that depicted Italian-Americans, Hispanic-Americans, Polish-Americans, and so many other ethnic groups as inferior. Some Protestants regarded Catholics as inferior. There were even status hierarchies between the different denominations of Protestants, some viewing others as less socially acceptable, less well bred. People with a great deal of money often regarded the lives of poor people as less important, while some with college degrees made it clear that they looked upon those with less education as less intelligent.

What else could all these attitudes be except a quest for a higher status, a means of fulfilling the quest to feel power and control? And who else could have created these hierarchical spectrums, these ladders of status in so many facets of life, other than those who had decided they were on top? Oddly enough, many of the methods used by cult leaders to diminish the value or worth of their members were all too similar to the methods used by those who claimed to be at the top of each hierarchy. It was to diminish the value or worth of the particular groups of people they had placed further down on the ladder. In one way or another they were all saying, "You should be more like me, but you can't." (pp. 16–17)

It should be noted that Merlin expresses similar thoughts in her groundbreaking pamphlet *Three Thousand Years of Racism* (New Sibylline Books, 1981). Addie continues to question and observe:

Why were people setting up these ladders on which to judge themselves and others in the first place? Why did people even think in terms of status and hierarchy? It was almost certainly a part of the quest for power and control, but then why the quest for power and control?

I had recently read an article about the serotonin levels in the brains of chimpanzees. It claimed that becoming the leader of a group had raised their levels of serotonin. Could the quest for power and control be fueled by an unconscious desire to have a higher level of some neurotransmitter rushing around in the brain? I felt the need to present these questions to the class, but it was frustrating to realize I didn't have any specific answers.

I could hear my mother saying, "Figuring out the right question is halfway to the correct answer." (pp. 243–244)

All this is in Dr. Addie Weaver's voice. In his memoir of his life with Merlin, Lenny Schneir notes how Merlin loved her mother greatly, though he notes a moment along the way where she wished her mother better understood her writing and publications. It seems fitting that Addie can "hear my mother" giving good advice.

For all the wisdom revealed in the nearly four-hundred-page manuscript of Merlin's novel, some of the best advice seems to be on how we relate to children. The comments are imparted during a scene describing Addie's class on cults and cult behavior:

> One of my deepest beliefs is that too many children are not encouraged to think for themselves, not only not encouraged but at times actively discouraged.
>
> "We know what's best for you. You're too young to understand. Just do as I say." I believe these phrases find their way into children's innermost belief systems and, without any attempt at explanation by the parent, weaken children in the long run. Encouraging a touch of skepticism in children may be as crucial to their safety as warning them to watch for cars when they cross the street.
>
> "Cult leaders use gullibility, naive innocence, to their advantage as they encourage people to trust them rather than themselves," I explained to the class. Some of the students nodded in agreement. Others looked puzzled. The message that a child should not trust his or her own judgment is a subtle, almost subliminal process that can even further discourage the child's trust in what he or she perceives. How is this form of undermining done to children? I'll use the word 'reflection' for want of a better one. By reflection I mean a subtle impact that a parent or caretaker is having on a child. Reflection often determines a child's sense of identity, their sense of the value or worth of their own perceptions and judgment....
>
> The idea is to gradually teach them to use and trust their own perceptions and judgment so they can learn to think and reason for themselves, and for us as adults to understand that they are in the process of learning to do this. The pattern of a so-called spoiled child is a pattern of being unreasonable. Encouraging children to use their own perceptions and judgment to think and to reason helps them learn to negotiate differences and decisions in a reasonable way. It results in just the opposite of a spoiled child. (pp. 38–40)

A biographical critic would have to delight in noting that Merlin's theories seem to work, as her own two daughters have gone on to lead happy, successful professional lives with solid families of their own. What Addie, in the novel, perceived must have helped in Merlin's life. A myth critic, finding the deeper, mythological roots for even the characters in contemporary novels, could delight in finding the archetypal Earth goddess in Addie's nurturing and bringing forth wellness and growth in Andrea and at least three other patients.

A psychological critic could, of course, psychoanalyze the author through her characters, asserting that, like dreams themselves, the fiction is a projection of the author's own deepest aspirations and beliefs.

However, here one need only operate as a simple literal reader, enjoying the words Addie herself uses to summarize the actions in the book:

> I suddenly found myself thinking that all quests might be a reaction to the infantile hunger of our insistent egos, an effort to satisfy their continual crying out for reassurance and a desperate clinging to a self-righteous security blanket of power and control. On the other hand, they could be a response to the call of our immortal souls that needs to feel the flow from where we began, our origins, and to where we might be going. This creates a deep desire to follow the gentle whispering voices as they try to help each of us build our own unique bridge between yesterday and tomorrow, inspiring us with a yearning to experience the exultant joy of sensing eternity in the here and now.
>
> The question was how to decide between the loud, driving passions of our egos and the gentle, tranquil guidance of our souls. As if in answer to my question, I could hear the voices… that someday all of us would naturally perceive our connections to everything and everyone, as well as a greater comprehension of time, as far backward and as far forward as each of us would be capable of envisioning. Perhaps it really was a matter of time, a matter of transforming ourselves, a

matter of reaching a level of human development that would make it possible for us to quiet our egos enough to be able to hear the quieter messages from our immortal souls telling us how to change ourselves so we might change the planet into that perfect, or at least a much better, place. (pp. 367–368)

Merlin, circa 1981.

the importance
of merlin stone

Merlin, New York City, 1988.

The Importance of Merlin Stone

by Lenny Schneir, with David B. Axelrod

*It is very spiritually strengthening to feel that women
have been made in the image of Goddess.*
—MERLIN STONE, *SAN FRANCISCO CHRONICLE* (APRIL 7, 1978)

*I*T WAS MERLIN STONE's work in sculpting and contact with Goddess
imagery that fostered her first interest in archaeological studies that
would rediscover and reclaim the thousands of years of lost matriar-
chal/Goddess history. She spent two years off and on in the Near and
Middle East and the Mediterranean, returning to London as required
to confirm the data for her groundbreaking books at the Ashmolean
Museum of Art and Archeology in Oxford and at the British Library's
Special Collections. Her research, however, began a decade prior. Her
quest was not just thorough but quite remarkable.

She visited such countries as Greece, Crete, Turkey, Lebanon, and
Cyprus. She was a single woman who did not speak any of the languages. She had limited financial resources and used not just public
transportation but even hitchhiked, camped out, and relied (before
computers and other technology) on taking hundreds of pages of handwritten notes. Yet she was able to amass all that she would need to return to London to write what would become two seminal, groundbreaking books.

First published in London by Virago in March 1976 as *The Paradise Papers: The Suppression of Women's Rites,* a book elaborating on the stories, rites, and rituals of the Goddess, Merlin's book was instantly recognized as an important work. Scholars responded with reviews praising the book as revelatory, even as others questioned and resisted the notion that thousands of years of Goddess tradition and worship preceded our present patriarchal societies and religions. An associate of Robert Graves wrote to Merlin from Mallorca soon after the publication of the book to praise her work, saying that Graves himself "might have nodded 'suitable grave assent' to *The Paradise Papers.*"

In 1976, Dial Press recognized the importance of her work and purchased the rights to publish the book in the United States, under its final, celebrated title, *When God Was a Woman.* In 1978, Harcourt Brace Jovanovich published the soft-cover version, which remains in print. Best estimates are that at least one million copies of the book have now been sold in its various versions in English as well as translations into French, German, Dutch, and Italian.

Following the success of *When God Was a Woman,* Merlin wrote a sister volume entitled *Ancient Mirrors of Womanhood: Our Goddess and Heroine Heritage* (New Sibylline Books, 1979; Beacon Press, 1984).

Merlin Stone's books became widely used texts in women's studies programs throughout the world, and the referenced resource of hundreds of other authors' articles, monographs, and books. Scholar upon scholar wrote to her to thank her for her original, classic work of Goddess reclamation and to acknowledge the place of her work in their lives and studies. The actual number of links back to Merlin are innumerable—so much so that a simple Google search of her name with her book titles will produce millions of links on any given day.

Among those acknowledging her in their works are Margot Adler, Barbara Walker, Erica Jong, Charlene Spretnak, Miriam Simos (Starhawk), Shere Hite, Lucy Lippard, Mary Daly, Luisah Teish, Riane Eisler, Carol P. Christ, Buffie Johnson, Marija Gimbutas, Elizabeth Davis, and Gloria Orenstein. The list is extensive. At the Clearwater,

Florida, ceremony commemorating Merlin's life, held on September 24, 2011, such notables as Olympia Dukakis and Gloria Steinem testified to the impact of her work.

Throughout her life, Merlin published articles, organized and moderated significant radio and other educational series and presentations, and appeared at hundreds of seminars and festivals. Most notable among her series was the Canadian Broadcasting Corporation's four-part presentation "Return of the Goddess" (1986), which was conceived, organized, and moderated by Merlin Stone.

She also wrote the chapter on Goddess worship in the Near East for Macmillan Publishing Company's *Encyclopedia of Religion*. She authored forewords for other books and met privately and appeared publicly as a scholar and advocate for women.

A documentary film and book, both entitled *In Search of Merlin Stone*, have been made but have not been produced or published. Merlin's work is now being collected and digitized to be preserved for the ages.

Millions of men and women in the United States have been touched by Merlin Stone's research, books, and spirituality. Because they no longer have to view the creator as exclusively male, people have a new perspective that collectively changed forever how women and men feel about themselves, their religion, and their roles upon the earth.

Merlin's efforts, in many ways, were heroic attempts to overcome the ill treatment of women in America who suffered from gender discrimination, patriarchal domination, and inequality in the workplace. In Merlin's early years of research, many scholars and religious leaders scoffed at the notion that there was an age when the deity was a woman. Such a view was, at best, vague mythology. With her travels and research, Merlin added extensively to the scholarly evidence of women's importance in history and society.

Prior to the publication of Merlin Stone's books in the United States, there were very few university women's studies programs. Those that did exist concentrated primarily on the early feminist movements of the nineteenth century and women's right to vote. Merlin's books have been cited as required reading in hundreds of curricula over the years. The publication of her books and her subsequent research unleashed a hidden force. In universities, in popular culture, and in women's studies programs, an unstoppable energy was set free. There is hardly an informed student of her field who doesn't know Merlin's work. Merlin's impact on present and future religious viewpoints of women and men in the United States is immeasurable.

The noted author Erica Jong said, on the back cover of *Ancient Mirrors of Womanhood* (Beacon Press, 1984):

> [This book is] an essential book for anyone interested in the female aspect of deity, the history of religion, and attitudes toward women—ancient and modern. I applaud Merlin Stone's research, her passion, her commitment.

Significantly, Merlin stated in an interview in *Aquarian Voices* magazine (November/December, 1989), "Mine was the first book to be written that gathered the material together and presented it from a feminist point of view." *When God Was a Woman* and *Ancient Mirrors of Womanhood* became touchstone books about the Goddess from a feminist viewpoint. They proved conclusively that the Goddess existed with many names, in almost all cultures, for at least eight thousand years, and more likely as many as twenty-five thousand years.

Because of Merlin's research and books, a very old religion began anew. Merlin was famous for saying that modern calendars were, in fact, eight thousand years behind. Perhaps Merlin said it best, starting in 1976: "The Goddess is back." Thereafter, she often dated documents by adding eight thousand years. Thus, according to Merlin, the year of composition for this article is not 2013, but 10,013.

Yet Merlin herself did not quest after fame. To promote the good work of Goddess and women's studies programs, she traveled internationally, lecturing and encouraging further research and translation of her work and the work of others, but video productions on the Goddess show her as glad to allow others present to be featured. In an article on racism in a Bay Area newspaper, she also said feminists should not develop an elitist cult that promotes themselves instead of the cause. Women throughout the world have engaged in further research.

Wherever women's rights and women's spirituality are championed, Merlin is there—and often in name, not just spirit. Yet, in keeping with her desire to see the truth triumph and not simply to promote herself, she did not espouse or encourage any single movement, let alone worship of the Goddess. Rather, she made the world-encompassing comment that "now is the time to think of the supreme being as both mother and father. It is kind of like having a broken home to think of God exclusively as male or female" (*Cleveland Plain Dealer,* 1977).

There are no borders that define female identity. Clearly, work of the kind that Merlin Stone accomplished has a vast, global outreach. The translation of her work continues. Most recently, an Italian edition has been released. Parts of her book and citations of it occur in dozens of languages.

To further demonstrate her global intentions, Merlin wrote and published *Three Thousand Years of Racism* (New Sibylline Books, 1981), which discussed "recurring patterns in racism" in conjunction with the movement "Women Against Racism." The monograph included "accounts of racism from ancient history; a myth-shattering analysis of racism, and vital information in the struggle against racism."

Merlin said, "We need to understand the history and concepts of the Goddess in order to understand the politics of today, specifically concerning women" (April 1979 Conference at California State University, Chico). By her own account, women throughout the world were to be the beneficiaries of her studies. She fought for all women; she fought for what she knew was right, and her weapon of choice was her typewriter.

It can be argued that, since the publication of Merlin Stone's books, there are now millions of men and women around the globe whose daily lives have improved greatly. As surely as Susan B. Anthony changed the face of democracy, Merlin Stone enfranchised women's spirituality. As surely as Margaret Mead provided the perspective that helped foster a sexual revolution, Merlin Stone empowered women as females, not just as the helpmates of men. As surely as Maya Angelou's gift with language has elevated all our language, Merlin Stone is the author of powerful perceptions—often voiced in poetry she composed and included in her books. Her technique was to first thoroughly research the facts and attributes of each goddess, and then write poems that convey the place the goddess held in the lives of her followers. Each poem reads like a prayer or sacred text—so much so that the reader may even forget that, using all her research and extensive knowledge, Merlin herself composed the verses.

Merlin Stone, increasingly, chose to let her writing speak for itself. For that modesty, she should be all the more recognized for her efforts. Unlike the enforced, diminutive position required of women even in the recent past, Merlin's willingness and ability to place herself in critical, useful, but background status in the movements she helped start bespeaks tremendous strength and self-confidence.

Merlin Stone found and documented, popularized and helped proliferate, a life-changing body of information. Her work is of national and global significance. No better words describe the importance of Merlin than the summation published and read at the presentation of her honorary doctorate by the California Institute of Integral Studies on September 26, 1993:

> A historian, feminist scholar, researcher, and artist, Merlin Stone is a pioneer of the women's movement and the reclaiming of the Great Goddess tradition for the Western world. Inherent in her work is an ecological vision for the future, based on an understanding of the Goddess as the flow of life energy that nurtures and sustains the planet.
>
> It was through her artistic work as a sculptor that she came in contact with ancient Goddess images and became interested in archaeology and ancient religion. Her book *When God Was a Woman* (Dial Press, 1976) reclaimed the Goddess and women's role in prehistory and laid the groundwork for those who continue to research pre-patriarchal history.

The reclamation of the Goddess has influenced the visual arts, literature, music, theological views, and feminist studies, as well as a movement of women and men who now celebrate Goddess reverence as the core of planetary consciousness and environmental conscience.

The day after Lenny met Merlin, September 21, 1976.
Key Largo, Florida.

Merlin, 1933.

Erasmus Hall High School, senior photo, 1949.

Mylar construction on canvas.

Merlin's painting of Jenny and Cynthia (acrylic).

Merlin in San Francisco, California, 1978.

Cynthia and Merlin in California, circa 1971.

Cynthia and Merlin in London, circa 1974.

Lenny and Merlin in Milady's Restaurant,
Prince and Thompson streets, New York City, 1991.

Grandma Merlin in Paris with Cynthia's
children, Oliver and Juliette. 1989.

Merlin in Phoenicia, New York, 1992.

Merlin in her room, circa 1995, when she finished her novel.

Merlin at home in New York City, 1995.

Merlin with her books.

Lenny and Merlin in front of their apartment at 184 6TH Avenue, New York City, 1999.

Merlin on the special bench she and Lenny shared ("our bench"), 6TH Avenue, between Prince and Spring streets, NYC, 1996.

Merlin, circa 1991.

merlin stone,
artist and sculptor

Merlin Stone, Buffalo Evening News, *May 5, 1962.*

Merlin Stone, Artist and Sculptor

by David B. Axelrod

THE TRAJECTORY OF MERLIN STONE's career as an artist pointed her clearly toward her studies of the Goddess and feminist causes. Born Marilyn Claire Jacobson, on September 27, 1931, in Flatbush, Brooklyn, New York, her early education showed signs of greatness. Her high level of talent was evident even in high school, where she received the first sculpting award ever presented by Erasmus Hall High School in Brooklyn. She graduated in 1949, and that September entered the State University of New York, Buffalo, where she continued her art studies. In 1950, she married and left school to work and raise a family.

In 1958, she completed her studies at SUNY, Buffalo, obtaining her BS in art with a teaching certificate, and a minor in journalism. She was soon employed as a junior high school art teacher and, in that capacity, was already showing signs of her desire to work outside conventional strictures. A reporter covering a Kenmore School Board meeting for the local paper in 1960 noted that Mrs. Stone of the Kenmore Junior High School art faculty had concerns that "giving the same test to everyone in an individualistic subject like art seemed like a bad idea.... To back up her position, Mrs. Stone wrote to leading art teachers and asked their opinions on standardized tests.... done up in a presentation... to the committee [that] won her case. Kenmore will continue to let teachers grade their own pupils on the basis of their classwork" (Dave White, *Buffalo Courier-Express*, 1960). Merlin, the reporter noted, "urged freedom of expression and not making them conform to set standards."

Marilyn Stone, not yet known as Merlin, was creating new and ever-more-innovative art. By May 1962, an article announced that she had received a commission to create a sculpture for a building on Delaware Avenue: "Sculptress Hired for New Building." The reporter described her as "the trim, dark-haired Mrs. Stone [who] will do the sculpture in her basement studio at home." Years later, when filling out an author's information form for Dial Press to assist in the promotion of the first American printing of her book *When God Was a Woman*, Merlin would complain that they were more interested in the way she looked or who was watching her children while she did her art than in the art itself.

"The City," a Merlin Stone sculpture placed at
Benderson Building, Delaware Avenue, Buffalo.

As for her actual creations, often they were large, ambitious welded-bronze constructions. Photos in the papers show Merlin welding—without gloves, sparks flying everywhere. In another article on her sculpture when it was placed in front of the new Benderson Building, she explained how "the work represents the juxtaposition of buildings along with the activity of people who live within the city" (*Buffalo Courier-Express*, Nov. 15, 1962). More indicative of her future research and authorship, she continued, "To just display the type of work that was popular four hundred to five hundred years ago indicates a lack of acceptance of life on the part of people today." Ms. Stone was refining her passion for new ways to see the world—new rules for shaping art and individual identity.

As Merlin's sculptures were commissioned, built, and placed in more buildings and public places, she wrote a commentary for an "Arts and Culture" section of a Buffalo newspaper explaining how she felt about her creative process, saying that for her, "there is a tension of Earthbound objects." In the relationships between people and objects, there is a kind of "magnetic push and pull that each of these things creates toward each other," which can be the truth that art captures. Merlin continues, "There is the encompassing relationship of a shell or cover protecting precious contents, a pregnant woman, a seed in the earth, a flower in its closed bud … There is the emanation from that which is precious, outwards into space" ("What Does It Mean," *The Buffalo News*, 1962, p. 9).

Merlin received commissions from some of the largest corporations in America, including Marine Midland Bank, Graphic Controls, Union Carbide Corporation, Bethlehem Steel Corporation, and the City of Buffalo.

One of Merlin's sculptures commissioned for outdoor placement in Upstate New York, circa 1965.

Another of Merlin's sculptures commissioned for outdoor placement in Upstate New York, circa 1965.

THE BUFFALO MUNICIPAL HOUSING AUTHORITY

JOSEPH J. KELLY GARDENS
HOUSING FOR THE ELDERLY

ROBERT TRAYNHAM COLES · AIA · ARCHITECT *architecture and urban design*
321 humboldt parkway/buffalo 8, new york/phone 884-4470

Merlin's welded-bronze sculpture is pictured to the left as part of
an advertisement for federal housing for senior citizens in Buffalo.

Reporters sometimes asked why she didn't title some of her creations. On the occasion of the unveiling of yet another massive work of welded, yellow brass, Merlin commented, "I didn't name the piece. After all the furor over the 'Spirit of Womanhood,' I decided to stay away from names." She was referring to a fourteen-foot bronze abstract sculpture of a woman by Larry W. Griffis Jr., which apparently generated a great deal of controversy over its name and subject matter when placed in a Buffalo park.

As an assistant art professor at State University College, Buffalo, in 1962, she was asked to lecture on the history of sculpture. Later, Merlin explained that her preparations for her lectures helped her discover lost Goddess cultures. Time and time again, she encountered figures of women from ancient civilizations, but their roles were either subordinated to a male patriarchal system or simply dismissed as not central to the cultures where they were found. Worse, they were characterized as lewd vestiges of female cults.

By the mid-sixties, Marilyn C. Stone was branching out, not just in sculptures that broke away from old forms, but with kinetic art and art constructions that escaped the frame. Divorced in 1964, she moved to a farmhouse in Upstate New York, where she continued to sculpt and create. Later, she worked out of her large studio on West Ferry Street in Buffalo, where she established herself as a force in the arts community. She became an instructor at the Albright-Knox Art Gallery, where her work was not only exhibited but won sculpture awards. Merlin exhibited widely in 1966, a banner year for her. She created a three-dimensional wall of eight floor-to-ceiling panels, which, she told the *Buffalo Courier-Express*, "should appear that the paintings are growing, like a wall-to-wall painting [with] implied motion" (Garcia de Campos, October 2, 1964, p. 24D).

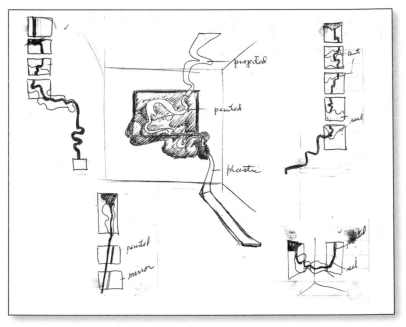

A sketch for a painting by Merlin that escapes from its frame.

Merlin with her creation in her backyard in Oakland, CA.

Spurred on by her increasing success, Merlin applied to and was given a teaching fellowship to study in the MFA program at the California College of Arts and Crafts (now known as California College of the Arts). Early in 1967, she moved to the San Francisco/Oakland/Berkeley area, where she soon began working with the San Francisco Bay Area chapter of Experiments in Art and Technology, Inc. (E.A.T.). The group itself was new to the area and had just published its first newsletter. E.A.T. promised to "emphasize the collaborative relationship between artists and engineers... [to] maintain a constructive climate for the recognition of the new technology and the arts... eliminate the separation of the individual from technological change" (*E.A.T. News*, vol. 1, no. 1, January 15, 1967, p. 1 and back cover).

Merlin appears in the foreground of this photograph, working with the Pacific Gas and Electric Company to create the entrance to an E.A.T. show entitled "The Machine as Seen at the End of the Mechanical Age."

In her MFA dissertation, entitled "The Energy Systems of Marilyn Stone," Merlin not only presented a summary of her multimedia environmental sculptures but also articulated some of the most basic concepts that would shape her future feminist work. Looking back on her art to that point, she stated: "My original concerns for the spatial and temporal aspects of our existence have led me to an exploration of what visually causes our sensory perceptions of space and time" (Dissertation, 3). Using the shift of mountains—too slow to perceive—and the spin of a propeller—too fast to perceive—she explains that "we do not see slow enough and we do not see fast enough to perceive other than a very narrow scale of temporal existence. This offers us a very limited definition of what we refer to as visual reality and that which artists have explored until now." But from that basic declaration of her need to seek new technologies that offer more dimensions for us to experience and perceive, she extrapolates to make a highly prophetic statement: "There appears to be a kind of humanistic provincialism or sort of religious fear of what 'The Powers That Be' intended for us to know, that has until now controlled our explorations of what is visually interesting" (Dissertation, 4).

In her quest to expand the media, Merlin came to believe that we are only able to advance if we can see the world in new patterns. In her summation of her environmental sculptures and her MFA, she stated, "The colors that we perceive are the eye's reception of photons of varying wavelengths. We may, then, begin to explore controlling these wavelengths with fluorescence, phosphorescence, diffraction gratings, fiber optics, polarization as we have until now explored controlling these wavelengths by mixing chemicals together that we refer to as paint." To that end, she constructed a series of four increasingly large environments that combined sound, music, and lighted objects turned on and off to create a feeling of motion, and projections of video and film images—all of which surrounded a person in a room-sized environment rather than simply presenting itself as a static object of art to be viewed.

Two light constructions that Merlin built for her MFA project. Above is a time-lapse photo showing light patterns for a room-sized environment. Below is a bench with a moving light pattern.

"I had become too concerned with static solid forms," Merlin declared, but the same disillusionment with conventions of art would imbue her later desire to change the way we look at the role of women. In her art she stated, "If new information is found that does not fit into the original system, a new system must be developed which will either negate or include the original one.... We start to think of evolution, anthropology, archaeology, cinematography and relativity. When the distant points of history force us to regard our own existence as another point in time, the comprehension of our own existence as another point in time, the comprehension of a fourth dimension is pressed upon us" (Dissertation, pp. 11, 13). Merlin's subsequent research into our forgotten and/or suppressed matriarchal societies would provide the stimuli, the building blocks, that helped create a new dimension of Goddess awareness and feminism.

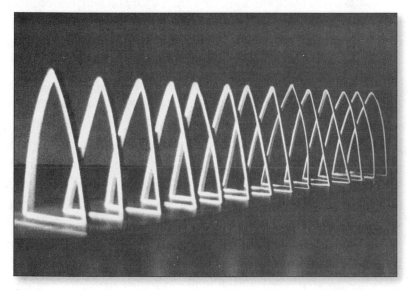

This flashing, fluorescent light sculpture, which Merlin created for her MFA, was later included in the University of California, Berkeley, "Energy of Art" exhibition.

After the completion of her MFA, by spring of 1969, Marilyn Stone, who was now known as Merlin, was the E.A.T. Bay Area coordinator, expanding and articulating the mission of E.A.T. in its newsletters. The University of California, Berkeley Extension, where she taught as an instructor, acknowledged her by her professional name, Merlin Stone, noting in their description of her course that "her own work with energy systems of electronically activated light-modules has led her into recent explorations of the electric waves of the human brain as a control device to activate light and sound environments" ("Energy Art: New Media of Art and Technology," E.A.T. spring catalog, 1969).

Merlin was, once again, a subject of newspaper articles, one headline declaring "She'd Light Up the Sky." A reporter, still as interested in describing Merlin's looks as her art, began her story, "A tall brunette who always dresses in black and wants to turn the City on with light configurations is behind a far-out happening now taking place at the San Francisco Museum of Art" (Virginia Westover, *San Francisco Chronicle*, 1969). The article chronicles Merlin's work on a project entitled "Outside/Inside," described as "an electronic video-audio performance that . . . picks up sights and sounds of the crowds as they walk through [and allows] participants to see themselves on large video monitors which also transmit pre-programmed images." At the time—when videography was anything but ubiquitous—the idea of putting art patrons into the art itself was highly innovative. The article, which later characterizes Merlin as "vivacious," makes note of Merlin's work with brain waves in art as well as plasma gas light sculptures, and ends by quoting Merlin as wanting "to laser-beam a light show on the moon" (Westover).

Marilyn Claire Jacobson's metamorphosis from Mrs. Stone, to Marilyn Stone, to Merlin Stone—a highly innovative artist and sculptor—did not end there, of course. In her own résumé, and in her informational sheet she provided to Dial Press, Merlin says that she began research for her book *When God Was a Woman* as early as 1962. She dates her specific independent studies for the book between 1970, when she devoted herself to research and writing, and 1976, including time at the Ashmolean Museum of Art and Archeology in Oxford, England.

She also spent time at the British Library's special collections in London, and traveled to Greece, Crete, Turkey, Lebanon, Cyprus, and other birthplaces of the Goddess to collect evidence and additional research material for her book. But beyond the actual dates of her career, the strains of her independence of thought and feminist beliefs were evident even in her demand that she and her junior high school colleagues be allowed to determine their own standards by which to measure their students. She bristled at those who reduced a woman's career to a hobby, or worse, those who described the physical attributes of the artist (as opposed to the art itself), and she asserted that art must be dynamic, not bound by past conventions or even contained within the measured space of a frame. That same inquisitive nature set in motion her Goddess research. After the appearance of and acclaim for her feminist writings, she continued to speak at conferences on women in the arts, moving easily between the art world and gender studies for the rest of her life.

List of Merlin's Commissions

Marine Midland Bank, Vassar branch. Turley, Stievater, Walker, Mauri & Assoc., Architects. "The Group"—welded bronze.

Benderson Building, 135 Delaware Avenue, Buffalo, NY. Harold Bell, Architect. "The City"— welded brass.

The Cloister Restaurant, 472 Delware Avenue, Buffalo, NY. James Di-Lapo, Architectural Designer. "Fountain"—welded brass.

Union Carbide Corp., Linde Air Division. House of Crafts. "Cage"— welded copper.

Marine Midland Bank, Wappinger Fall, NY. Turley, Stievater et al, Architects. Divider screen—welded bronze.

Graphic Controls Corp., Buffalo, NY. Arthur Carrara, Architect. "Three"—welded bronze.

Continental Inn, Delaware Avenue, Buffalo, NY. James Sapienza, Interior Designer. "Furnace"—brass and bronze.

Marine Midland Bank, Syracuse main office. Turley, Stievater et al, Architects. "Wall Squares"—brass, bronze, and copper.

Milky Way Restaurant, Williamsville, NY. James DiLapo, Architectural Designer. Forty-foot screen divider—welded brass.

Buffalo Dental Supply building, Amherst, NY. Suburban Galleries, Interior Designers. Series of three: "The Odyssey"— brass, copper, and enamels.

Federal Housing Project for the Elderly, Cornwall Avenue, Buffalo, NY. Robert T. Coles, Architect. "Fountain and Screen."

Merlin's graduate school transcript from what is now
California College of the Arts.

Merlin sculpting, 1964. Buffalo, New York.

CIIS

California Institute of Integral Studies

March 8, 1993

Ms. Merlin Stone
Box 266
201 Varick Street
New York, NY 10014

Dearest Merlin,

It is with the deepest and most profound pleasure that I inform you that the California Institute of Integral Studies has decided to award to you an honorary doctorate in recognition of your outstanding scholarship and leadership in the field of women's spirituality. We will be presenting the degrees at our 25th Anniversary Gala celebration on September 26, 1993 here in San Francisco. We will of course cover your expenses and we hope that your schedule is free so that you will be able to participate.

We will be honoring both you and Thomas Berry with these honorary degrees; I feel that it is most appropriate that the two of you are being recognized in concert as you represent a recovery of the voice of the earth, the voice of the feminine which has been suppressed and ignored for so long.

Robert McDermott and the entire faculty, Board of Trustees, Staff and students join me in extending our appreciation for the lifetime of work that you have contributed to women's scholarship. Robert will be writing his personal wishes to you under separate cover.

Merlin, you know how pivotal you have been in my life, and it is with great happiness that I bring you this news of your honorary Ph.D.. I look forward to speaking with you before too long, and I hope all is well with both you and Lenny.

Love,

Pamela Westfall-Rosen
Director of Program Development

765 Ashbury Street, San Francisco CA 94117 (415) 753-6100 FAX (415) 753-1169

*Letter to Merlin informing her she'd been awarded an honorary PhD
from the California Institute of Integral Studies.*

Merlin in her studio, circa 1964. Buffalo, New York.

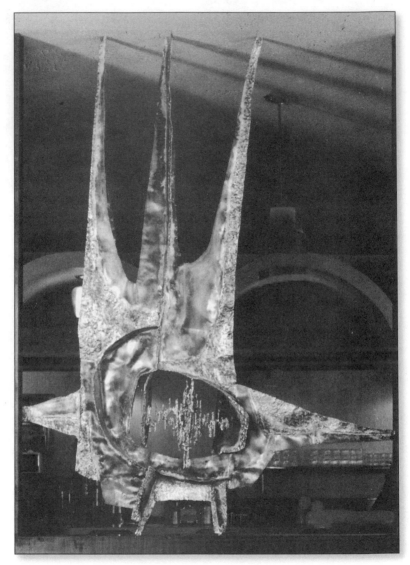

Bank installation, welded bronze.

ROBERT F. KENNEDY
NEW YORK

110 EAST 45TH STREET
NEW YORK 10017

United States Senate

July 29, 1965

Mrs. Marilyn Stone
531 Potomac Avenue
Buffalo, New York

Dear Mrs. Stone:

Since the works of art which have been on loan in my New York
City office from the Albright-Knox gallery are now going back,
I would like to take tnis opportunity to thank you for
permitting us to show your sculpture.

Enclosed is a copy of a story in a recent New York Times
about our show which I thought you may find of special interest.

All of the art work have attracted the attention of the many
people who come into the office, and I understand from my New
York staff that they too have enjoyed being surrounded with
exciting works of art.

With good wishes.

Sincerely,

Robert F. Kennedy

Letter from Robert F. Kennedy thanking Merlin for her art
he exhibited in the lobby of his New York City Senate office, 1965.

KENNEDY'S OFFICE HERE SHOWS ART

Works Are Exclusively of Senator's Constituents

By GRACE GLUECK

A small art gallery exclusively for the work of New York State artists has sprung up in the city offices of Senator Robert F. Kennedy.. . .

A small abstract sculpture, "Flight," by Marilyn Stone, sits on a conference table, and in Mr. Kennedy's office at the far end of the suite are water-colors by Margaret Etenger and Louis Vastola.

'Lots of Room'

In setting up the art display Mr. Kennedy is following other Washington officeholders. Senator Jacob K. Javits, a cosponsor of the recent bill establishing a National Arts Council maintains displays of borrowed art in all three of his public offices. Yesterday, he said:

"I welcome the fact that my colleague is similarly engaged There's plenty of art and lots of room for everyone."

The New York Times (July 23, 1965).

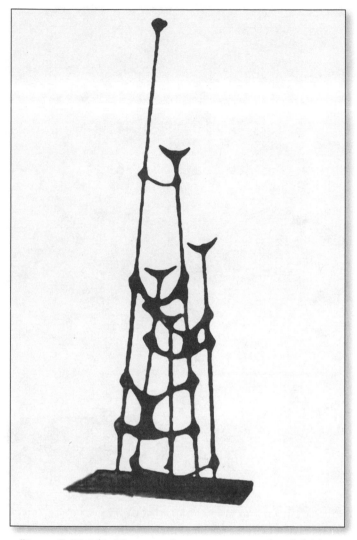

"Struggle." Welded brass. 26th Western New York Exhibition.
Albright-Knox Gallery, 1960.

Welded bronze, 1964.

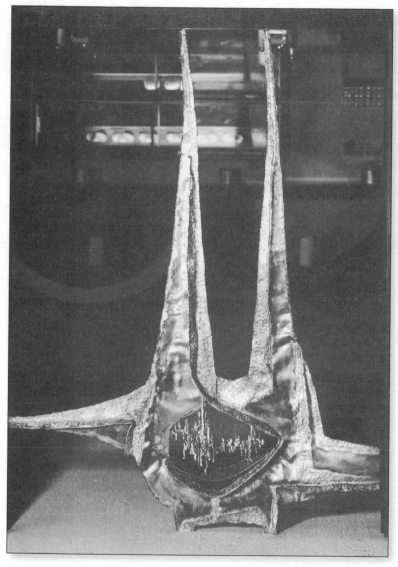

Detail of panel/wall (displayed on next page). Welded brass, 1966.

Milky Way Restaurant, Williamsville, New York.
Forty-foot screen divider. Welded brass.

Welded bronze, circa 1965.

Mylar construction on canvas.

*Merlin Stone embracing a lighting column
as final photo in her 1968 MFA dissertation.*

i remember merlin

Jenny and Cynthia, Merlin's daughters.

I Remember Merlin

by Cynthia Stone Davis

*F*ROM MY EARLIEST RECOLLECTIONS, she sang. The songs that I remember the most were "Summertime," "Que Sera Sera" (Whatever Will Be, Will Be), and "Tura Lura Lura" (that's an Irish lullaby), but there were many others. She didn't have an incredible voice, but I loved it when she sang.

She sewed. She used to make matching dresses for my sister, herself, and me. My favorite one was the black velvet dress with the red rose application, but it was the mini-dress with the big bell sleeves (the one she called "the Merlin dress") that won her the nickname "Merlin."

She was born into the Jewish religion, though I don't think either of her parents were very religious. She raised us as atheists. We did, however, have a number of Christmas trees and an attempt at a Passover dinner, which ended abruptly because one of our Egyptian girlfriends was attending, and she felt uncomfortable with the prayer book text. Despite the lack of organized religion, Merlin raised us with many values that I cherish and have tried to pass on to my children.

We had a big brown book when I was a kid called *The Epic of Man*. It was filled with photos and descriptions of all sorts of primitive cultures. I loved it so much that she gave it to me years later. I guess her interest in ethnological studies had already been there in the early sixties.

Merlin with Jenny and Cynthia, circa 1959.

Merlin inserted the word "Woman"
on the cover of this Time Life Ancient History Book.

Merlin's painting of Jenny and Cynthia (acrylic).

My strongest memories of Merlin are as an artist. She painted when we were very little. People might remember Merlin as a writer, but I can't forget the wonderful moments spent as a child playing with the various materials she had lying around her workshop while watching her weld these huge metal sculptures. It's amazing looking back now on all the commissions she received. As I pored through her boxes of old clippings, I found so many articles and letters praising her unique artistic talents and personal style. I just saw her as my mom working away at what she enjoyed doing.

Later, when we moved to Oakland, California, when I was about twelve, she constructed an enormous sort of "womb" in the garage. It was made out of canvas, fiberglass, and fur. She called it an "environment," and one could enter and sit inside it. She left it all behind when we moved, but then, she wasn't very attached to things.

I remember when we moved from Buffalo, New York, to California. The Bay Area in the late sixties was rather magical. Merlin, who had always had to fight for what she believed in, suddenly found a town full of people who shared similar values, although she was always too intellectual to be a real hippie.

Cynthia and Merlin in California, circa 1971.

When I was seventeen, I decided to go to England with a girlfriend. We weren't sure how long we would stay or what we would do there. Merlin surprised me by saying that she would come along too, but that she wouldn't stay with us. So in 1972, the three of us flew off to London. I had no idea at the time that she wanted to do research about Goddess worship, though I do remember her spending a lot of time at the British Library and traveling to different Middle Eastern countries. Anyway, the rest is history.

Cynthia and Merlin in London, 1974.

I moved to Paris in 1984. Neither of us traveled very often, so our weekly calls were a great joy to me. We would discuss politics, literature, ideas, and how the kids were getting along. When she became ill and found it harder and harder to speak, I suffered from the lack of feedback. Then, when she couldn't speak at all, I knew it was the end of something very special that we had shared.

Grandma Merlin in Paris with Cynthia's children,
Oliver and Juliette, 1989.

It wasn't always easy being Merlin's daughter. When I was younger, I often wished that she were a bit more traditional like other mothers. I guess she was "too busy being free," as the song says. These recollections would not be complete without mentioning Merlin's encounter with Lenny Schneir in Florida in 1976. They were so different and yet made for each other, real soulmates. He always supported her in her work and was so proud of all her accomplishments. He taught all the grandchildren how to play pool and poker. He took care of her right till the end.

a gallery of merlin stone photos and artifacts

Merlin's birth certificate. Note the motto:
"Remember thy Creator in the days of thy youth."

Merlin's earliest photo. Brooklyn, 1931.

Merlin, 1933.

Merlin, circa 1939.

Sister Myrna; Merlin; Aunt Alice; Merlin's mother, Anne;
Grandma Betty Marcus; and Uncle Abe, circa 1946.

Erasmus Hall High School, senior photo, 1949.

Merlin at home before her senior prom, 1949.

Merlin with Jenny, 1953.

Merlin in Buffalo, New York, 1960.

Merlin in San Francisco, California, 1978.

Merlin, 1969.

Merlin in Miami Beach, 1969.

Merlin and her younger sister, Myrna, 1975,
on the occasion of their parents' fiftieth wedding anniversary.

British Library card, used while researching When God Was a Woman.

Lenny and Merlin in Milady's Restaurant,
Prince and Thompson streets, New York City, 1991.

Merlin at home in New York City, 1995.

a great sense of hope:
letters to merlin stone

Lawrence, IN 46226

January 4, 1995

Dear Ms. Stone,

I have had your book _When God was a Woman_ in my possession for three years. I began reading it, but discontinued due to being involved in such a hectic schedule. However, I began continuing to read it again on my Christmas vacation. I found I could not put it down. I "knew" it was for me I simply didn't realize to what extent.

I cannot begin or fully express my gratitude to you for all the time, research and personal energy you extended on the writing of this truth-finding treasure.

The correlations made between the male myths, to conform to their desires, and what you unearthed, is to me, absolutely incredible.

These realistic findings are what I and every woman, if listening to their heart, "know" to be true.

Your book confirms our "knowing". I could not refrain from writing and saying thank you!

Sincerely,

D. P.

One of the hundreds of letters received by Merlin,
thanking her for her work on behalf of women.

San Francisco, CA 94115, November 7, 1995

Dear Ms. Stone,

Thank you so much for writing *When God Was a Woman*. It's one of those rare and wonderful books that permanently alters the way you see the world. It left me with a great sense of hope: If we created a Goddess-centered world once, surely we can create one again! Years after reading it, I find myself still quoting facts from it in conversations, and I've recommended it more times that I can count. I was also fascinated by *Ancient Mirrors of Womanhood*.

~

Cremorne NSW 2090, Australia, June 25, 1992

Dear Ms. Stone,

I am 42 years old and have just discovered the Goddess. I watched a television programme on one of our public networks here in Australia 12 months ago which very briefly talked about the Goddess and which mentioned Robert Graves' book "The White Goddess." I am a great admirer of Robert Graves' work and was, to put it mildly, blown away by his book. Even though it is a very scholarly study of ancient myths and poetry and a little bit above my head in many places, it gave me so much information that my quest to learn more truly began.

After visiting various bookshops here in Sydney without any luck, I went to my local library and the only book they had available was your book *The Paradise Papers*. Having never been personally involved in political activities within the feminist movement which may have allowed me to discover all of this much sooner, your book opened my eyes to such a great extent that I cannot thank you enough for affording me the opportunity to discover the truth. I must say that my initial reaction was one of seething anger to put it mildly. One of my closest friends is a young and intelligent 25-year-old lady, who has become most concerned at the reaction to my discovery and feels that I am beginning to sound like a "man hater."

This could not be further from the truth. I'm angry at the system that our patriarchal society has created rather than against men themselves. What really concerns me is that younger women, such as my friend, have no idea of feminist principles or any interest in participation in women's rights as regarded by society. In general these days some even being in the movement is an indication that "she must be a lesbian." I watched a programme recently where many young women were asked if they were feminists and they all replied in a negative fashion because they didn't want it to be seen that they could be lesbians. A frightening concept indeed.

Recently, I finally found a bookshop with many books about the Goddess. I purchased "The Goddess Re-awakening" and there you were again. I felt immediately that I had to thank you personally for passing on your knowledge to me and for putting me on track. It has greatly increased my understanding of my decision (made before I discovered the Goddess) to get out of this depressing rat race and buy some land in the country where I intend to live a life as self-sufficient as I can make it and get back to nature as they say. Needless to say, I am saving madly. My family and friends all believe I've gone crazy this time.

After reading the "Paradise Papers," I typed out and framed one of the prayers to the Goddess mentioned in your book as I found it to be very beautiful and it now sits in a place of honour in my living room. When I am finally living in the country (hopefully in about three years time), I intend to make a shrine to the Goddess in the most beautiful place available to me. I am also a little sad that, having visited so many of the archaeological sites mentioned in your book, at the time I had no idea of their significance.

Once again, thank you so much for the knowledge you have passed on to me through your writings and I will continue, in my own way, to hopefully, make more people aware (particularly women) of the truth.

Best regards.

~

Barrington, MA, September 17, 1981

Dear Merlin,

I want to tell you how much I appreciate your book *Ancient Mirrors of Womanhood*.

I am a feminist poet, actively seeking new images of women and a continuity between our past and present. I have never gained so much pride and inspiration from a book as I did from yours. I must have made a hundred of those little connections that are the seeds of poetry.

I am especially interested in the concept of the triple nature of women in myths—for example the Greek Fates and Graeae. I wonder if you could possibly give me the names of other triple women and perhaps tell me where I could find more information on each group.

Thank you very much. Yours,

~

St. Paul's Episcopal Church

13 May 1977

Dear Mrs Stone,

    I have just finished your book, "When God was A Woman" and want to thank you for a book of great & profound thought. It was a joy to read & I could hear my good friend & teacher's voice ring out in so very much of your work, more so when you Quated him — Jame Pritchard. It made me wish I had paid more attention in his classes & Continued reading in his books & the ones he referred us to.

    I am happy to say, as you no doubt know by now, that Bishop Myers, after much prayer, thought & study, has changed his mind about women priest & has ordained four of them in his diocese.

    May your book be read by many people all over the world, as you have what needs to be heard. Gods image is female & male genesis 1: 26-27.

        Faithfully yours,

          T

Early intimations of changes in the clergy.

Correos, Deya, Mallorca, May 15, 1976

[Sent to a director of Virago Press, the first publisher of Merlin's book.]

Re: The Paradise Papers

Beryl, Robert Graves' wife, lent me this book because it has bearing on work I'm doing on mythology. Graves himself is now too old to concentrate on any work, and the book has come into my hands. I don't mean to speak for Graves, nor has anyone asked me to; but I feel I must comment on it, and I think he would agree in general with what I will say....

I've always thought that *The White Goddess* was inspired, like E. G. Davis' *The First Sex*; and it struck me that Merlin Stone's book has the same quality; so does her journeying in search of evidence. The amateurism—in the best sense—of *The Paradise Papers*, seen in the lack of typical scholarly hallmarks of over-professionalism and hesitancy of speech, bespeaks of one who was led into unfamiliar ways by forces beyond her control. This doesn't compel me to agree with it all, any more than I do with Graves' work, but the importance of the book, especially at this point in history, is clear to me. The advance in religion and the status of women go together surely. Besides, it is quite difficult, if not impossible, to find an equivalent to Stone's book, at least in print.

Stone's book helps me, not because it has a theme I don't support already, and could not have sketched from my own reading, but because it collects and evaluates the evidence supporting this theme in a way which is clear, conscientious, unanswerable (so far as I know), educative, and prophetic. I envy the author her travels and her access to references. The job needed doing badly and she certainly didn't fall down on it. Further, it is good to see women taking over areas of scholarship where their insights and morality greatly exceed men's, and where something more than angry disputes about how to pronounce the letter 'c' in Latin is due to be said if the world is ever to make sense again.

Graves might have nodded 'suitably grave assent' to the *Paradise Papers*, and added that his *Hebrew Myths* and *Adam's Rib* have direct bearing on the Adam-and-Eve contrivance that forms the cornerstone of Protestant Christianity and the degradation of women in societies dominated by varieties of Judaism.

If a whiff of my own anger at the position forced upon women over the last 3 or 4 millennia comes off in this letter, it is because that anger has a good deal to do with the form my own work has been taking over the last 4 or 5 years. I hope the book does very well.

Yours sincerely.

0266 Oslo 2, Norway, February 14, 1992

Dear Merlin Stone,

When I was a teenager, your book, *When God Was a Woman*, aroused my interest in history, a subject which until then I had loathed wholeheartedly as I felt it had nothing to do with me as a woman. It also gave me a deep sense of gratification to be able to refute arguments which until then had been the word of God, so to speak and therefore conclusive.

For me, this issue was very important because I was brought up in a rather strange and confusing environment. I was born in Iran from Armenian/English parents. My mother, as a reaction to her strict Catholic upbringing, brought me up as a complete atheist. My father died when I was very young. So, I was cared for by my mother, my grandmother and my four aunts. Thus, I was surrounded by able, strong and vital females at home, while at school, and in society I was taught that women were really an afterthought in the cosmic structure.

These conflicting informations were very frustrating and isolated me completely because I chose to believe more in my own experience than what others told me. And my experience being subjective and limited was not good enough an argument. Therefore, when I discovered your book it was like being able to speak after having been mute all my life.

~

Oakland, CA 94610, January 22, 1987

Dear Ms. Stone,

I cannot easily describe to you what *Ancient Mirrors of Womanhood* means to me. When I was twelve, in my 7th year at a Fundamentalist Protestant day school, I learned that we were not to study the gods and Goddesses of Ancient Greece because they were pagan, and we studied the one true God. I can remember accepting this at the time—there was no other acceptable outward behavior—but I can remember registering a deep question and curiosity about the idea of Goddesses. It was the first I'd heard of such a thing. That year, my routinely "straight A" report card was marred by a "C" in "Bible." I had begun a rebellion that was to last more than fifteen years. Today I am thirty two and my emotion and wonder about the Goddess is no longer a rebellion against a solely male-principled way of anthropomorphizing the Greatest Force. Instead it is a sweet and challenging practice.

~

Weehawken, NJ 07087, October 5, 1978

Dear Merlin,

When God Was a Woman blew my mind. I first got interested in the subject when Monique Wittig's *Les Guérillères* was translated into English. I wanted to review it for *Ms. Magazine,* but my friend there said it was too radical for their readership. That book made me realize that without the mythic or spiritual dimension, something would be forever missing from consciousness-raising.

I've always had difficulty affiliating totally with one group or another. Your book clarified for me why I could never bring myself to practice Judaism, the "faith of my fathers." This "clarification" felt like a punch in the stomach. I sat for a day immobilized with rage. I realized that I had, on some level, always known what you were saying, but had never wanted to face all the implications of it (i.e., the rejection of my heritage) until you forced me to look. Some of that anger has passed; I feel now more compassion for my foremothers and concern that the lies not be passed along to the next generation.

$\sim$

New York, NY 10023, June 12, 1980

Dear Ms. Stone,

I am both fascinated and moved by your book *When God Was a Woman* which I am starting to read all over again to catch up on all the details which the emotion of reading made me overlook.

I was fascinated because you seem to have been motivated to do your research by the very questions, intuitions, inexplicable feelings, which have pushed me to keep reading more and more material on the subject of the place of women in all societies.

$\sim$

Brentwood, NY, February 9, 1980

Dear Merlin,

I have just started *Ancient Mirrors of Womanhood—Volume I*. I love it already. Your point about the definition of myth and theology is well taken. I had never thought of that and yet it is so clear. I also read *When God Was a Woman* twice and loved it. It is especially important in these books of woman-loving and woman-strength that there is no man-hating. I just came out a couple of years ago and felt much relief to let go of so much hate. (Hating half the world takes up a lot of energy!)

Do you ever give lectures or make appearances? I would love to hear you speak and know of several others who would want to hear you. How do I find out if such an occurrence will be taking place?

Thank you, thank you, thank you for the years and energy you have given to bringing the Goddess back into our lives.

Blessed be,

P.S. This is the very first fan letter I have ever written! Now I hope I mail it!

Olympia Dukakis

March 17, 1993

Dear Merlin,

I was so happy to hear from you over the holidays. I was out of town almost three months doing a play in Providence, R.I.

The last two years have been full of travels — Egypt, Mexico, Australia, Greece. I've really missed you and would be so pleased if we could meet, share a meal, just talk. If this is to your liking and pleasure, please do give me a call. There is so much to share! You are so often in my thoughts and regardless, you'll always be in my heart.

Love,

Olympia

Merlin and Olympia Dukakis were longtime friends and associates.

Amherst, MA 01002, October 9, 1991

Dear Merlin,

You were my first embodied Goddess teacher, Merlin, and I hasten to add, one of the few Real Teachers I've ever had. It really feels essential to include you in this first issue. You created such a sage (typo: I wanted to type "safe" but it works) classroom that I was able to overcome my shyness and request the space to read my poem about Demeter and Persephone. Do you remember?

Baltimore, MD 21217, December 8, 1980

Dear Merlin Stone,

It was with tremendous admiration and excitement that I recently completed your book *When God Was a Woman*. A number of women in Baltimore and I have all been involved in our own independent research of matriarchal history and participated in a workshop which was held this year and last at the Women's Growth Center. We were thrilled to see that your research confirmed much the same material that we had unearthed.

Plano, TX 75075, December 22, 1993

Dear Merlin,

Seven months ago, I read *When God Was a Woman* and today I am about to finish *Ancient Mirrors of Womanhood*. In between these two books, I have read more than a score of others on the same topic. I have also watched, several times, the film done by Canadian public television in which you appeared. All this has been life-changing for me, but you must know the impact of your work already.

Since reading your first book I have been on a women's retreat, joined a women's drumming group, been to a Cradle Basket ceremony, an Earth Blessing ceremony and had myself officially unbaptized by a group of women friends. Where all this is leading, I do not know. But I do know that it is leading me where I am supposed to go.

My first reaction to *When God Was a Woman* was anger, why had I never learned this information before? I have both a bachelor's and a master's degree, the master's is from a women's university. I have read thousands of books in my life, many of them histories. Yet, nothing I had read or learned contained my own story. This makes a travesty both of education and written histories.

My second reaction was joy. Here, at last, was what I had always known deeply, below consciousness. You, and others, have given me myself. So, I thank you from the bottom of my heart.

~

Oxford OX2 6JA, United Kingdom, August, 1993

Dear Merlin Stone,

I would like to try to tell you how much your book has meant to me. Reading it was like unraveling a fabric which I had long suspected was flawed and coming apart—the basic 'God the Father' construct I had been brought up with.

More importantly, your book has been part of putting something infinitely more empowering in its place. The perspective I have now got on human spirituality, namely that we have worshipped female deities for at least four times as long as we have worshipped male, has also changed my feminism. From having been involved in an apparently endless effort to establish equality, I now have a feeling of the strength and authority of thousands of years behind me, meaning that the task in front of us is to integrate what women do well with what men do well.

〜

Satellite Beach, FL 32937, July 9, 1977

Dear Merlin,

I read your book, *When God Was a Woman*, with interest and joy. It was an affirmation of feelings I've had for as long as I can remember, that the idea of a male god, condemning women to perpetual subservience to men, must be total nonsense, and terribly damaging to men as well as women. I have talked about your book and recommended it to anyone who will listen to me; since my friends are feminists, their response would warm your heart. I'm not sure how many books it will sell, but have a hunch that your work will become a classic.

〜

Created as a thank-you for a quotation used to promote
the comic strip Mother Goddess Funnies.

the legacy of merlin stone

Merlin in Phoenicia, New York, 1992.

The Legacy of Merlin Stone:
One Feminist's View
by Carol F. Thomas

*F*OR ME, MERLIN STONE was one of the most remarkably gifted artists, sculptors, and writers this country has ever known. Her books, *When God Was a Woman* and *Ancient Mirrors of Womanhood*, exploded on college campuses, in women's consciousness groups, and among millions of other women who wondered how they had come to a place of proscribed subjugation, patriarchal mandates, and limited choices and opportunities. Until Stone's first book, *When God Was a Woman*, appeared in 1976, there was only one prevailing and uncontested myth in contemporary American culture: the creation story of Adam and Eve and that of male supremacy, divinely ordained male domination in all political, educational, financial, and, most important, religious institutions. In all the major contemporary religions, except perhaps Hinduism, there is a prevailing male deity. There is no deity representing the qualities of the mothering, nurturing, and nourishing one, known by her many names and images as Goddess.

Yet, her values, principles, and perspective of the universe had endured and sustained a cooperative, all-encompassing artistic, peaceful, and imaginative way of life long before patriarchy. For at least eight thousand years and as much as twenty-five thousand years, people all around the globe had known of her creation of the universe, a profound valuing of life, compassion, equality, love for each other, all of which had been part of a vital life force. The Goddess was integral in understanding the meaning of life and an individual's place on Earth.

The Goddess fostered our desire to care for the earth and respect the planet in all of its infinite splendor.

For a majority of Americans, this mythic patriarchal structure is still validated by a prevailing male deity. What a man wants and what a deity living in the sky wants are precisely the same. In a very real sense, Merlin Stone singlehandedly exposed and exploded this mythic hoax—a hoax that nonetheless still remains the prevailing belief system in contemporary American life. It was Merlin who, through her archeological and historical evidence, revealed an extremely complex theological structure in which the woman was seen to be the autonomous creator of new life and was, therefore, understood to be sacred, divine, to be honored and revered. Stone points out the development of later male-worshipping religions, and the ideological inventions and masculinist mythic structures associated with them, which erased from history the earlier communities associated with the leadership, perspective, and values of the feminine. Having definitively established the earlier matrilineal communities, Stone goes on to submit the bleak regard, the irritable and narcissistic perspectives, of patriarchy, with a need for mastery, competition, tribal warfare, and deficit definitions of women.

To those of us subjected to these masculine mandates, based on power and subjugation, the emergence of Merlin's voice provided us with an alternative to bondage in wedlock, adherence to patriarchal rules and mandates, mores and regulations derived from the Old Testament, and male deity notions and beliefs. Merlin's fastidious and precise research illuminated and explicated ancient texts that determined, without a doubt, the authenticity and veracity of a time during which the values, precepts, and concepts of women were predominant—women who, in their own language, artifacts, behaviors, principles, and perspective, ruled their world.

The emphasis within these matrilineal communities was on the essential nurturing values. Merlin Stone revealed a deep, expansive, and capacious consciousness. As she points out in her essay "Ruminations on Gaia Consciousness and Goddess Reverence":

It is the consciousness that knows there are no fences, no black borderlines, no names of countries in the view from the moon. This is a period of time in the history of humans and of a consciousness of the ecological relationship of humans to our environment, whether that environment is natural or human made. It is time to observe and question what we have so far developed to better life on the planet, and to decide which directions are valuable and which are destructive if life on planet Earth is to continue to exist at all. We have arrived at a time that allows us a planetary consciousness and, along with it, a planetary conscience. (Stone, 44)

Words such as these were a call to action for me and for all women. In the twenty-first century, contemporary American culture has the opportunity, the responsibility, and the obligation to encourage its population to move away from the delusions and distortions of patriarchy and more fully examine the complexity, intellectual gifts, and heightened awareness and sensibilities with respect to saving the habitat of humanity. Stone shifts our attention to saving Mother Nature, saving Mother Earth. Where and how, we might ask, did we lose the historical and prehistorical basis of knowing the fullness of our planet, constellations, and our own capacities for both destruction and enhanced creation? Merlin Stone speaks of women's immanence. "Immanence" is associated with the knowing, being, intuitive, profoundly affective, and spiritual connection to the universe. In a very real sense, we are but bits of the universe—brothers and sisters of each and every feature of the cosmos and each and every species on Earth.

However, writing in 1976, Merlin Stone pointed out that without the "female principle, the nurturing, nourishing, caring, compassionate, cooperative energy that allows life to continue," our planet will die. She concludes, "Mother Nature is all. Mother Nature is the essence of life and it is this idea that we must really begin to understand in terms of time and in terms of space" (Stone, 44–45). It is time for another "Great Awakening," not of the frenzied, primitive, superstitious ceremony to make supplications to a great Father God who has chosen us for special privileges and protection. Rather, it is time for an awakening of the human consciousness—pre-, sub-, and unconsciousness, fully aware of the nature of the real world and its true character.

As I read Merlin Stone, here is what strikes me as the bedrock of her discoveries—what gave so many of us a new ground on which to rebuild our lives and to build a women's movement. According to Merlin, there was a time when male Homo sapiens did not have any knowledge or understanding of their material participation in the creation of life. Therefore they worshipped the female life force as singularly responsible for reproduction and continuity of the species. As Stone points out in her discussion of "history" and "prehistory," there have been egregious errors in understanding these terms. Her reworking of the human chronological "calendar" uncovers two thousand years of recorded history prior to the world of fifth-century Greece and the works of Homer. Matrilineal communities, such as the one on the island of Crete, flourished for thousands of years. When men discovered their power and their stake in the process of reproduction, then the assertions of male ownership, hierarchy, primogeniture, and animal husbandry began. Men introduced ownership of women and children and heightened competition between and among different cultures, fostering constant war and violence.

It is liberating and empowering to recognize the earlier epochs during which life on Earth was not just matriarchal but was reflective of an entirely different value system. Merlin went on to expound, and my own observations and studies confirm, that contemporary American culture remains wedded to the puritan trope that denigrates and disparages women. Women are perceived as immanent, carnal, and created by the male deity to be subservient and obedient to men. Men are purportedly superior and transcendent, and spiritually aligned with a Father God, a deity who protects them and directs their warring and violent activities. We are, in fact, engaged in perpetual warring activities. Merlin Stone intrepidly points out the facts and then offers another way of living, submitting that if we do not admit the fantasy, folly, and foolishly antiquated myths of patriarchy, our planet will be destroyed, and with it, its human population. As she observes in the preface to the 1990 edition of *Ancient Mirrors of Womanhood*:

> The perceptions and values of women's spirituality and Goddess reclamation hold the vision of a truly humane and life-nurturing future. I realize now that my original hopes and goals while doing my research were identical to the hopes and goals of so many others. They are far from fulfilled, but by rejoicing in our gains and keeping a protective watch over our garden, it may yet bear the fruit of a better tomorrow. (p. xix)

Merlin Stone invites us back in time chronologically from eight thousand to twenty-five thousand years ago, when an extraordinarily different matrix of principles and values existed. It was a time when "the coin of getting psychological or material benefits from regarding others as less important, less intelligent, less creative, less moral, *even less real* [emphasis added] than oneself" (*Mirrors*, xi) had no conceptual framework. Such views were, indeed, anathema to a culture of equality that led many women to feel that "we are experiencing and observing the birth and childhood of a spiritual philosophy... which could transform life on this planet" (*Mirrors*, xii).

As a clinical psychologist, I sense that, psychoanalytically, Americans remain an "Old Testament" nation. As Merlin Stone points out, in order to save planet Earth and ourselves, we must become increasingly mindful of the fact that "the Earth is a sphere, textured with snow and with grass, with water and with mountains." She continues:

> We see that the sphere is inhabited by life forms of all kinds, made possible by the nature of the sphere itself. The further we get, the wider the view, until we see the sphere spinning around in space, a part of a much larger cosmological system. The life forms that exist on Earth have developed in a continual evolutionary process, and are still evolving. There is the intuitive belief that this evolution will be toward humans of greater consciousness, to a species of people, perhaps already evolving,

who do not see physical combat and violence as the solution to the myriad problems of existence on the planet. (Stone, "Ruminations," p. 43)

It was precisely this view that I and so many women who read Merlin's books responded to, personally, with completely life-changing results.

In the early 1980s, and while I was teaching at Saint Leo University in Florida, I experienced the great pleasure of discovering the work of Merlin Stone. Ironically, I was just completing a doctor of ministry degree at Pittsburgh Theological Seminary. My dissertation focused on the gospel of Saint John and Jesus's conversation with the Samaritan woman at the well. It seemed at the time a tentatively "feminist" way to understand the relation between the sacred and the profane. As I continued to explore and examine this passage, it continued a dialogue essentially based on patriarchy. The holy man is purportedly able to telepathically "see" the promiscuity of the woman before him, but accepts her cup of water and sends her on her way to engage in a more ethical, moral, and "religious" way of life. In terms of all the topics we were given for a dissertation, this passage seemed to me to begin perhaps a more equitable relationship between the transcendent and the "immanent."

Having spent four summers at the seminary, I was increasingly shocked at the patent absurdities of both Old and New Testaments, their various authors, and the ongoing redaction. This is to say nothing of superstitions, egregious historical miscalculations, misogyny, and rigid patriarchal interpretations. When I finished my DMin degree, I decided to pursue a PhD at Union Institute and University, which went beyond the traditional dissertation to allow a "creative project" focusing on the body of knowledge I derived from my research. Having explored the Western metaphysical colleges and universities, I sought more knowledge with respect to a broader understanding of the human condition and the individual's place in the world.

In order to accomplish this objective, I chose, for my dissertation, a focus on five aspects of women's experience. First, I would complete the required traditional dissertation, but then I would choose five different areas of contemporary American women's lives. During my studies in ministry and while teaching at Saint Leo University, tremendous changes in ideologies, politics, and religious perspectives were taking place. Merlin Stone moved the rock from the cave's door, and the Goddess was resurrected. Given the static nature of the prevailing "totalitarian" epistemologies, new voices, new perspectives, and new knowledge were being excitedly disseminated. This was the time of renewed feminist theoretical and epistemological knowledge.

The five women's studies courses I created for my creative project were designed to provide a fledgling undergraduate course in women's studies. The five courses included "The Psychology of Women," "Inventing the American Woman," "Early American Literature by Women," "Creative Writing and Poetry: Our Own Voices, Our Own Stories," and "Contemporary Women's Spirituality: Heart, Soul, and Spirit." My inquiries indicated that these were the areas of greatest interest and utility to women. The courses were one semester each in length and consisted of night and weekend classes to accommodate the women's families and work lives. Each class contained approximately fifteen to thirty students and was centered heavily on class participation.

By far the most popular class was the Women's Spirituality class, in which female students carefully read and discussed Merlin Stone's works. The goals and objectives of the class were rigorous. We encouraged one another to move toward a richer, fuller perspective of what constitutes divine encounter and experience. Following Merlin's scholarship and commentary, the students heightened their awareness and became more mindful of the world from a feminist perspective. They even gained a spiritual strength from their Goddess studies.

Because Stone's research is fastidious, precise, and so amply documented, we were encouraged—each and every one of us—to engage in a close and careful reading of the text, to cultivate a more compassionate and empathetic mode of being-in-the-world, and to perceive spirituality as compassion. Merlin challenged us to critique gender asymmetry, to work for true equality for all, and to never to see "the other," except as a part of ourselves. Further, she encouraged us to embrace pluralism, diversity, and the radically dynamic components of the sacred with a completely open acceptance. Within the class there was a growing sense of validation and affirmation. We were increasingly able to claim the validity of our own experiences and speak with strong voices. We read and studied, and told our stories. Our narratives became liberating texts in dialogue with others, appreciating the fullness of women's experience as a source of knowledge, empowerment, imagination, and compassion.

Indeed, as I have continued to teach my class on women's spirituality, Merlin Stone is ever present in my classroom—her spirit guiding us with her own intrepid courage and deep desire to uncover the truths of women's experiences. She is the lever of change for women's lives, work, and knowledge, fostering a new way of living in harmony with the earth and one another. Each and every individual in the class is essentially awakened, sustained, and supported in her journey to increased self-knowledge, history, and voice.

In Merlin's exhumation of women's history—anthropologically, archeologically, ethnologically—sifting through the very artifacts of the women's lives, she illuminates twenty-five thousand years of lost time, lost stories. Merlin explicates the crucially important contributions of women to the development of an enhanced perspective of humanity, community, cooperative and peaceful in nature. She encourages us to develop what Milton called "right reason," but with a feminist twist. Long before anyone else dared to suggest what patriarchy had attempted to annihilate, she, with her assiduous research and energy, provided the knowledge and tools, the paths to understanding a deeper reality than what patriarchal myth proselytized as fact, as truth.

My students and I are continually dazzled by Merlin Stone's work. We read her books in the eighties and nineties and into the twenty-first century. Then, and even now, so many of us grew up with patriarchal mandates concerning female behavior, sexual mores, and mandates based on deficient definitions of womanhood. When looked at through the lens of Merlin's writing, we come to see our childhood and its patriarchal regulations as a terrifying "hoax." Thankfully, some of the trepidations of the eighties and nineties, when I first taught women's studies, are gone. The bright, dedicated students of ethnological and anthropological studies have themselves gone on to further the cause of women.

What we see now, and will continue to experience, is the tremendous impact and influence of Merlin Stone's work. She revealed the deliberate erasure of women's epistemologies, philosophies, literature, and ways of living in (and finding their place in) the world. My students and I were forever changed by her courage and her convictions—convictions that lived in our own hearts, souls, and bones intuitively. She brought us truth, validation, and a resounding affirmation to believe in ourselves. We left those classes inspired to believe that there was another way to live, cooperatively, creatively, artistically, among all the species on the planet, to heal the earth. Merlin has shown us the way to live in peace. May we follow her wisdom and work toward a truly humane and life-nurturing future.

What follows, in the next section of this book, are two poems I have written in response to Merlin Stone's work, my studies, and my classroom experiences. I, like so many who discovered Merlin at a critical time in their lives, have been transformed in a way that not only changed my own path but allowed me to help other women. The poems reflect the awareness that Stone's work can foster in all of us. My students were not simply students, but women in the cause of Merlin's better perceptions. Thus it is a privilege to be able to include two poems of mine in this book—as a way to honor the world-changing work of Merlin Stone.

Two Poems for Merlin Stone by Carol F. Thomas

Life Studies: Natural Law

No one ever told us we had to study our own lives,
make of our lives a study as if learning history,
linguistics, or cultural anthropology, examine artifacts
and rituals, as if field studies of the Aka, Yanamama,

!Kung or Mudurucu. No one ever told us how to deconstruct
gazed alterities; examine old men's ringing declarations—
their frayed and tattered pseudo life; past economies of
commerce, husbandry; past myth and fetishistic horn

and chalice, cloven-hoofed containers for our darknesses.
No one ever told us where to learn the million quiet
nuances of heartbeat's antiphon in sync with ancient
world's incessant undersong; to light upon each note

as meadow larks might light upon a branch—twig-flexed
and tensile, anchored and yet not, but ready for flight.
No one ever told us to embrace the chaos, quarks and
patterns, and that perhaps, they never were designed

for us in particular. Or how to love life's murmuring,
rumbling, moiling, boiling evolutionary soup, in which
we dream, desire to be the song itself. No one ever told
us we held aphrodisiacs and anodynes; could summon

desire unkempt to trample through our souls at will.
All heaven and Earth boiled down to one sweet drop
and we hold it in weltered and love pummeled hearts—
a legend for our crinkly map of terra incognita,
becoming now vaulted, origamied liberty.

New Origin Story

We suffer now, bewildered and bamboozled, alienated
from the Earth, the sky, the universe, our *mea culpas*
projected onto stone, like gargoyles gouged from marble.

Are we angry, bitter children out to punish what we thought
was ours forever, and the planet and the Earth diminished now,
betrayed us with false promises, just like the father-god-myths

of dying white old men? Read Stevens on the patriarch, his
"no, no, no, yes, no's," his bleak regard for Earth, for life.
It was Nietzsche who asked, perhaps with irony,

"What if the women are right?" What if Homo Sapiens are two
species seemingly alike, but not the same, each sui generis,
singular, genders as multiple as you could ponder?

We live in different matrixes, and don't usually agree. The
Manichean Paranoids have been with us since history began,
hiding in the Puritan's old trope—unsavory sinners, blest

saints, this rule applied to economics exaggerates and tidies up
a complex, messy world. Even as the planet dies, Earth is
depleted, that wondrous little word, "renewable," euphemistically

softening the deaths and crimes that have reified Earth and
all her species, women, children, those different, those they
call superfluous. Patriarchs are oligarchs, alchemizing Earth

into objects to be destroyed, prison with its ill and maimed.
Look around, the prison is our metaphor for mental health
and rehabilitation.

We do not deserve another chance.
Beyond this vale of tears awaits an adolescent's dream,
except the adolescents are old men who will soon die.

epilogue

Epilogue

by Carol F. Thomas

WE ARE LIBERATED AND uplifted by the work of Merlin Stone. As teachers, we each have wonderful stories of our students' journeys from subjugation to a voice of their own and a newfound freedom. Merlin Stone's intrepid, courageous, and unaccompanied travels to research her books, her fieldnotes, her heuristic research, respecting and listening to women from dozens of different cultures and times, essentially cracked the code of the Western metaphysical tradition, exposing its lies, delusions, and distortions of truth and reality. Other fine scholars followed Merlin Stone's lead, but it was she who, at a critical moment, provided the grounding of scholarship that exposed patriarchy's great hoax. We have so very much to thank her for—so many more women are free, are empowered to speak the truth of their lives without strife of tongue or stuttering of words not their own. When I think of my women's studies classes, I inevitably think of Merlin Stone and her impact on my hundreds of students. And somehow, for me I also think of Harriet Tubman, about whom Susan Griffin in one of her most famous poems wrote, "There is always a time to make right what is wrong," and Merlin Stone has provided us with the tools to disinter our heritage as women and speak truth to power. Indeed, she encouraged us to make right and true what has been delusional and duplicitous. As Muriel Rukeyser has observed, "What would happen if one woman told the truth about her life? The world would split open." Merlin Stone has told the truth about thousands if not millions of women's histories around the world. It is time to celebrate with awe and wonder the liberating power of her work.

Acknowledgments

THANKS TO CYNTHIA STONE DAVIS for her guidance with this book and for the personal photos and papers she shared. Thanks to Nili Weisman for sending us so much material on Merlin that we thought was lost. Thanks to Gloria Orenstein for her expertise and generosity in writing the introduction to our book. Thanks to Daniel Axelrod for his editorial assistance and skills in proofing this book. A very large measure of thanks to Linda Winburn Walker, whose devotion to the project went far beyond her assistance as typist, researcher, and advisor. Thanks to Z Budapest for inspiring the creation of this book, and to Laura Vaughan for her many key contacts and enduring faith. Thanks to Selena Fox for introducing us to Elysia Gallo and all those at Llewellyn Publishing for their genuine interest in Merlin Stone, which we believe has helped us to produce a fine book. Lastly, thanks to all the endorsers who took the time to read our early manuscript.

Bibliography and Works Cited

Anderson, Mike. "The Lord Is My Shepherdess." *Pittsburgh Press* (January 1977).

"The Awakening of the Goddess." *Los Angeles Inner Resources* (Summer 1987).

Bear, Euan. "Great Goddess: Merlin Stone Discussion and Workshop, October 18–19." *In Print.* Burlington, VT: Vanguard Press, 1986.

Booher, Barbara. "Reclaiming the Goddess: An Interview with Merlin Stone." *Common Ground* (Winter, 1989–90).

California Institute of Integral Studies. Gaia Consciousness: A Conference and Celebration of the Re-Emergent Goddess and the Living Earth. April 6–10, 1988. San Francisco, CA.

Diner, Helen. *Mothers and Amazons: The First Feminine History of Culture.* Anchor/Doubleday, 1973.

The Globe and Mail. United Kingdom (December 27, 1991).

Gould Davis, Elizabeth. *The First Sex.* Penguin Books, 1971.

Holland, Darrell. "'God Was Woman' to Ancients." *Cleveland Plain Dealer* (January 22, 1977).

Kennedy, Robert. Personal letter included in this book. July 29, 1965.

Long, Asphodel P. "Feminism and Spirituality: A Review of Recent Publications 1975–1981." Women's Studies International Forum 5:1 (1982), pp. 103–108. www.asphodel-long.com/html/feminism _and_spirituality.html.

"Messenger of the Goddess, Merlin Stone." *Aquarian Voices* (November/December, 1989), pp. 10–12.

Orenstein, Gloria. Preface by Merlin Stone. *The Reflowering of the Goddess.* Oxford, England: Pergamon Press, 1990.

Ostling, Richard N. "When God Was a Woman." *Time Magazine* (May 6, 1991), p. 73.

Patai, Raphael. Foreword by Merlin Stone. *The Hebrew Goddess.* Detroit, MI: Wayne State University Press, 1990.

Seltzer, R. M. "Goddess Worship in the Ancient Near East" by Merlin Stone. *Religions of Antiquity.* New York: Macmillan, 1990.

Sowers, Leslie. "Feminists Revive Ancient Goddess Worship." *Houston Chronicle* (February 17, 1990), pp. 1E–2E.

Stein, Ruthe. "In the Image of the Great Goddess." *San Francisco Chronicle* (April 7, 1978), p. 25.

Stone, Merlin. *Als Gott eine Frau war.* Stuttgart, Germany: Goldmann Buch, 1991.

Stone, Merlin. *Ancient Mirrors of Womanhood.* Boston: Beacon Press, 1984.

————. *Ancient Mirrors of Womanhood, Vol. I.* New York: New Sibylline Books, 1979.

————. *Ancient Mirrors of Womanhood, Vol. II.* New York: New Sibylline Books, 1979.

————. *Eens was God als Vrouw belichaamd.* Netherlands: Servire, 1979.

————. "The Goddess and Evolution." *Green Egg: A Journal of the Awakening Earth* XXI: 81 (Beltane/May 1988), p. 8.

————. "Goddess Reverence in the Ancient East." *The Encyclopedia of Religion.* Vol. VI. New York: Macmillan, 1986.

————. "Inner Voice: Intuition." A lecture at a conference on "Feminist Visions of the Future," delivered by Merlin Stone: Chico, California, 1978.

————. Juror. "The Goddess Show." Printed announcement/flyer. Washington Women's Arts Center, Washington, DC (February 28– March 31, 1984).

————. *Quand Dieu était femme.* Montreal, Canada: Éditions l'Étincelle, 1978.

————. "Ruminations on Gaia Consciousness and Goddess Reverence." *Goddess Thealogy: An International Journal for the Study of the Divine Feminine* I: II (December 2011), pp. 41–49.

————. *Three Thousand Years of Racism.* New York: New Sibylline Books, 1981.

————. *When God Was a Woman*. New York: Dial Press, 1976.

————. Unpublished lecture notes. 1978.

Toms, Michael. "When God Was a Woman: An Interview with Merlin Stone." *At the Leading Edge*. Burdett, NY: Larson Publications, 1991.

Woman of Power: A Magazine of Feminism, Spirituality, and Politics 15 (October 1989), pp. 16–18.

To Contact the Authors

If you wish to contact the authors or would like more information about this book, please write to the authors in care of Llewellyn Worldwide Ltd. and we will forward your request. You may also leave a message for the authors on the Contact page of www. merlinstone.org. Both the author and publisher appreciate hearing from you and learning of your enjoyment of this book and how it has helped you. Llewellyn Worldwide Ltd. cannot guarantee that every letter written to the author can be answered, but all will be forwarded. Please write to:

David B. Axelrod, Carol F. Thomas, Lenny Schneir
℅ Llewellyn Worldwide
2143 Wooddale Drive
Woodbury, MN 55125-2989

Please enclose a self-addressed stamped envelope for reply,
or $1.00 to cover costs. If outside the U.S.A., enclose
an international postal reply coupon.

Many of Llewellyn's authors have websites with additional information and resources. For more information, please visit our website at http://www.llewellyn.com.